A Peaceful Patch of Earth

A Peaceful Patch of Earth

Blacks in Jamestown, Rhode Island, in a Time of Racial Turbulence in America, 1850–1920

Peter Fay and Valerie J. Southern

HAMILTON BOOKS

HAMILTON BOOKS

Bloomsbury Publishing Inc, 1359 Broadway, New York, NY 10018, USA
Bloomsbury Publishing Plc, 50 Bedford Square, London, WC1B 3DP, UK
Bloomsbury Publishing Ireland, 29 Earlsfort Terrace, Dublin 2, D02 AY28, Ireland

BLOOMSBURY and the Diana logo are trademarks of Bloomsbury Publishing Plc

First published in the United States of America 2026

Cover image Jamestown Historical Society, P2009.001.001.

Bloomsbury Publishing Inc does not have any control over, or responsibility for, any third-party websites referred to or in this book. All internet addresses given in this book were correct at the time of going to press. The author and publisher regret any inconvenience caused if addresses have changed or sites have ceased to exist, but can accept no responsibility for any such changes.

Library of Congress Cataloging-in-Publication Data
Names: Fay, Peter (Writer on Rhode Island,) author | Southern, Valerie J., author
Title: A peaceful patch of earth : Blacks in Jamestown, Rhode Island, in a time of racial turbulence in America, 1850-1920 / Peter Fay and Valerie J. Southern.
Other titles: Blacks in Jamestown, Rhode Island in a time of racial turbulence in America, 1850-1920
Description: New York, NY : Hamilton Books, 2026. | Includes bibliographical references and index.
Identifiers: LCCN 2025038364 (print) | LCCN 2025038365 (ebook) | ISBN 9780761880752 pb | ISBN 9780761880769 epdf | ISBN 9780761880783 ebook
Subjects: LCSH: Free Black people–Rhode Island–Jamestown–History | African Americans–Rhode Island–Jamestown–History–19th century | African Americans–Rhode Island–Jamestown–History–20th century | Jamestown (R.I.)–Race relations–History–19th century | Jamestown (R.I.)–Race relations–History–20th century
Classification: LCC F90.B53 F39 2026 (print) | LCC F90.B53 (ebook)
LC record available at https://lccn.loc.gov/2025038364
LC ebook record available at https://lccn.loc.gov/2025038365

ISBN: PB: 978-0-7618-8075-2
ePDF: 978-0-7618-8076-9
eBook: 978-0-7618-8078-3

Typeset by Deanta Global Publishing Services, Chennai, India

For product safety related questions contact productsafety@bloomsbury.com.

To find out more about our authors and books visit www.bloomsbury.com and sign up for our newsletters.

Contents

Preface

This work is the culmination of a shared commitment by its authors to preserve the history of the Black community in Jamestown. Its purpose is to affirm the community's existence and legacy. Its impetus was the discovery by one of its authors that the histories of her white childhood friends and families were well documented in town archives, but those of her civic-minded family and other island Blacks were not. Documentation on Black life in earlier centuries was also limited.[1] This is the first in a series of publications intended to affirm and inform on the legacy of the Jamestown Black community.

The challenges encountered when pursuing research were instructive. Despite comprising one-third of the Jamestown population in the mid-eighteenth century and almost 10 percent in 1895, Blacks appear to have been forgotten. A perusal of the most popular histories of the town bears this out. A forty-page chapter recounting 250 years of island history by historian J. R. Cole mentions neither the colored community nor even slavery.[2] The classic History of Jamestown on Conanicut Island in the State of Rhode Island, published in 1949, remembers the Resort Era but neglects to mention the persons of color who contributed. It chronicles the island's religious life, enumerating in eleven pages the history of the five white churches, but fails to mention the more than half-century of Black religious services.[3]

Newer histories fare little better. One written in 2010 dedicates fourteen pages to the Resort Era and eight pages to white churches, but the Black community is not mentioned, although there is one sentence acknowledging the existence of a Black church.[4] Even today, a local society dedicated to the history of the Dutch Island Lighthouse discusses its role in the Civil War but fails to mention the hundreds of soldiers of the 14th Rhode Island Heavy Artillery Regiment (Colored) stationed on Dutch Island from 1863 to 1865.[5] This omission is also in contemporary articles.[6]

Historical society and municipal archives likewise offer meager evidence of Black life. The common records and artifacts of the island's white residents—

their businesses, churches, estates, wills, civic activities, accomplishments, letters, diaries, family Bibles, and photographs—chronicle their lives from 1657 to the present day. There is little documentation of these life-affirming milestones and markers for Jamestown Blacks. The paucity suggests persons of color were either not valued or simply ignored, though research affirms their presence and contributions to commerce, growth, and development. The few archival photographs of Blacks on the island appear accidental, such as a dark-skinned child astride a horse, an animated couple briskly walking, and a male in business attire, gazing. Their names, places, associations, and deeds are mostly unknown or forgotten. The authors resorted to oral histories and combing military service records, government documents, census data, and historical narratives for sporadic matches with newspaper articles, photographs, periodicals, town meeting minutes, and church, court, and property records. Through deduction, association, and the assemblage of facts, members of the island's past Black community have begun to emerge.

The time period for this book, 1850 to 1920, was chosen because this is a time when Jamestown Blacks were no longer enslaved. Their numbers grew significantly and their community blossomed. This also was a transitional period for all persons of color in America. It begins with the Fugitive Slave Act of 1850 and the Civil War in 1861 and ends with the migration of millions of free Blacks from the South to every region of the country, including New England and Jamestown.

Chapter 1 describes the island's colonial origins and its engagement in the business of slavery. Chapter 2 presents first-ever profiles of the Black personages that walked and lived free in Jamestown from 1850 to 1920. Chapter 3 tracks the notable episodes and events in American, State of Rhode Island, and Jamestown history over the seven decades. The appendix shows the Jamestown locations, homes, and structures of colored persons in the period. It also provides census data with their names, ages, occupations, and origins.

Future publications will cover other periods in the 350-year history of the Jamestown Black community. To support this work, the Friends of Jamestown Black History (FJBH) was launched in 2019 out of concern that the history may be lost forever. FJBH strives to contribute to the growing body of reclaimed American Black history and to educate on Jamestown's legacy.

Friends of Jamestown Black History

Founders
Peter Fay, Jamestown
Valerie J. Southern, Jamestown
Supporters
Bari Freeman, Bike Newport
John Doty, Jamestown
Keith Stokes, Rhode Island Black Heritage Society
Kimberly Conway Dumpson, Rhode Island College
Lorén Spears, Tomaquag Museum
Marcus Nevius, PhD, University of Missouri
Marjory Gomez O'Toole, Little Compton Historical Society
Ray Rickman, Stages of Freedom
Richard C. Youngken, Historian
Richard Ring, Rhode Island Historical Society
Rosemary Enright, Jamestown Historical Society
Theresa Stokes, Rhode Island Black Heritage Society
Timothy Cranston, Town Historian, North Kingstown

Scholars, historians, and concerned citizens have joined the authors in support of this goal.

Notes

1 The Jamestown Historical Society has updated its archives with emphasis on slavery in the colonial period. See "From the Collection—Slavery in Jamestown," *Jamestown Historical Society*, accessed 12/4/2024, https://jamestownhistorical society.org/2021/02/08/from-the-collection-slavery-in-jamestown/. The Society also, in 2017, archived photographs and narratives of persons of color that lived in Jamestown in the 1960s, contributed by the author. Other New England towns have begun documenting their Black histories. See *Map and Guide, African American Sites in the Village of Deerfield, Massachusetts, 1695–1783*, Pocumtuck Valley Association, African Americans in Early Rural New England Project, 2013,

and Elena Sesma, "A Web of Community: Uncovering African American Historic Sites in Deerfield, MA," *Journal of Community Archaeology and Heritage* 2, no. 2 (2015): 121–36, accessed 12/2/2024, https://www.tandfonline.com/doi/abs/10 .1179/2051819615Z.00000000033.

2 J. R. Cole, "Town of Jamestown," in *History of Newport County, Rhode Island,* ed. Richard M. Bayles (New York: L.E. Preston, 1888), 723–51.

3 Walter Leon Watson, *The History of Jamestown on Conanicut Island in the State of Rhode Island* (John F. Greene, 1949), 42–5, 73–84.

4 Rosemary Enright and Sue Maden, *Jamestown—A History of Narragansett Bay's Island Town* (History Press, 2010), 65–9, 71–84, 109–11. One architectural preservation book of 1995 mentions only one of the two dozen historic Black homes and the AME Church. See *Historic and Architectural Resources of Jamestown, Rhode Island* (Rhode Island Historical Preservation & Heritage Commission, 1995), 41.

5 "From Settlement to World War II," *Dutch Island Lighthouse Society,* accessed 12/4/2024, https://dils.support/2021/03/09/from-settlement-to-world-war-ii/.

6 "The Allure and Dangers of Rhode Island's Dutch Island," *GoLocal Prov News Team*, March 7, 2021, accessed 12/4/2024, https://www.golocalprov.com/news/The -Allure-and-Dangers-of-Jamestowns-Dutch-Island.

Introduction

The town of Jamestown is located on Conanicut Island, 2 miles west of Newport and 26 miles south of Providence. The island is bounded on the north, east, and west by lower Narragansett Bay and on the south by the Atlantic Ocean. It is a peaceful setting with bedrock outcroppings lacing the shoreline and panoramic vistas of the bay and ocean. Recognized for its grazing grass and abundant fields, the island was purchased from Native Americans by white settlers in 1657.[1] Jamestown was incorporated in 1678 and encompasses Conanicut Island and the smaller islands of Dutch and Gould.[2]

In the mid-1800s, the island was a rural outpost measuring nine miles long and one mile wide. It could only be accessed by boat. The Black community, once numbering over 160 enslaved persons, had dwindled to a handful of free laborers and families rooted there since the days of slavery. Their numbers would grow again in the early twentieth century, suggesting a welcoming environment for Blacks migrating primarily from the South. However, the island had not always been welcoming. One hundred fifty years of slavery in Rhode Island could not be quickly forgotten, nor the earlier wars against Indigenous peoples.[3]

Historian Christy Clark-Pujara describes Rhode Island as a small prosperous colony that invested heavily in "the business of slavery."[4] Initially a provisioner of goods to the British slave colonies in the south and West Indies, it soon became a profitable producer of rum, made from imported molasses processed with slave labor.[5] In the early eighteenth century, traders and merchants in Newport sought a larger market for their exports, finding it in the African triangular trade.[6] Their expansion into the trade resulted in the capture, transport, and sale of 63,163 Africans to the Americas from 1701 to 1775, averaging 854 per year.[7] After American independence, human chattel was in such demand an additional 48,995 Africans were transported from 1775 to

Conanicut Island in Narragansett Bay. Source: D. G. Beers Atlas of the State of Rhode Island, 1870.

1808 at 1,960 per year, double the rate of the previous seventy-five years. Other colonies engaged in the trade, but Rhode Island volumes exceeded those of Delaware, New Jersey, New York, Pennsylvania, Virginia, and the Carolinas combined.[8] Because the colony controlled as much as 60 to 90 percent of the market, the American slave trade would have been better named "the Rhode Island slave trade."[9] According to Clark-Pujara, slavery was foundational:

> Enslaved people lived and labored in Rhode Island from the birth of the colony, in 1636, until slavery was abolished in 1842. . . . Their work . . . reflected the business of their enslavers.[10]

On Conanicut Island, white settlers soon found the purchase of slave labor critical to cultivating their fields. Their quest was made easier by the island's two-mile proximity to Newport, a prolific slave port. Ownership of enslaved people, in addition to enriching their agricultural enterprises, created personal wealth and prestige for the settlers. Rhode Island Governor Caleb Carr (1695) and the grandson of one of the island founders, Benedict Arnold, were among the original Jamestown families that enslaved Africans and Native Americans and profited from their labor.[11]

By 1748, seventy years after the town of Jamestown was incorporated, one-third of its residents were enslaved Africans and Native Americans. By the mid-eighteenth century, the island held the largest percentage of enslaved persons of any town in New England. By 1774, over 160 persons of color—most, if not all, enslaved—worked in the fields and homes of Jamestown whites.[12] They were captive to their daily demands and lived in crude ancillary spaces, basements, and garrets close to and within the enslaver's home.[13]

As agriculture declined after the War of Independence, slavery itself began a slow decline.[14] In 1784, Rhode Island enacted a Gradual Abolition Act, which did not free any existing enslaved persons.[15] The children of enslaved mothers after 1784, however, were legally free after the child served a period of indentured servitude until adulthood. Despite this act, or perhaps because of it, it took a full half-century after the war for all of the enslaved in Rhode Island to be freed. Well into the nineteenth century, they were often returned to bondage of another type, indentured servitude. If they were believed to be indigent and unable to support themselves, Rhode Island towns including Jamestown used poor laws to "warn out" undesirables under threat of fines and whipping. Hundreds of Blacks and Native Americans, many once enslaved in these towns, as well as poor whites, were pushed into cities or out of state.[16] According to historian Douglas Harper:

> Rhode Island, having ended slavery . . . sought to make it difficult for blacks to remain in the state or move there. Rhode Island towns . . . turned to the old New England custom of "warning out" . . . to purify themselves racially. The custom continued to have as a stated goal the removal of poor and undesirable strangers . . . [b]ut blacks were increasingly its targets, out of proportion to their numbers and without regard to whether they were long-term residents or not.[17]

"Warning outs" persisted until the late nineteenth century when Jamestown and other localities awakened to the new reality that they would soon need laborers of all races for the growing economy.

No evidence of race-related riots or violence was discovered in Jamestown for the seven decades from 1850 to 1920. While it is certain that the fledgling free Black community endured daily discrimination and race hatred, no apoplectic acts of white terrorism, prevalent in America at this time, threatened its survival.[18] This, the island's tranquility and beauty, and its growing tourist economy may have enticed Blacks migrating from the South. They eventually arrived by boat in unprecedented numbers, many directed by recruiting networks reaching from Newport into the southern states.

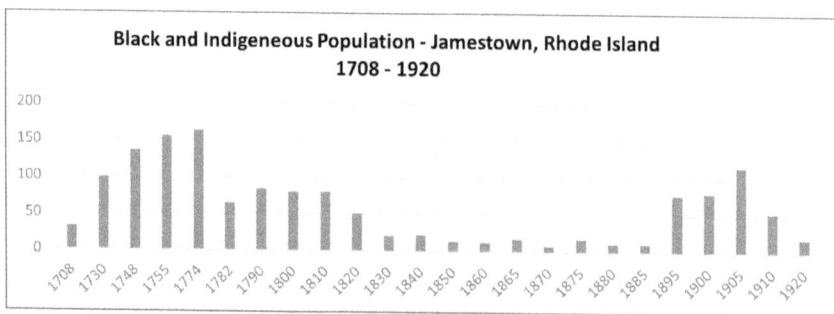

Black and Indigeneous Population - Jamestown, Rhode Island 1708 - 1920

The ebb and flow of persons of color in Jamestown from eighteenth-century enslavement to nineteenth- and twentieth-century freedom and independence. Sources: US Census, RI State Census.

The island's community of color gradually grew from 14 in 1850 to a peak of 116 in 1905.[19] Those new and arriving provided labor and services, established businesses and farms, purchased homes, nurtured families, engaged civically, and contributed to the building of the island's roads, infrastructure, and economy.[20] For many, their time on the island's peaceful patch of earth was a temporary stop, a way station, a pause; their ebb and flow emblematic of the masses of American Blacks freed from bondage, in search of better lives. Those who chose to stay and settle in Jamestown are the subject and substance of this research.

Notes

1 The terms *Native American* and *American Indian* reference Indigenous peoples living within what is now the United States prior to European contact. For the 1657 Jamestown purchase agreement, see Walter Leon Watson, *The History of Jamestown on Conanicut Island in the State of Rhode Island* (John F. Greene, 1949), 6–7. The agreement among the colonists to purchase Conanicut Island is in the Jamestown Historical Society archives, 1657, A2006.461.001.

2 Town of Jamestown, Rhode Island, *2015 Comprehensive Community Plan* (Town of Jamestown, 2015), 5.

3 For Indigenous Wars see "King Philip's War, 1675–1678," *National Park Service, Roger Williams National Memorial*, accessed 11/29/23, https://www.nps.gov/rowi/learn/historyculture/kingphilip.htm; Lisa Brooks, *Our Beloved Kin: A New History of King Philip's War* (Yale University Press, 2019).

4 Christy Clark-Pujara, *Dark Work. The Business of Slavery in Rhode Island* (New York University Press, 2016), 3–5, 13, 18.

5 Rhode Island had twenty-eight rum distilleries. See Jay Coughtry, *The Notorious Triangle: Rhode Island and the African Slave Trade, 1700–1807* (Temple University Press, 1981), 20–1, 81; Clark-Pujara, *Dark Work*, 4; Khalil Gibran Muhammad, "Chap 3—Sugar," in *The 1619 Project A New Origin Story*, ed. Nikole Hannah-Jones (New York Times Company, Penguin Random House, LLC, 2021), 80–1.

6 The Triangular Trade involved shipping Newport rum to the African coast for the purchase and enslavement of African men, women, and children. The captives

were shipped as human cargo to the West Indies or North America and sold for bills of exchange on European banks. Sugar cane, ground by enslaved Blacks and refined into molasses, was the principal commodity purchased in the West Indies for shipment back to Newport for distilling into rum which, in completing the triangle, was shipped to the African coast. The cycle included coastal trading between Newport and West Indies ports with foodstuffs, materials, and supplies shipped to West Indies plantations for enslaved laborers. In many cases, before the mid-eighteenth century, the enslaved Africans were shipped directly to Newport for shipment to the South or for sale in Newport and neighboring towns. See Richard C. Youngken, *African Americans in Newport. An introduction to the Heritage of African Americans in Newport, Rhode Island, 1700–1945* (Rhode Island Historical Preservation and Heritage Commission and Rhode Island Black Heritage Society, 2nd Printing, 1998), 6.

7 Compiled from David Eltis, *Trans-Atlantic Slave Trade Database*, accessed 11/19/24, https://www.slavevoyages.org/voyages/VKU76vyq.

8 Clark-Pujara, *Dark Work*, 13–17, 18—Table 1, 21—Table 2.

9 Rachel Chernos Lin, "The Rhode Island Slave-Traders: Butchers, Bakers and Candlestick-Makers," *Slavery & Abolition* 23, no. 3 (2002), accessed 12/20/23, https://www.tandfonline.com/doi/abs/10.1080/714005253.

10 Clark-Pujara, *Dark Work*, 3.

11 Edson I. Carr, *The Carr Family Records. Embacing [sic] the Record of the First Families who Settled in America and their Descendants* (Rockton, IL: Herald Printing House, 1894), 19. The will of Governor Caleb Carr, 1694, bequeaths to his son Edward, "Fifty acres and half acre of land at Connanicut . . . and my Indian boy named Tom," and other "negros" to other children. Governor Carr participated in the King Philip's War against the Native American tribes in New England, possibly acquiring human property as proceeds of the war; Richard M. Bayles, *History of Newport County, Rhode Island* (New York: Preston & Co., 1888), 217–18. Benedict Arnold, grandson of Jamestown founder of the same name (but not the traitorous Revolutionary War officer of the same name), left his enslaved male and female property—Eben, Hagar, Jenny, Rose, York, Sarah, Rogers, Lancaster, and Clero—to his descendants. See "Will of Benedict Arnold," *Newport Historical Magazine*, July 1883, 21–49.

12 Evarts Greene and Virginia Harrington, *American Population Before the Federal Census of 1790* (Columbia University Press, 1932), 61–9.

13 Marian Mathison Desrosiers, *John Banister of Newport: The life and Accounts of a Colonial Merchant* (McFarland & Company, Inc., 2017), 96, 200n68; Becky Little, "Slavery Persisted in New England Until the 19th Century," *History.com*, June 29, 2020, accessed 3/22/23, https://www.history.com/news/slavery-new-england -rhode-island.

14 Clark-Pujara, *Dark Work*, 75–80.

15 "An Act authorizing the Manumission of Negroes, Mulattoes and others, and for the gradual Abolition of Slavery, February 1784," *Rhode Island State Archives Repository*, accessed 5/14/23, https://sosri.access.preservica.com/uncategorized /digitalFile_cb907aee-887d-4c77-9cdd-88ac56b0ec9c/. The first anti-slavery statute in the US colonies was passed in Rhode Island on May 18, 1652. It applied to whites and Blacks and, in 1676, to Native Americans. The law was ignored. After the referenced 1784 Act for the gradual abolition of slavery, an official abolition was adopted in the state constitution in 1843. See Olivia B. Waxman, "America's First Anti-Slavery Statute Was Passed in 1652. Here's Why It Was Ignored," *Time Magazine*, May 18, 2017, https://time.com/4782885/rhode-island- antislavery/ and Samantha Boss, *Hidden Truths: Slavery and the Slave Trade in Rhode Island*, Roger Williams University, https://www.theridirectory.com/blog/ at-what-time-was-slavery-abolished-in-rhode-island/.

16 Joanne Melish, *Disowning Slavery: Gradual Emancipation and Race in New England, 1780–1860* (Cornell University Press, 1998), 190; Margaret Creech, *Three Centuries of Poor Law Administration: A Study of Legislation in Rhode Island* (University of Chicago Press, 1936), 134–63. For narrative on the warning out of the Black Champlin family in Jamestown, see Chapter 2—Hannah Elizabeth Champlin.

17 Douglas Harper, "Slavery in Rhode Island," *Slavery in the North*, accessed 6/24/23, http://slavenorth.com/rhodeisland.htm.

18 The prevalence of terrorism and assaults by whites against American Black communities is discussed in Chapter 3—Historical Context.

19 US Census 1850–1920; Rhode Island State Census, 1865–1915.

20 Shirley Teixeira Quattromani (comp.), *History of the Portuguese of Conanicut Island*, ed. Catherine M. Wright (Jamestown Philomenian Library, 1980), 219. Construction manager Alton Head of Jamestown ordered the services of Black quarry and road workers in the 1920s through Culpepper, Virginia employment agencies.

2

Profiles of Blacks in Jamestown, 1850–1920

Jamestown in 1850 was no longer an island of white settlers and enslaved Africans. With freedom, many left but some members of the Black community stayed and continued on as laborers, domestics, and farmers. They would see the island gradually awaken from its rural slumber and attract new residents, Black and white alike. The newcomers of color would merge with those who never left and build a solid foundation for the free Black community. Profiles of several of these pioneers are presented in this chapter.

James Howland (1756–1859): One of the Last Survivors of Rhode Island Slavery

In Jamestown in 1756, an enslaved couple, Great Peter and Cylvy, bore a son named James. Their child's death certificate reveals his parents were born in Africa and therefore were likely captured, transported by ship to Rhode Island, and enslaved.[1] Their son, James, was born in Jamestown and owned by the white Howland family. First as human property and later as a free man, when he chose "Howland" as his last name, James Howland worked for three generations of the Howland family until his death at 103 years of age. Little did Great Peter and Cylvy know their son would live such a long life and enter the annals of Rhode Island history as one of the last survivors of slavery. He endured the indignities of the institution for seven decades and lived his remaining thirty-three years, free. Historical societies, scholars, and newspapers across the nation took note of his passing, which marked the end of an era.

Up to the hour of his death he retained all his faculties unimpaired, and on the night of January 2nd attended to his usual duties about the house. On the morning of the 3rd he arose, dressed himself, and was about to descend the stairs from his chamber, when he fainted and expired in a few moments.[2]

His longevity and earlier life of bondage were likely well-known to the small enclave of island Blacks at the time. Two families were undoubtedly aware: the Champlins, who had lived on the island since the early 1800s, and the Rices, long-term residents whose grandfather was a leader of the Newport Anti-Slavery Society.[3]

The story of James Howland is unique, but his experiences were shared by hundreds of Blacks in Rhode Island history. His life spanned the height of the state's African slave trade and its gradual abolition of slavery. He died sixteen months before a little-known Illinois senator, Abraham Lincoln, was nominated to run for the US presidency, presaging a Civil War that, when won, liberated Mr. Howland's race.[4] His father, Peter, was born in 1725 and likely lived on the Gold Coast of Africa in what is today Ghana. At the age of fifty-two, his father was recorded only once as the human property of "Mr. Howlin" (likely Isaac Howland) in an enumeration of enslaved males of working age

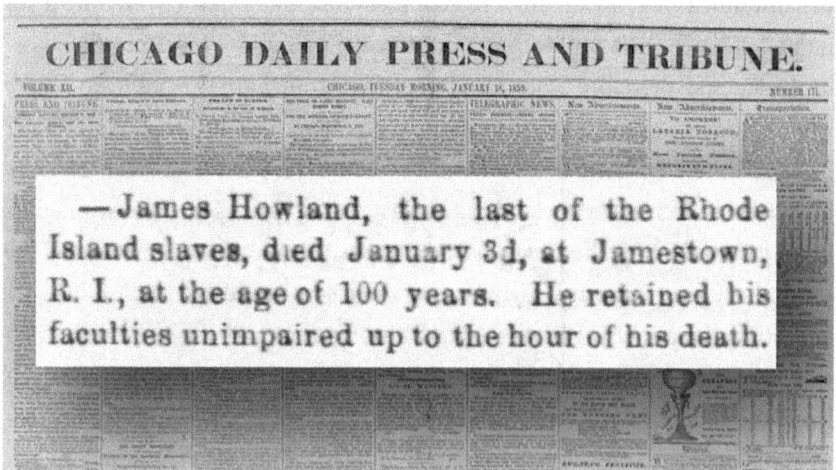

CHICAGO DAILY PRESS AND TRIBUNE.

—James Howland, the last of the Rhode Island slaves, died January 3d, at Jamestown, R. I., at the age of 100 years. He retained his faculties unimpaired up to the hour of his death.

James Howland's death was reported in newspapers across the country. Source: Personal and Political, Chicago Daily Press and Tribune, January 18, 1859.

RETURN OF A DEATH.

State of Rhode Island.

1. Date of Death. — *January 3 A 1859*
2. Name. - - - - *James Howland*
3. Age. - - - - - *100* Years. ✗ Months. ✗ Days. ✗
4. Place of Death. *Jamestown*
5. Street and No.
6. Sex. - - - - - *Male*
7. Color. - - - - *Black*
8. Condition. - - ~~Black~~ *Single*
9. Occupation. - *Laborer*
10. Where Born. ◦ *Jamestown*
11. Father's Name. *Great Peter*
12. Mother's Name. *Dylvy*
13. Parentage. - - Fa. *African* Mo. *African*
14. Where Buried. *Commons Jamestown*

John Howland Informant.

N. B. At No. 8, state whether married or single, widow or widower. At No. 13, state whether parents were American, Irish, French, German, Scotch, &c.

PHYSICIAN'S CERTIFICATE.

Name? ....

Date of Death? ....

Disease? 1. Primary. ....

    " 2. Secondary. ....

....

Physician.

UNDERTAKER'S CERTIFICATE.

I certify that the above is a true return, to the best of my knowledge and belief.

Undertaker.

the last slave of Rhode Island died under the act of 1792.

Death Certificate of James Howland, 1859. Courtesy: Jamestown Historical Society Collections, T2013.501.055.

The location of the James Howland residence at the Howland Farmhouse in Jamestown (marked as X). Source: Daniel Watson Map, 1875 overlaid on Google Earth Map. [Lionel Pincus and Princess Firyal Map Division, "Map of Conanicut Island, opposite Newport, Rhode-Island in Narragansett Bay," New York Public Library, New York, NY, 1875, accessed 3/23/21: https://digitalcollections.nypl.org/items/7c302910-c546-0134 -f338-00505686a51c.]

in Jamestown, made by the British military during the War of Independence in 1777.[5] The other enslaved Howlands listed were Cuff and Quam, whose names in the Akan language of Ghana mark the day they were born: Friday ("Kofi") and Saturday ("Kwame"). This was the only time in the one and one-half centuries of slavery in Jamestown that there was a census of the proper names of those enslaved. Ironically, it was created by the British rather than by the American slaveholders.

James Howland likely lived on the Isaac Howland farm with his parents from his birth in 1756 and then bequeathed as human property to Isaac's son, Daniel Howland. When Daniel died in 1837, Mr. Howland was again passed, this time as a free servant, to the third-generation son, John Howland.[6] He is believed to have gained his freedom between 1820 and 1830, his name appearing for the first time in records at age seventy-eight in his former enslaver's will: "I order the old Black man James to be surported out of my Real Estate as long as he Livs."[7] The phrase, "*the* old Black man," is revealing. Now free, James

Howland could no longer be referred to as "*my* old Black man" which would have denoted possession.

It is not known whether Mr. Howland purchased his freedom or was granted it, but he was first listed a free man at age seventy-five, about a decade before slavery was finally abolished in Rhode Island in 1843. The 1820 Federal Census lists one enslaved male over forty-five years of age owned by Daniel Howland of Jamestown. By 1830, two free Black inhabitants were listed in the Howland household, one between fifty and 100 years of age. This is believed to be James Howland. Later, the 1850 Census identifies Mr. Howland by name as a ninety-four-year-old laborer in the house of Daniel Howland's son, John.[8]

James Howland lived the remainder of his life as a servant at the now demolished John Howland farmhouse near Green Lane and High Street.[9] His death certificate records his burial place as "Commons Jamestown," which is RI Historical Cemetery #JM002 located in the town center on the northeast corner of North Road and Narragansett Avenue. There is no tombstone marking his grave.[10]

14th Rhode Island Colored Heavy Artillery Regiment (1863–5): Black Civil War Troops at Camp Bailey, Dutch Island

The outbreak of the Civil War in 1861 brought dramatic changes to Black life in Rhode Island and America. For the first time since the War of Independence, hundreds of soldiers of color took up arms to serve their country. In Rhode Island, they mustered at their training camp on Dutch Island, a 100-acre island in Narragansett Bay roughly one mile west of the Jamestown shoreline.

At first, the war was fought only by white soldiers, sent into battle against the rebel confederacy. Blacks had been excluded since the discriminatory Militia Acts of 1792.[11] For two years, President Lincoln resisted calls from Frederick Douglass and other abolitionists to allow Blacks to fight, fearing defections of the border slaveholding states to the rebels and thinking the war would soon end. But by 1863 it was clear there was no end in sight. White enthusiasm for the war waned and states could not fill their recruitment quotas. But Black enthusiasm grew as the North refused, in defiance of the Fugitive Slave Act, to return the thousands of enslaved men streaming into Union camps. Their desire to join the Northern cause helped build support for the signing of the Emancipation Proclamation in January 1863, which authorized Blacks in combat roles and ultimately bolstered Union forces by 200,000.

With recruitment open to Blacks, Rhode Island Governor James Youngs Smith requested permission to recruit colored soldiers, noting the state's "historic right to this regiment" having created a Black regiment during the War of Independence.[12] A consequence of the new policy was that Dutch Island became the training camp for an armed Black regiment. While sanctioning colored recruits, Union troops were largely led by white officers. Later some 110 outstanding Black recruits won commands. Far more passed officer exams but were never promoted, such as Quartermaster Sergeant George W. Hamblin of Providence.[13]

When the war erupted, there was popular excitement among people of color in joining the fight against slavery. In 1862, before the Emancipation Proclamation was signed, church members at the Colored Baptist Church in Providence with few exceptions "were in favor of taking up arms, as their grandfathers had done" in the fight for independence. One member avowed, "I should lose my life rather than have the southern confederacy rule over me."[14] They assembled again the day the Emancipation Proclamation was expected. In his autobiography, Black community leader William Brown wrote:

> . . . the hall was packed, and at the hour of nine, when the bell was tolling, a man rushed into the room with a telegram from the President that the proclamation was issued. No one that was at that meeting can ever forget the sensation it produced . . . our prayers were heard and our country was free.[15]

In the summer of 1863, a battalion of four companies was commissioned in Providence and soon recruiting facilities at Camp Smith on the western outskirts of the city were overwhelmed with volunteers. Disturbances between whites and armed Black troops in the city and worries about white reactions like those in the New York draft riots led the governor to post heavily armed guards at the Camp.[16] In September, the Black unit was moved to the larger isolated facilities of Camp Bailey on Dutch Island.[17] There, they built earthworks to defend Narragansett Bay from Confederate vessels reported offshore.

Word of Black recruitment spread across the country and two more Rhode Island battalions were raised, mostly from residents of twenty-three other states, constituting a regiment of twelve companies of Black and brown soldiers.[18] The 14th Rhode Island Heavy Artillery Regiment (Colored) would eventually total 1,703 Black and Native Americans including 679 from Rhode Island.[19]

On November 19, 1863, the day President Lincoln delivered the Gettysburg Address, Rhode Island Governor Smith, accompanied by members of the State Legislature and invited guests, traveled to Dutch Island, reviewed the troops, presented their stand of colors, and proclaimed:

> It affords me much pleasure to present to your regiment, our Fourteenth Corps d'Afrique, this flag, and I feel confident that it will be entrusted to as brave men as ever enter the service in our defense of our country and its liberties.[20]

A white officer, Colonel Nelson Viall, on behalf of his command accepted the flag. Remarks by Rhode Island senator Henry B. Anthony and Brown University president, Reverend Dr. Barnas Sears, followed. Finally, the regiment wheeled into column and marched in review before the governor.

The only known photograph of a 14th Regiment soldier is that of John N. Sharper, a twenty-two-year-old printer's apprentice from Herkimer, New York. The eldest son of a family of five, he traveled to Providence in October 1863 to volunteer for the 14th Regiment, Company G and trained at Dutch Island until leaving for the South. He served as a printer for the military post.[21] While serving, he became ill and was discharged in September 1865 with tuberculosis, which the army declared a preexisting condition. He died within the next year.

In December, the first battalion left Dutch Island for Texas and in January another to New Orleans. Then in January, upon the anniversary of the Emancipation Proclamation, the 14th Regiment troops "showed their appreciation of the efforts made by President Lincoln to free the oppressed, by celebrating New Year's Day with addresses, singing and prayer."[22] In February, when the US transport *Daniel Webster* traveled to Dutch Island to collect the third battalion, smallpox broke out and delayed its departure for Camp Parapet, New Orleans until April. Despite a quarantine, Jamestown residents

Only known photograph of a 14th Rhode Island Regiment soldier. John N. Sharper arrived in 1863 and trained at Camp Bailey on Dutch Island. Courtesy: Library of Congress (https://www.loc.gov/item/2010647911/).

In foreground, the graves of soldiers of the 14th Rhode Island Heavy Artillery Regiment (Colored) at Dutch Island; later moved to Long Island, New York. Courtesy: Jamestown Historical Society Collections, P1973.050.

were terrified—"alarmed lest the waters of the Narragansett convey contagion to the hearths and homes."[23] There was no such contagion. Just two soldiers succumbed to smallpox.[24] Sadly, the more common respiratory diseases such as measles, pneumonia, and tuberculosis took eleven lives.[25] Cramped quarters and unhealthy winter conditions worsened their plight.[26] Sixteen soldiers in all died and were buried on Dutch Island. A greater number deserted the camp and the military altogether. More deaths would await the soldiers at their destinations in Texas and Louisiana swamps. Of the entire regiment, 438 died of disease or were discharged as invalids. Eighty deserted, although this rate was far lower than for white troops.[27]

The Black men who died while training on Dutch Island and were buried there include: William Betson, twenty-two years of age, a farmer from Prince George, Maryland; Dennis Carroll from Washington, DC, "where he was very respectfully connected"; Frederick C. Grames, a farmer from Poughkeepsie, New York, "buried with military honors"; Joseph H. Whitfield, a waiter from Buffalo, New York; and Lemuel H. Smith of Windsor, Connecticut, father of three boys and one girl.[28]

Compounding the health problems at Dutch Island was a massive financial swindle. Recruiting agents skimmed bounties that were due Black soldiers for joining the regiment, often paying them $50 while pocketing the remaining $250 to $300 and promising the soldiers they would be paid later. The *Providence Journal* reported the findings of a House of Representatives investigation on "How the colored soldiers were robbed of their bounty." It reported "$127,835.76 of the State's Money [was] Paid to one Recruiting Agent for the 14th Regiment."[29] The equivalent of that value today is $2,118,607.[30] The 428-page report included depositions of the Black soldiers who were swindled. Some, like Samuel McGowan, a private of Company M of the 14th Regiment, were formerly enslaved southern Blacks. He reported:

> I certify that I was enlisted in Providence by Major Engley . . . and was promised a bounty of $350 . . . Of my first installment, I only received $50. I received none of my last installment. I was brought up in South Carolina and was a slave before the war.[31]

After leaving Dutch Island, further turmoil, protests, and courts-martial ensued when the soldiers found that promises of pay equal to that of the white soldiers were not honored. In March 1864, Companies A, C, and D refused to accept their pay—three dollars a month less than the white troops—resulting in their arrest.[32] Some suffered severe penalties of up to one year imprisonment with hard labor for what other commanders called a minor technical violation.[33]

The 14th Regiment established its own newspaper, *The Black Warrior*, under the motto "Freedom to all. Death to Copperheads and Traitors." Its first issue was published at Camp Parapet, Louisiana in May 1864 by Sergeant George W. Hamblin, who published the first Black newspaper in Providence before joining the war.[34]

That spring the regiment was transferred to the Department of the Gulf,[35] changing its designation to the 8th US Heavy Artillery (Colored) and then to the 11th US Heavy Artillery (Colored) Regiment.

After the war, the 11th US Heavy Artillery (Colored) Regiment mustered out of service in October 1865 at Camp Parapet, Louisiana and sailed aboard the steamer *North Star* for New York. They then sailed via the steamer *Doris* to Providence where they were met with parades, cheers, and celebration.[36] In total, 200,000 Black soldiers enlisted in the Union Army and Navy nationwide. Nearly 40,000 died during the war, mostly of disease.[37]

The Black Warrior, official newspaper of the 14th Rhode Island Heavy Artillery Regiment (Colored), Camp Parapet, New Orleans, La., Vol. 1, No. 1, May 17, 1864. Courtesy: Wisconsin Historical Society Collections, Pamphlet Collection, 01-4180.

Hannah Elizabeth Champlin (1855–1925): Lifelong Resident, First Black Family Farm, Extensive Native American Lineage

A century ago, an elderly woman of seventy years of age passed away quietly at her home on North Road in Jamestown.[38] Hannah Elizabeth Champlin was the last in a long line of Champlins of African and Native American descent.[39] According to news accounts, she was remembered as having "a very reserved nature and never went to Newport without [her employer Mistress Carr] and had few callers."[40] She was laid to rest on the land comprising her family's farm which would later become Cedar Cemetery, the official burial ground for many islanders, Black and white, to the present day.

Hannah Champlin was born in 1855 into a nation on the precipice of war over slavery and would be a witness to the crisis. At age eight, she would see segregated troops preparing for war, 1,000 white cavalrymen quartered in the town center and over 1,700 Black artillerymen on Dutch Island.

Ms. Champlin was born free, but her understanding of slavery would be informed by the presence of James Howland, one of fourteen island residents of color who earlier in his life was enslaved. Moreover, her mother and grandmother, named Hannah like her, descended from the Black and Native American Weedens who, generations earlier, had been enslaved on the white Weeden Farm only a short walk from her home.[41]

Hannah Champlin's close-knit family on her father's side can be traced back two generations to her grandparents, John Henry and Hannah Brown Champlin.[42] Her grandfather—John Henry Champlin—moved to the island and first appeared in the 1810 census when he was counted as the head of a family of four living there.[43] He was a free man who likely labored on island farms like the Thomas Hazard farm, alongside other laborers who were still enslaved.[44] Since he was not born in Jamestown, he was twice "warned out" by the town council, afraid they might become obligated to support him, but he either returned or never left.[45] The town later dropped the order perhaps because his labor was critical to the local farmers. Ms. Champlin's paternal grandmother, Hannah Brown Champlin, worked as a free laborer for the Borden Watson farm and the John Carr farm throughout the early 1820s, performing household chores including whitewashing walls for 30 cents a day.[46]

John and Hannah Champlin had two sons. The first—Hannah Champlin's father, George W. Champlin—was born in Jamestown in 1809. When he died in 1890, at age eighty-one, the local newspaper reported "the oldest colored citizen of the island, was found dead in his bed by a member of his family. He had been in poor health for some time, but his death was unexpected."[47] Their second child—Hannah Champlin's uncle, John Henry Champlin Jr.— was a sailor when young. He later worked as a farm laborer and servant at the Hazard Farm in Jamestown for the remainder of his life. He died in 1876 and is buried next to the Champlin family gravestone.[48]

Throughout the nineteenth century, the Champlins lived on the north end of the island on Eldred Avenue. When Hannah Champlin was three, her mother passed away, leaving her husband, daughter, and four sons who worked on the

Champlin family farm and home in Jamestown, 1874–1913, precursor of today's Cedar Cemetery.

surrounding farms of George W. Carr, Arnold and Jeremiah Hazard, John and Edward Hammond, and Thomas Carr Watson.

Hannah Champlin never married. There is no record of her attending school. From the time she was a teenager until her death, she worked as a domestic for white families.[49] In a rural society where slavery existed only one or two generations earlier, occupations for women of color were often limited to domestic service. Their choice of employers was also limited. At age twenty,

Ms. Champlin labored as a servant at the neighboring Edward Hammond Farm in 1875 and the adjacent Thomas Arnold Hazard Tefft farm in 1900.[50] She later worked as a domestic for the John Carr family for over twenty years.

In 1872, the Champlin family achieved some financial independence when brother Alexander purchased farmland on Eldred Avenue and established a homestead for the extended family. The purchase was a milestone event, a first for Blacks in Jamestown. The seven-acre property was purchased from Walter Watson in 1872–3 for $290, the equivalent of about $6,300 today.[51] The next year, brother William Champlin purchased an adjoining plot of 3–1/3 acres, expanding the family farmstead to 10–1/2 acres.[52] The property remained in the Champlin name for four decades until sold in 1913 to create most of what today comprises Cedar Cemetery.[53] The farm afforded the family needed staples and perhaps extra income. In 1880, it produced 20 bushels each of Indian corn, potatoes, and oats.[54] One milk cow produced 90 pounds of butter. Their chickens laid 160 dozen eggs. Maintaining the farm was likely backbreaking work, but the family made full use of their land while also working on other farms. For a time, they leased five acres to a Black neighbor, Isaac Rice Jr.[55]

In this period, males were afforded the right to vote if they owned land. According to town records, Hannah Champlin's brothers George, Alexander, and William voted in 1883. George and Alexander Champlin also voted in 1885. They were the only Blacks on the town's eligible voters lists in 1883 and 1885.[56] This marked the first known time in Jamestown history that Blacks voted in local elections.[57]

Hannah Champlin's siblings began passing away in the early 1900s, leaving her as the last surviving family member. According to local newspapers, in 1901, her forty-nine-year-old brother Alexander Champlin, a "well-known colored resident of the island," after working his entire life as a farm laborer, was "at work for Mr. E. N. Hammond and complained of not feeling well and went home," then expired.[58] Her brother Charles Champlin died at age forty-four in 1902 of typhoid fever.[59] Brother George Champlin died in 1903 at age fifty-six after having "lived in Jamestown practically all his life, and was a farm laborer, being well known among the farmers on the island."[60] Like their sister, the brothers never married.[61]

Her immediate family was now gone. The small Black community of a dozen locals that Hannah Champlin had known since childhood increased to 116, now mostly couples, families, widowers, and singles from the South, seeking better lives. With this critical mass came two Black churches and a broader sense of community. Though described by her employer as "reserved and reclusive," Ms. Champlin likely interacted with the community of color and with members of her extensive network of family connections with deep ancestral roots descending from generations of Champlins and Weedens in Jamestown and southern Rhode Island.

The depths of Hannah Champlin's local ancestral roots were only learned after her death in 1925. She had saved her earnings and proceeds from selling her family farm and because there was no will and no known living family members, the executrix of the estate (her former employer, Caroline A. Carr) awarded the proceeds to a small number of Champlin relatives. The executrix excluded all Weedens, the maternal relatives.

Strongly asserting their familial ties, the Weedens objected and appealed to the state probate court, which opened an inquiry seeking to identify all relatives. Newspapers reported a flood of witnesses attesting to their ties to the Champlin family. "The heirs were so numerous that [estate] shares are as small as one hundred and sixty seconds," the news reported.[62] Champlin second cousins traveled from across the state and the Narragansett Indian Weedens on the maternal side arrived to assert their familial ties. One John S. Weeden claimed to be the closest relative and recounted the family history of York Weeden and London Weeden, who had been enslaved in Jamestown and manumitted in the 1786 will of their owner Daniel Weeden.[63] The court agreed, finding John Weeden was in fact Hannah Champlin's nephew.[64] Court hearings on Hannah Champlin's estate stretched across years with family witnesses arriving "from Peacedale to Pittsburgh" and from far-flung ports across the eastern seaboard.

In the end, the court concluded all parties were in fact related though often no written proof existed other than the detailed memories of the family members.[65] The recognition and rights of the Weeden descendants, like the Champlins, were won in a state court which only a century earlier did not recognize the rights of colored and Indigenous peoples.

Family gravestones: John H. Champlin Jr. (foreground right); George W. Champlin, his wife and children (background). Cedar Cemetery, Jamestown. Photograph: Peter Fay.

The family gravestones stand on the boundary of what was the original Champlin Farm of 1872, now Cedar Cemetery. They are permanent reminders of the Champlin family's existence.

Frank Horton Clarke Rice (1869–1937) and Olivia Johns Rice (1880–1973): Descendants of Civil Rights Champions; Landowners; Island Matriarch

Frank and Olivia Rice were well-known in Jamestown, having for decades been the caretakers of Ledgehurst, an estate at 89 Walcott Avenue and the summer home of Daniel Lyman Hazard of Newport.[66] The Rices lived in a cottage on the estate with their children, Lois, Olivia, Ethel, and Viola.[67]

Frank H. C. Rice of Jamestown. [1869–1937]. Courtesy: ancestrylibrary.com/family
-tree/person/tree/1527295/person/1283095380.

Frank H. C. Rice was born in 1869 in Wakefield, Rhode Island to a Black
father, Isaac Rice Jr., and an American Indian mother, Hannah Noka of the
Narragansett. The family moved to Jamestown when he was a child. His brother,
Fred Rice, one of his five brothers and two sisters, attended school on the
island.[68] By age eighteen, Frank Rice worked as a laborer while his father farmed
five acres in town.[69] At age twenty-two he married into a prominent Maryland
family, wedding Cornelia Johns in 1891. Her father, Reverend Reading B. Johns,
was minister of the Harlem Presbyterian Church in New York City and one
of the first graduates of historically Black Lincoln University.[70] Cornelia Rice's
brother, Paul Johns, was a graduate of Howard and Yale universities.[71]

After marriage, Frank and Cornelia Rice moved to Newport where for two
decades he worked as a coachman, likely for the Daniel Hazard family.[72] They
had three girls in succession.[73] Sadly, after her third child, Cornelia Rice died
from tuberculosis. In 1910, Frank Rice married Olivia Johns, the sister of his
deceased wife, a common practice at the time.[74] Continuing his employment

with the Hazard family, he returned to Jamestown in 1915. The couple had two daughters and moved into the Hazard's caretaker house on Walcott Avenue.[75]

In 1922 at age fifty-three, Frank Rice was appointed to the office of special policeman by the Jamestown Town Council, a post he held for about a decade.[76] For his last forty-four years he was employed by the Hazard family until his death in 1937 at age sixty-eight. He is buried at Cedar Cemetery.[77]

His second wife, Olivia Johns Rice, was born in Cleveland, Ohio, in 1880. She is remembered as a businesswoman and matriarch to the Black community. In 1920, she was one of the first women of color to register and vote in Jamestown

Olivia Johns Rice of Jamestown [1880–1973]. Courtesy: Rhode Island Black Heritage Society.

after the passage and ratification of the 19th Amendment.[78] She purchased two properties while married: a lot on the corner of Columbia and High Streets in 1925 and, in 1932, a 16-acre farm on the north end of the island, purchased with her brother on Rosemary Lane off North Road. From the farm, Mrs. Rice ran a successful poultry business.[79]

Throughout her long tenure, Olivia Rice welcomed and hosted new generations of Blacks to Jamestown at the Rosemary Lane farmhouse, which still stands. One such encounter is remembered from the early 1960s:

> Mrs. [Elizabeth] Hodge invited me to Olivia's. We went up [the] Dump Road and turned onto a side dirt road. [Mrs. Rice] was elderly. She showed us around, we had a snack, and she was very friendly. She welcomed me [and my family] to the island. There were chickens and we could see the water from her porch. She talked . . . about the old days, when most of the colored people came with the whites, just for the summer.[80]

Olivia Rice died in 1973 at the age of ninety-three. She is buried at Cedar Cemetery with her husband.

Olivia Johns Rice farmhouse on Rosemary Lane in Jamestown. Photograph: Valerie J. Southern, 2020.

The Rice family represents a celebrated lineage noted for their advancement of civil rights, fight against slavery, and advocacy for equal education. In 1977, a *Newport Mercury* article described the Rices of Jamestown as "a black family with roots in Rhode Island before the American Revolution, which held strong beliefs in self-employment and recognized the need for education."[81]

Frank H. C. Rice's father, Isaac Rice Jr., enlisted in the Civil War Navy to aid the fight against slavery. He joined in Philadelphia in 1862 as a steward and later as a seaman on the Navy vessels *Princeton* and *St. Louis*. He was discharged in 1863 and married Hannah Noka of the Narragansett in 1879.[82] They settled in Jamestown and tilled a five-acre tenant farm which in 1880 yielded 40 bushels of corn and oats, 20 bushels of potatoes, and 90 pounds of butter. Their twenty chickens provided fresh eggs for the family.[83] Isaac Rice Jr. also worked as a carpenter for extra income. Within a few years, his sons Frank H. C. and Frederick were teenagers, also working as laborers.[84] He died in Newport at the age of seventy-one in 1902 and is buried at the Common Burial Ground.[85]

Frank H. C. Rice's grandfather, Isaac Rice Sr. was born free in 1794 in Narragansett, Rhode Island and married Sarah Ann Connor of New York, fathering seven children.[86] He was an abolitionist and the leader of the African Benevolent Society in Newport which in 1807 replaced the Free African Union Society, the first Black mutual aid society in America. As secretary in 1824, he purchased land for a church and school building for the society. The congregation, originally called the Colored Union Church, survived 139 years until it disbanded in 1963.

The Compromise of 1850, with its Fugitive Slave Law, made harboring and aiding enslaved persons a crime punishable with a $1,000 fine and six-month jail sentence.[87] Freedom seekers nonetheless found food and shelter in Isaac Rice Sr.'s Newport home, said to be a stop on the Underground Railroad.[88] The house at 23 Thomas Street is still owned by the family.[89] He frequently hosted renowned abolitionist and friend Frederick Douglass there in the 1840s. In the 1850s, his church urged defiance of the Fugitive Slave Act and he fought for decades for equal education legislation. By 1859, he was elected vice president of the New England Convention of Colored Citizens which petitioned "the oppressors of our countrymen let the oppressed go free."[90] Isaac Rice Sr. was also a well-known caterer and owner of the Alhambra restaurant in Newport.[91]

```
                        Newport, R. I.,  May 31st.1899.
            Central Baptist Church.
            Jamestown R I.
Dear Bretheren.
In behalf of a large number of my people who are baptists
and spend the season in your town as servants, I renew my
appeal to you again this season for the use of your house of
worship,  for these brotheren. You know the larger portion
of them are waiters and their work is of such that they can-
not get to the meetings at the hours that you have service.
You will remember 10 years ago you first granted us the use
of your h ouse of worship to hold meetings for the benifit
of your help,    I then organized a mission known as the
Shiloh Centralmission of Jamestown ,ever since then you have
been  kind hearted and allowed us to have services Sundays
during the season from 4 to 5 PM.and one evening in the week.
We have been careful in the use of your church.
       Part of the collection we have given you for the use
of your church.We hope that you will continue to let us have
use of the church.In addition to the hours mentioned we would
like to have Sunday    evenings
At the close of your ev ning meetings  for you will be through
by the time our people get through their work and ready for
church. We would like to have about one hour for service in
the evenings.
            Yours In Christian Fellowship
                  H. N. Jeter   Pastor of Shiloh
                  Baptist Church, NewportR. I.,
```

Rev. H. N. Jeter 1899 letter to Jamestown Central Baptist Church requests use of church building by Shiloh Baptist Mission. Courtesy: Jamestown Historical Society Collections, A2018.1704.011.

Colored Baptist Church (1889–1945) and Mount Zion African Methodist Episcopal (AME) Church (1896–1988): Sacred Ground for the Black Community

The church was central to the Jamestown Black community for over 100 years and provided a sacred place for its religious, political, and social expressions. Several Black families were drawn to and purchased homes around the church. Community fairs, dances, recitals, concerts, and rallies were held on its grounds. Pastors, orators, and guest dignitaries spoke under its roof.

Jamestown Colored Baptist Church

The Shiloh Baptist Central Mission was first organized in Jamestown in 1889 by Rev. Henry N. Jeter, D. D.[92] It was an outgrowth of Newport's African American Shiloh Baptist Church organized in 1864. Beginning in 1889, Rev. Jeter led services every Sunday afternoon during the summer using the facilities of the Central Baptist Church.[93] Rev. Jeter explained the name Shiloh Baptist Central Mission was taken from the Shiloh Baptist Church in Newport and the white Central Baptist in Jamestown and provided benefit for "many of our Baptist people who work there in the families and hotels" during the summer. He reported the church often had "a larger congregation on the island of Jamestown than we had here" in Newport.[94] In a letter of 1899 to the Jamestown church renewing a request to use the church during the summer, Rev. Jeter notes, "a large number of my people who are Baptists spend the season in your town as servants."[95] Fifteen years later, the Central Baptist Church declared in its by-laws that "membership shall be composed of persons of both sexes and any nationality or race," although some Blacks had already joined the church as early as 1888.

At the turn of the century, the Jamestown Town Council permitted the church to meet in the Town Hall for almost two decades.[96] The Colored Baptists reported holding services there during the summer, meeting as "Shiloh Central Mission," led by Joseph Dunn, a graduate of the Gordon Mission School in Boston. "We feel under many obligations to the Town Council who so kindly let us use the hall," they noted.[97] Reverend Dunn and Anna B. Dunn purchased two lots on Pemberton Avenue and North Road, settling in a home one block from the site of the Baptist services.[98]

In 1920 the church met under the name "Jamestown Colored Baptist Church" at 10 Cole Street, home of the AME Zion Church.[99] By 1945, it was meeting as the "Negro Fellowship" at the Central Baptist Church again.[100]

Mount Zion AME Church

In July 1896, a certificate was filed with the Office of the Rhode Island Secretary of State for incorporation of the Mount Zion African Methodist Episcopal (AME) Church in Jamestown. The incorporation was filed by William H. and

Mt. Zion AME Church, 10 Cole Street, Jamestown. Courtesy: Jamestown Historical Society Collections, P1968.146.

Harriet Holliday, Mary Cox, Isaiah Burton, and Herminta Wilson.[101] The same year, Mr. Holliday purchased a lot at 10 Cole Street for the church.[102] For nearly a century, the Mount Zion AME Church was the welcoming religious home for the free Black community. It was most active in spring and summer when a great number of service and domestic workers arrived in the peak tourist season. Prior to 1896, there was the unincorporated Zion AME Mission which held services in the afternoon and evenings as early as 1895.[103] At the church, Rev. William H. Thomas was deacon, a graduate of historically Black Lincoln University where he earned his Doctorate of Divinity.[104] In 1896, visiting speaker Rev. J. E. Harper of Lincoln University preached at the AME Zion Mission.[105] Visiting speakers were common for the AME denomination. The same year, for example, the namesake of the Jamestown church, the AME Zion Church in Providence, hosted renowned abolitionist Harriet Tubman.[106]

With its incorporation filed and lot purchased in 1896, the Jamestown Mount Zion AME Church building replaced the AME mission as the place of

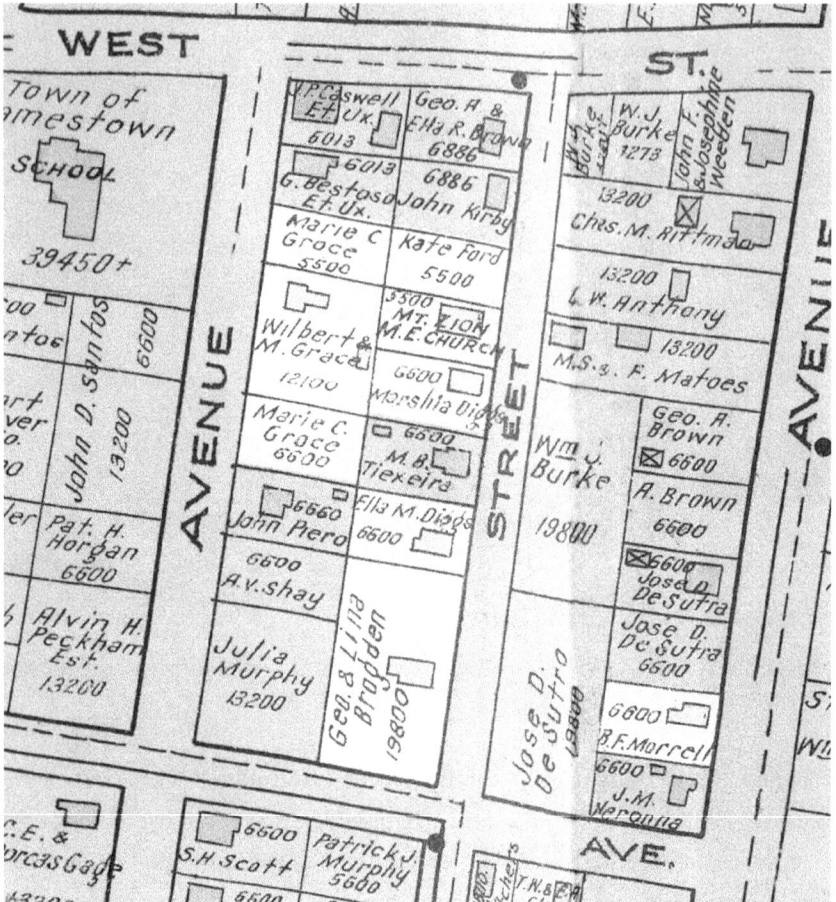

Several Black-owned properties (highlighted) were located near and around the Jamestown Mt. Zion AME Church at 10 Cole Street. Source: Sanborn Fire Insurance Map, 1921.

worship. It had been built in 1868 on Four Corners as a white Baptist Church, then sold in 1889 to a white family, moved to Cole Street, and later sold to the AME pastor.[107] The structure was a plain white meeting house of one and one-half stories with a gable end. The central entry had a molded cap in a three-bay facade and near the front, a small square belfry. After nearly 100 years of service, it officially closed in 1988. Its structure stands today as a private residence.[108]

Mt. Zion AME Church building today as a private island residence. Photograph: Valerie J. Southern, 2023.

There were strong ties between the Newport and Jamestown AME churches. In 1905, the Newport AME arranged to bring performers to the Jamestown AME for a concert. On July 12th, "under the management of D. Ernest Gibbons," there were piano solos, vocals, readings, and a "graphaphone" played. "It was well attended, the little church being filled. All who attended reported that they were well pleased," reported the *New York Age*. The party had chartered launches from the Champlin & Sons ferry service in Newport, returning home at 12:35 am.[109] Again, in August, the choir from Newport AME sang in Jamestown "at a grand rally at the church."[110]

Typical Sundays were spent in Sunday School in the early afternoon and in the chapel where there was "a large attendance, both in the afternoon and evening."[111] In 1906, the Jamestown Mount Zion AME hosted a fair with speakers such as Attorney J. L. Mitchell on Richard Allen, the national founder of the AME Church who had been enslaved. Joyous open-air dances were scheduled "every Tuesday and Friday for the young ladies and Gentlemen who visit that place during the hotel season."[112]

Benjamin F. Morrell (1847–1930) and Lucy J. Morrell (1868–1932): Army Officer; Educator; Civil Rights Advocates; Proprietors

Born enslaved in Madison County, Kentucky, in 1847, Benjamin F. Morrell lived a notable life, overcoming human bondage, rising through the US Army during the American Indian Wars to the highest enlisted rank of Sergeant Major, and retiring with Mrs. Lucy Morrell in Jamestown to create a hospitality business for distinguished Black patrons.[113]

In his formative years, Mr. Morrell lived enslaved with his family on the Caldwell Campbell plantation southwest of Richmond, Kentucky.[114] His parents Sarah and Benjamin Moran, brother George, and half-sister Easter Miller labored with thirty-three other enslaved persons on the 1,800-acre plantation.[115] The land was said to be "the best . . . in Central Kentucky" and valued at $160,000, the equivalent of $3 million today.[116]

According to his sister, when Benjamin Morrell left the plantation, he eschewed his slave name (Moran) and chose Morrell. He did not return to the plantation for thirty years. Two years after the Civil War in which Kentucky was contested between the North and South, he enlisted in the US Army in 1867 along with 15,000 fellow Black Kentuckians.[117] He spent the next five years in the 9th Cavalry distinguishing himself as an accomplished marksman

Sergeant Major Benjamin F. Morrell of Jamestown [1847–1930]. Source: *Pastor Henry N. Jeters' Twenty-five Year Experience*, 1901.

and as a Buffalo Soldier engaged in the nation's brutal wars against the Comanche and Apache peoples in the Southwest. In an interview later in life, he said he witnessed "the most beautiful maneuvers that could be performed" on horseback by the Comanche and their "greatest exhibitions of stoicism." He sought a transfer from the cavalry, saying, "I had enough of it" and joined the 25th Infantry, re-enlisting six times.[118] By 1878, records of his military unit document that he was ranked the best marksman in his company and eighth among the hundreds in his regiment.[119]

It is not known where or when he was educated, but Sergeant Morrell's exceptional literacy landed him a position teaching officers' children.[120] He recalled:

> I had an average attendance of about thirty-five children [. . . some of whom became] commissioned officers in the regular army. I was the first colored man to teach a white school in Texas, and never heard of any other instance of the kind in the United States.[121]

Sergeant Morrell recounted that by 1885, "I received my promotion May 27 of that year, being the first colored man ever appointed ordnance sergeant in the United States Army."[122] Transferring to Fort Meade, Dakota Territory, he was appointed speaker at the town's Emancipation Day celebration in 1882, reciting the Emancipation Proclamation to a crowd of 2,000.[123]

In 1886, Sergeant Morrell transferred to Rhode Island from Fort Yates, Dakota Territory to Fort Bailey, Dutch Island, just west of Jamestown. There he

Morrell cottage home, 60 Clarke and High Street, Jamestown. Photograph: Peter Fay, 2021.

lived on the same island and training ground occupied by the 14th RI Heavy Artillery Regiment (Colored) during the Civil War just decades earlier. He likely visited the graves of the sixteen Black soldiers still buried there, having died of disease in 1864. He served as the sole soldier of the garrison on Dutch Island in charge of unused armaments and lived there with his first wife Nannie A. Morrell, born in 1848 in North Carolina.[124] They occupied a cottage atop the island, "high among the upland trees and the grassy fortifications."[125] Historians concluded that the other structures were vacant by then, such as "a mess house, a blacksmith shop, a carpenter shop, two barracks, and former officers' quarters."[126] In one dramatic event, while rowing ashore in a December ice storm, Sergeant Morrell's boat became trapped by ice and unable to move. He remained stranded in Narragansett Bay for three hours before help finally arrived.[127]

When the Morrells settled in Jamestown in 1888, they purchased two lots on Clarke and High Streets. They built a cottage home there and later adopted a son, Frederick G. M. (White) Morrell.[128] After his first wife died, Sergeant Morrell married Lucy Johnson Giles of Virginia, twenty-one years his junior, in 1906.[129] Ms. Giles was active in the Women's Clubs in Newport and attended the Rhode Island Union of Women's Clubs convention in 1906.[130] She was financially secure, owning properties at 3 Elm and 66 and 68 John streets in Newport, purchased before her marriage. At that time, the properties were valued at $4,000. In 2024, they were appraised at $1.1 million and $1.7 million.[131] They produced rental income for her before and after her marriage.[132] In addition, Ms. Giles was bequeathed a large sum of $2,000 upon the death of her employer, Newport millionaire Frances Hoyt, having served her as a "lady's maid" for eleven years.[133]

The newly married Morrells merged their real estate holdings then expanded them with purchases on Pleasant View and Howland Avenue. Their holdings now totaled seven dwellings in Jamestown and Newport with a value of $6,577.[134] In 2024, the 60 Clarke Street home still stands and is assessed at $656,000.[135]

With property holdings now established, Lucy Morrell launched a successful vacation resort business in Jamestown called the "West View Cottage." Every summer for at least a decade she advertised to Black vacationers in the African

1908 Advertisement, Morrell West View Cottage, Jamestown. Source: *New York Age.*

American newspaper *New York Age,* offering "weekly hops, tennis, croquet, swings, private bath houses," "all comforts of a refined home," and "ferry to Newport and Narragansett Pier . . . every half hour."[136]

The "hops" or dances were a common form of entertainment at the Jamestown hotels in the early 1900s and often featured Black musicians and performances.[137] The New York Black society pages reported the "refined patronage" and "society people" visiting the Morrell cottage with guests including Dr. S. E. Courtney, a Harvard-trained physician and a founder of the National Negro Business League; William H. Lewis, a Harvard-educated US Attorney in Boston and later Assistant Attorney General appointed by President Taft; and one of the foremost Black leaders of the time and founder of the Tuskegee Institute, Booker T. Washington, reputed to be Lucy Morrell's relative.[138]

Benjamin Morrell was active politically in Jamestown as a member of the Republican Town Committee. At times he occupied the speaker's platform at political rallies.[139] He served on town committees overseeing taxes, roads, and the fire department. He performed jury duty, administered estates, and contracted with the town to supply lighting.[140] The respect for Mr. Morrell was evidenced by an American Legion meeting honoring him, at age eighty-two, as guest of honor.[141]

Town leaders, however, espoused views that likely contradicted his own beliefs and experiences. Dr. Lincoln Bates, a revered community leader and descendant of the Carr family which had enslaved Blacks just over a century earlier, wrote for the Jamestown Historical Society:

> The owners of slaves in Newport, as a general thing, were indulgent masters, so much so that the blacks were not conscious of being in bondage but were treated with every mark of kindness befitting their station.[142]

Mr. Morrell, having been enslaved and having lived through the Civil War, would hardly have agreed with this view or, further, Bates' statement that Newporters were honorable to "never join in a crusade against the South," nor interfere in "the institutions of the South [i.e., slavery]" which "was a matter which belonged exclusively to themselves."

Sergeant Morrell was deeply committed to racial justice in a time of Jim Crow segregation and lynchings. In 1895 and 1896, he penned letters to the *Richmond Planet* and sent contributions in the defense of three Black women he felt unjustly accused of murder in Lunenburg County, Virginia.[143] He decried the handling of the "innocent colored women . . . so cruelly and maliciously treated by a court of so-called Justice in Virginia." His contributions to their defense were $2.50 and $2.25, respectively, including $1.00 from Mrs. Morrell and $0.25 from son, Frederick.[144]

Sergeant Morrell often published letters in the Black press in New York, congratulating, for example, Fred R. Moore, editor and publisher of *New York Age* and a founder of the National Urban League, for "the good work that you have been doing in . . . Harlem in particular . . . wresting of political control from . . . white politicians and establishing colored leadership . . ."[145]

In 1928, as a member of the National Association for the Advancement of Colored People (NAACP), he paid $20 for a gift subscription to *The Crisis* magazine for the Jamestown Public Library. He wrote to the editor, "I would like to have people here . . . know more about the NAACP and what it is doing all over the country." Scholar and founder of the NAACP, W. E. B. Du Bois, replied, "I am glad of your interest. Perhaps you could send us names of persons white and colored who might subscribe . . ."[146]

For over a decade the Morrells lived in both Newport and Jamestown, perhaps to manage their properties in both towns and also to spend time with

Letter from W. E. B. Du Bois to Benjamin F. Morrell, 1928. Courtesy: University of Massachusetts Special Collections.

Mr. Morrell's half-brother, Gabriel B. Miller, who resided in the Morrell's Elm Street property. The two men had come a long way from their birthplace on the slave plantation in Kentucky. Gabriel B. Miller had married Louise van Horne, sister of Dr. M. Alonzo van Horne, the first dentist of color in Rhode Island and founder of the Newport NAACP.[147]

Having lived a long and storied life, Sergeant Major Benjamin F. Morrell died in Newport on February 8, 1930, at the age of eighty-nine when returning from visiting his wife in the hospital. Lucy Morrell died two years later in 1932 in Roxbury, Massachusetts.[148] In a *Newport Mercury* obituary, Sergeant Major Morrell was remembered as a "Retired Army Man, Outstanding Type of Negro Soldier." He was buried in Cedar Cemetery with military honors which included "a squad from Fort Adams firing a volley over the grave and a bugler blowing taps."[149] When news of his death reached New York City, the *New York Age* noted the loss and reported pall bearers for the funeral service included Dr. M. Alonzo Van Horne.

William H. Netter Sr. (1865–1938) and Mary F. Netter (1868–1928): Close-Knit Extended Family; Property Owners; Business Entrepreneurs

The Netter family of Jamestown was emblematic of the generation of Black southerners who migrated to the Newport area after the Civil War, following opportunities in the growing tourist economy. William and Mary Netter left their Maryland birthplace and built a new life and an extended family in Jamestown, eventually putting down roots across four generations. Their children Sherwood, Edith, Marie, and William Jr. were raised in their downtown Jamestown home that grew even fuller with the arrival of Mary Netter's mother and grandchildren. They resided for decades on the island, purchased land, established businesses, and voted in elections.

Likely Ella Netter, wife of William Netter Jr., with sons William D. Jr. and Shelly. Circa 1924. Courtesy: Jamestown Historical Society Collections, P2009.001.001.

William H. Netter Sr. was born in 1860 in Maryland, a year before the Civil War. He left Baltimore after the war, arriving in Newport in the 1870s as a laborer.[150] Hundreds like him were recruited from the former slave states of Maryland and Virginia by Newport intelligence offices, which filled the demand for labor in the area's booming economy. Some of these offices were owned by colored persons, drawing on their contacts in the South.[151] By 1885, Mr. Netter was employed as a hostler, managing horses at Hayward's Livery on State Street in Newport. Hayward's Livery boasted, "elegant single and double turnouts to let with experienced and careful drivers" and "Ladies and Gentlemen's saddle horses."[152] Mr. Netter's vocation in transportation placed him in a role vital to area commerce. His family would continue in this business for three generations, driving horse-drawn carriages and later motorized taxis in Jamestown, and working on the ferries.

His wife, Mary Frances Netter (née Reister), was born in Maryland in 1862 and lived in Baltimore after the war.[153] She and her parents, Henry and Maria Reister, had relocated to Newport by 1875. Mrs. Netter's mother was a laundress and cook, while her father was a hostler like her soon-to-be husband.[154] Her father may have been enslaved in Baltimore before the war. Newspapers reported a "Henry Reister, a slave of William McCann, coachmaker," was arrested for participating in a disturbance in 1842, when he would have been sixteen years of age. Later that year, according to the Baltimore newspapers, he was "locked up for strolling" with a Black woman, apparently violating an 1804 Maryland law which forbade enslaved persons from "strol the streets at night" without permission.[155] These experiences may have shaped his decision two decades later to join the 7th US Colored Infantry Regiment in Maryland in 1863 when Black troops were admitted into Union ranks in the war against the southern states.

In 1877, William Netter and Mary Reister married and by 1900 they lived in Jamestown with children Sherwood, Edith, and Marie. They were later joined by William Netter Jr., grandchildren, a niece, and a grandmother all under one roof on Narragansett Avenue.[156] The traffic generated by hotel visitors and their carriages in this period had reached a peak. The Jamestown & Newport Ferry Company reportedly carried 300,000 passengers in 1910, many upon landing

William L. Netter Jr. (front row, second from left), son of William and Mary Netter, Newport Shipyard, Newport, RI. Courtesy: Jamestown Historical Society Collections, P1972.194.

in Jamestown relied on horse-powered transit and coachmen.[157] Seeing this, their son Sherwood Netter entered the working world as a third-generation hostler and drove an "express wagon" conveying luggage and supplies from the East Ferry wharf to downtown hotels and estates across the island.[158] He later was appointed a special police officer, obtained a license, and opened a stable and garage on Clinton Avenue, eventually converting it to an auto service for the motorcars appearing on the island.[159]

The Netters also recognized the growing demand for domestic services. Matriarch Mary Netter, with help from daughter Edith, managed a successful laundry for three decades, initially from her home. With more clientele, she moved the business into a Caswell Block storefront opposite the downtown ferry wharf.[160] The Netter men likewise operated out of Caswell Block as

16 Cole Street, former home of William Netter Jr. and family (left); and 11 Antham Street, former home of Sherwood Netter and family (right). Photograph: Peter Fay, 2024.

hostlers for the hotels or as expressmen. When William Netter Sr. grew older, he established a less demanding shoe shine and repair parlor at the wharf.[161] Their son, William L. Netter Jr., worked as a laborer or cobbler for years, later becoming an employee of the Jamestown & Newport Ferry Company.[162] He worked alongside other Jamestowners at the Newport shipyard and repaired the ill-fated *Ferry Beavertail*, which was destroyed in the 1938 hurricane.[163]

With their growing families, the Netter sons purchased homes near Mount Zion AME Church. William Netter Jr. and wife Ella mortgaged a home in 1923 on two lots at 16 Cole Street. The structure still stands today.[164] Sherwood Netter had only $300 in tangible property in 1921 but a decade later he and wife Ruth mortgaged a home on two lots at 11 Antham Street, which also still stands.[165]

Matriarch Mary F. Netter passed away in 1928 at age sixty-two while visiting in Brooklyn, New York, and is buried there. William H. Netter Sr. passed in Jamestown in 1937 at age eighty-one and is buried at Newport City Cemetery.[166]

Andrew W. Lodkey (left) with Oliver Sprague in fanciful costumes for a local community event. Circa 1920. Courtesy: Jamestown Historical Society Collections, P1971.023.

Andrew W. Lodkey (1850–1936) and Milissa Lodkey (1855–1936): Chief Steward; Notable Restaurateurs; Property Owners

Andrew and Milissa Lodkey were successful entrepreneurs and members of the Jamestown business community from 1913 to 1936. Born in Georgia before the Civil War, they arrived in New England in the 1890s with Mr. Lodkey providing steward services and later opening his own restaurant in downtown Jamestown. Prior to moving to Rhode Island, he worked in New York in 1880

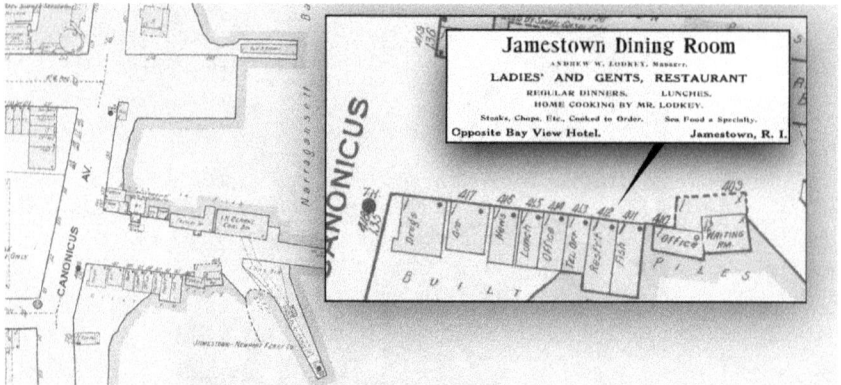

The Lodkeys advertised their "Jamestown Dining Room" in the Jamestown Directory, 1922. Source: Sanborn Fire Insurance Map and Jamestown Directory, 1921.

as a servant, then in Newark, New Jersey, as a waiter in the late 1880s.[167] By 1891, he opened a restaurant and advertised in the Newark city directory.[168] He moved to Newport in 1894 and immediately advertised as a steward in city directories.[169] There he provided dining services to banquets including one memorable celebration in 1899 honoring African American diplomat and US Consul to St. Thomas—Mahlon Van Horne of Newport.[170]

Mr. Lodkey was a caterer or steward for several white social clubs such as the Mianetuck Golf Club of Fall River, the Business Men's Association of Newport, and the Newport Country Club. He solidified his reputation and business acumen with each encounter.[171] By 1900, he was the chief steward for various vessels and sloops in the area, providing meals to the wealthy. He also served in Black fraternal organizations as secretary of a Masonic Lodge, steward of the Benjamin Gardiner Commandery of the Knights Templar, and as trustee of Mount Olivet Baptist Church.[172] A 1906 *Newport Mercury* article recounted a formal dinner where "an excellent menu was served by Andrew Lodkey, formerly steward of the County Club, and all did ample justice to it."[173]

These accomplishments were noteworthy considering the Newport society in which he lived, largely segregated by race. For example, in Newport in 1888, the pastor of the Jamestown Shiloh Baptist Central Mission, Reverend Henry Jeter, was ordered not to park his carriage on the waterfront, as it was reserved for whites.[174] Many economic opportunities were barred to people of color during Mr. Lodkey's rise, their employment limited to subservient roles.

By 1906, Andrew Lodkey again became a proprietor, opening a cookhouse at Cozzens Court in Newport, later moving it to 14 Franklin Street and then to 2 West Marlborough Street.[175] In 1914, he relocated the cookhouse to downtown Jamestown opposite the Bay View Hotel, advertising it as *The Jamestown Ferry Wharf Lunch Room*.[176] As the business grew, he selected a more formal name, the *Jamestown Dining Room* featuring "Home Cooking by Mr. Lodkey—Steaks, Chops, Etc. Cooked to Order. Sea Food a Specialty."[177]

The Lodkeys first purchased land in Jamestown in 1913 at 49 Calvert Place on the west edge of the Bryer Farm. Later Andrew, Milissa, and daughter Etta Lodkey settled on three lots at 14 and 20 Clinton Avenue, valued at $1,688 in 1921. In 2020, the property was valued at $1,250,000.[178] Andrew and Milissa Lodkey managed their restaurant starting in 1912 on Ferry Wharf for a decade, then relocated it to their 14 Clinton Avenue home for another decade, serving hundreds of ferry travelers, visitors, and island residents. Theirs was the first and only known Black-owned restaurant established in Jamestown. Recognition of Mr. Lodkey's accomplishments continued to grow and by 1917 he was elected Generalissimo of the Benjamin Gardiner Commandery of the African American Masonic Lodge.[179]

At age eighty, Andrew Lodkey's health declined. He moved into the Bates Sanitarium on Conanicus Avenue and died in 1936. He was memorialized in newspapers as "a well-known steward and restaurant keeper." His wife, Milissa Lodkey, died the same year. They are interred together in the Jamestown Cedar Cemetery.[180]

Notes

1 Jamestown Historical Society, "Death Certificate of James Howland of January 3, 1859," T2013.501.055. The identification of the parents as "African" (line #13) rather than "Black" (line #7) which is used to identify the son indicates James Howland's parents were born in Africa. The death certificate has a notation, "The last slave of Rhode Island freed under the act of 1792"; however, there was no act of 1792 that freed any enslaved person in Rhode Island. Only in 1843 was slavery abolished in the state, and several were freed by that act, but Mr. Howland was already free if the census is accurate.

2 "Last of the Rhode Island Slaves," *Providence Daily Tribune*, January 10, 1859, quoted in Samuel Greene Arnold, *History of the State of Rhode Island and Providence Plantations Vol. II* (Providence: Preston & Rounds, 1894), 32; *Proceedings of the Rhode Island Historical Society, 1873-74* (Providence, 1874), 37; "The Last Rhode Island Slave," *Detroit Free Press*, January 19, 1859, 2; "Little Rhody's Last Slave," *Weekly Oregon Statesman*, Salem, OR, March 1, 1859, 2, Newspapers.com database.

3 Joey La Neve DeFrancesco, "Abolition and Anti-Abolition in Newport, 1835-1866," *Newport History* 92, no. 281 (Spring 2020): 13. In this Chapter 2, see profiles of the Champlin and Rice families.

4 "With Malice Toward None, The Abraham Lincoln Bicentennial Exhibition, The Run for President," Library of Congress, accessed 12/26/23, https://www.loc.gov /exhibits/lincoln/the-run-for-president.html; "Abraham Lincoln, 16th President of the United States, 1861–1865: Remarks to Committee of the Republican National Convention Accepting the Presidential Nomination, May 19, 1860," *The American Presidency Project*, accessed 12/26/23, https://www.presidency .ucsb.edu/documents/remarks-committee-the-republican-national-convention -accepting-the-presidential-nomination.

5 "Return of the Owners' & Negroes' Names on Conanicut Island," January 28, 1777, Hugh Percy Papers, January-March 1777, Alnwick Castle, Alnwick, Northumberland, England. The list was prepared by Major Edmund Eyre of the British 54th Regiment; Christian M. McBurney, "Freedom for African Americans in British-Occupied Newport, 1776–1779 and 'The Book of Negroes,'" *Newport History* 87, no. 276 (2017): 7.

6 US Census, Jamestown, RI, 1850. If James Howland's age in the 1850 census is correct (94), then he died in 1859 at age 103; not 100 as reported on his birth certificate by his employer, John Howland.

7 "Daniel Howland Will," *Jamestown Probate*, October 3, 1837, 3: 270.

8 US Census, Jamestown, RI, 1820, 1830, and 1850. No manumission papers have been found, but the 1830 census shows no enslaved persons in the household.

9 "Map of Conanicut Island, opposite Newport, Rhode-Island in Narragansett Bay," *Daniel Watson Publisher*, 1875, accessed 3/22/21, https://digitalcollections .nypl.org/items/7c302910-c546-0134-f338-00505686a51c.

10 "Rhode Island Historic Cemeteries, #JM002," *RI Historical Cemetery Database*, accessed 11/27/23, https://rihistoriccemeteries.org/newsearchcemeterydetail .aspx?ceme_no=JM002.

11 For full reading of Military Acts of 1792, see "Militia Acts of 1792," *George Washington Mount Vernon.org*, accessed 4/24/23, https://www.mountvernon .org/education/primary-source-collections/primary-source-collections/article/ militia-act-of-1792/.

12 Cameron Boutin, "The First Rhode Island Regiment and Revolutionary— America's Lost Opportunity, The War Years 1775–1783," *Journal of American Revolution*, January 17, 2018, https://allthingsliberty.com/2018/01/1st-rhode -island-regiment-revolutionary-americas-lost-opportunity/; "African Americans in the Revolutionary War," *National Park Service*, accessed 11/25/2024, https:// www.nps.gov/chyo/learn/historyculture/african-americans-in-the-revolutionary -war.htm.

13 William H. Chenery, *The Fourteenth Regiment Rhode Island Heavy Artillery (Colored) in the War to Preserve the Union, 1861–1865* (Providence: Snow & Farnham, 1898), 48; Herbert Aptheker, "Negro Casualties in the Civil War," *The Journal of Negro History* 32, no. 1 (January 1947): 12; "The Civil War's Black Soldiers—Black Officers," *National Park Service*, accessed 1/22/23, https://www .nps.gov/parkhistory/online_books/civil_war_series/2/sec14.htm.

14 "Meeting of Colored Men," *Providence Journal*, August 8, 1862, 2.

15 William J. Brown, *The Life of William J. Brown, of Providence, RI* (Providence: Angell & Co., 1883), 187.

16 Kenneth S. Carlson, "Black & White, The Third & Fourteenth Rhode Island Heavy Artillery Regiments 1861–1865," *Rhode Island College*, 1992, 24; "Riotous Proceedings—A Boy Shot," *Manufacturers' and Farmers' Journal*, September 3, 1863, 2; "A Very Serious Disturbance," *Manufacturers' and Farmers' Journal*, September 14, 1863, 4. See Leslie M. Harris, *In the Shadow of Slavery: African Americans in New York City, 1626-1863* (University of Chicago Press, 2003) and "The New York City Draft Riots of 1863," *University of Chicago Press*, accessed 4/19/23, https://press.uchicago.edu/Misc/Chicago/317749.html&title=The+New +York+City+Draft+Riots+of+1863&desc=.

17 "Parade of the Colored Battalion," *Providence Daily Journal*, August 29, 1863, 2.

18 State of Rhode Island, *Report on the Committee on Finance of the House of Representatives on Bounty Frauds, etc.* (Providence: H. H. Thomas & Co., 1865), 5.

19 Carlson, "Black & White," 40, 50.

20 Chenery, *Fourteenth Regiment*, 14.

21 John Sharper / S. B. Brown, photographer, 101 Westminster Street, Providence, RI, Library of Congress, retrieved 6/19/20, https://www.loc.gov/item

/2010647911/. Sharper was a printer from Herkimer, NY, joining Co. G in November 1863; "US Civil War Pension Index to Pension Files," *Ancestry.com*; "US Adjutant General Military Records, 1631–1976," Ancestery.com *for John N. Sharper*; Gravesite, accessed 4/18/21, https://www.findagrave.com/memorial /52290273/john-n_-sharper.

22 "The Members of the 2d and 3d Battalions," *Providence Journal*, January 15, 1864, 1.

23 "The 3d Battalion, 14th R.I.H.A," *Providence Journal*, March 5, 1864, 1.

24 As of March 5, 1864 "none have died" of smallpox, "Letter from Dutch Island," *Providence Journal*, March 8, 1864; By March 12, "two [. . .] have died of small pox, and ten [. . .] are in the hospital," *Providence Journal*, March 12, 1863, 2. The two were Pvt. John Henry, died March 18, and Pvt. Philp Cole, died March 11. All other deaths were recorded as other causes; Chenery, *Fourteenth Regiment*; Brigadier-General Elisha Dyer, *Annual Report of the Adjutant General of the State of Rhode Island for the Year 1865* (Providence: Freeman & Son, 1895). For mistaken accounts of cause of death, see Walter K. Schroder, *Dutch Island and Fort Greble* (Acadia Publishing, 1998), 7–8 and Rosemary Enright and Sue Maden, *Historic Tales of Jamestown* (Acadia Publishing, 2016), 147.

25 "Disease & Infection in the American Civil War," *The American Biology Teacher* 60, no. 4 (April 1998): 258–62.

26 "Vaccination," *Providence Journal*, February 10, 1863, 3.

27 Carlson, "Black & White," 50–1.

28 "Notable Persons," *Long Island National Cemetery website*, accessed 6/19/20, https://www.cem.va.gov/cems/nchp/longisland.asp. For William Betson, see "Death of a Colored Soldier," *Providence Journal*, January 11, 1864, 2. For Frederick C. Grames, see "In Hospital, in Camp Bailey," *Providence Journal*, November 11, 1863, 2. For Lemuel H. Smith, see William H. Chenery, *Fourteenth Regiment*, 199.

29 "An Important Report," *Providence Journal*, March 7, 1865, 1; Richard F. Miller, *States at War, Volume 1–A Reference Guide for Connecticut, Maine, Massachusetts, New Hampshire, Rhode Island, and Vermont in the Civil War* (University Press of New England, 2013), 512.

30 Peter H. Lindert and Richard Sutch, "Consumer Price Indexes, for All Items: 1774–2003," *Historical Statistics of the United States, Millennial Edition* (Cambridge University Press, 2006).

31 State of Rhode Island, *Report on the Committee*, 69.

32 "Guide to the Rhode Island 11th United States Heavy Artillery (Colored), 1853-1913," *Rhode Island Archival and Manuscript Collections Online*, accessed 6/19/20, https://www.riamco.org/render?eadid=US-RPPC-us11regiment.

33 Dyer, *Annual Report*, 589; Howard Westwood, *Black Troops, White Commanders, and Freedmen during the Civil War* (Southern Illinois University Press, 2008), 142–66; Ira Berlin, Joseph P. Reidy, and Leslie S. Rowland, *Freedom: A Documentary History of Emancipation: 1861–1867, Series II, The Black Military Experience* (Cambridge University Press, 1982), 366.

34 "A New Paper," *Providence Evening Press*, April 9, 1862, 2.

35 The Department of the Gulf was established in February 1862 by US Army General Orders No. 20. It patrolled and serviced "all of the coast of the Gulf of Mexico west of Pensacola harbor, and so much of the Gulf States as may be occupied by the forces under Major General B.F. Butler." See "General Orders, No. 20 (Headquarters of the Army)," *American History Central*, https://www .americanhistorycentral.com/entries/general-orders-no-20-headquarters-of-the -army/. The 14th Regiment served in Louisiana and Texas defending the coast under the command of Lieutenant Colonel Nelson Viall.

36 Chenery, *Fourteenth Regiment*, 147.

37 "Black Soldiers in the U.S. Military During the Civil War," *National Archives*, accessed 6/19/20, https://www.archives.gov/education/lessons/blacks-civil-war.

38 "Hannah Elizabeth Champlin, Death Certificate," *Town of Jamestown*, RI, May 19, 1925.

39 "John Champlin, Negro," *US Census*, Jamestown, RI, 1810; Will of Daniel Weeden, 1784, Ancestry.com.

40 "Jury Does Not Agree," *Newport Daily News*, Newport, RI, May 8, 1928, 3.

41 "Probate trial of Hannah Weeden estate," *Newport Mercury*, May 11, 1928, 3, 6; *Newport Daily News*, January 11, 1929, 1, 2, 6. Amintus Weeden was earlier in life enslaved by John Weeden. See Franklin Dorman, *Twenty Families of Color in Mass* (New England Historic Genealogical Society, 1998), 457; Nelson Tamakloe, "Sarah Charles, Josias Budgel, Her Husband, And Their Children," *Rhode Island Roots* 39, no. 4 (December 2013): 177–80. For York Weeden, see Weeden, "Last Will."

42 "Hannah Elizabeth Champlin file, Family Tree," *Jamestown Probate Records*, Jamestown, RI.

43 US Census, Jamestown, RI, 1810.

44 US Census, Jamestown, RI, 1800. Two enslaved persons were in the Hazard
    household in 1800. Thomas Hazard posted a reward for a "Runaway Negro
    woman" in 1809. See "Five Cents Reward," *Newport Mercury*, December 2,
    1809, 3.

45 Jamestown Town Council and Probate, 1815, 3: 21; Jamestown Historical
    Society, 1817, T2007.016.002.

46 Jamestown Town Council and Probate, 182326, 3: 80, 89, 100, 102, 103.
    Whitewashing was applying unslaked lime to whiten walls, especially kitchens,
    to brighten and clean them.

47 "John Champlin, non-white family of four," *US Census*, Jamestown, RI, 1810;
    "George W. Champlin," *RI Census*, Jamestown, RI, 1865; *Newport Journal*, April
    19, 1890.

48 John Henry Champlin of Jamestown was a seaman in Newport in 1834 and
    1835. "Register of Seaman's Certificates," *Mystic Seaport Museum*, accessed
    1/26/20, https://research.mysticseaport.org/databases/protection/. According
    to the *Newport Daily News*, May 22, 1876, 2: "Under the influence of liquor left
    Newport on the one o'clock boat for his home . . . [Mr. Champlin's] body was
    found in a small stream. His hat and bundle were on the bridge; it is presumed
    that he sat down to rest and fell off. . ." The Champlin name is the most common
    surname of any in the Narragansett Tribe in the nineteenth century. See *Report
    of the Commission on the Affairs of the Narragansett Indians Made to the General
    Assembly, 1881* (Providence: E.L. Freeman & Co., 1881), 133–41.

49 US Census, Jamestown, RI, 1900, 1910; RI Census, Jamestown, 1875, 1925.

50 RI Census, Jamestown, 1875; US Census, Jamestown, RI, 1900.

51 Lindert and Sutch, "Consumer Price."

52 Jamestown Land Evidence, 6:396, 6:431, 7:324, 7:319, 7:324. Farm sold in
    1913 to John J. Watson, Jr., Jamestown, RI Land Evidence, 18:126–7; *Atlas of
    Southern Rhode Island* (Philadelphia: Everts and Richards, 1895), Jamestown and
    Prudence Island, 39; US Census, Jamestown, RI, 1880; RI Census, Jamestown,
    1885.

53 Jamestown, RI Land Evidence, Volume 6, 396–7, 431–2; "Birth Certificate,
    Walter Weeden, February 9, 1858," *Jamestown Historical Society*, Jamestown, RI.
    US Census, 1850 shows George Champlin, 28, laborer on Arnold Hazard Farm.
    US Census 1840 lists two males of color there between ten years and twenty-four
    years. US Census 1880 lists George Champlin at 67, laborer, living next door to
    Hannah Hazard, widow of Arnold Hazard.

54 "Isaac Rice" renting Champlin Farm, US Agricultural Census, Jamestown, RI, 1880.

55 US Agricultural Census, Jamestown, RI, 1880 and US Population Census, Jamestown, RI, 1880. Isaac Rice rented five acres of farmland (likely Champlin's) next to Hazard Farm. He resided between Hannah Champlin and Walter Watson, the site of the Champlin Farm. The Rice family is profiled in this Chapter 2.

56 Brothers George W., Alexander, and William H. Champlin are listed in the 1883 "Eligible Voter Roster" certified by Thomas Carr Watson, president of the Town Council, April 2, 1883. As property owners, they were marked as qualified to vote on all items except Governor. George W. Champlin was also marked as qualified to vote "on all questions excepting upon a proposition to impose a tax or for the expenditure of monies." In the 1885 "List of All Persons Entitled to Vote Under Article 2 Section 1st of the Constitution of Rhode Island," verified by John J. Watson, Clerk, brothers George W. and Alexander Champlin were declared qualified to vote. Source: Town of Jamestown, 1883 and 1885 Voter Records, accessed 4/1/22. It is noted that a Charles W. Champlin is listed in the voting rosters but he is not believed to be a member of the Black Champlin family as the Charles in that family had an "H" middle initial.

57 In 1842, Blacks fought and won the right to vote in Rhode Island, resulting in an amendment to the state constitution. See Joanne Melish, "Introduction," in William Brown, *The Life of William Brown of Providence* (University of New Hampshire Press, 2006), xxxiii–xxxiv. See also, "The Life of William Brown of Providence," *Google Books*, https://www.google.com/books/edition/The_Life_of _William_J_Brown_of_Providenc/O1SFYLxLSs0C.

58 "Jamestown Deaths," *Newport Daily News*, Newport, RI, September 25, 1901.

59 Town of Jamestown, RI, Death Registry, 1902, 60.

60 *Newport Daily News*, Newport, RI, February 18, 1903.

61 RI Census 1865 through 1925; US Census, Jamestown, RI, 1880, 1890, 1900, 1910, and 1920. The brothers worked for E. Hammond, T. Watson, and other wealthy white families.

62 "Jury does not agree," *Newport Mercury*, May 11, 1928, 3.

63 Will of Daniel Weeden, 1784, Ancestry.com; RI Wills and Probate Records, 1751–1841; Jamestown Town Council Probate Records and Index, Volumes 2–4, 1767–1874, image 233. Fifteen years after manumission, there were two Black Weeden families in Jamestown, those of Charles Weeden, 10 members, and

Mint (Amintus) Weeden, 5 members, US Census 1800, Jamestown, RI, 3, 34. For London Weeden, see James N. Arnold, ed., *Narragansett Historical Register* II, No. 1, 1883 (Narragansett Historical Publishing Co., 1883), 136; Work Projects Administration, *Inventory of the Church Archives of Rhode Island: Baptist* (Historical Records Survey, 1941), 186.

64 John S. Weeden from Mooresfield, South Kingstown claimed to descend from the enslaved London Weeden of Jamestown. London Weeden of Moorestown was reportedly a "prominent member" of the Colored Baptist Church. See "Order in Weeden Appeal," *Newport Mercury*, February 15, 1929, 7.

65 The white Carr family, for whom Hannah Champlin worked for over twenty years and in whose house she lived, claimed ignorance of her heritage. Her employer, Caroline A. Carr, administratrix of her estate, testified she knew of only one Champlin relative and rejected the claims of the Narragansett Weedens. She professed no knowledge of Hannah Champlin's maternal lineage from the enslaved Weedens in Jamestown, but the court confirmed it. In fact, the Carr family had for generations intermarried with the white Weeden family who had enslaved Hannah Champlin's ancestors. See Reporting of probate hearings, *Newport Mercury*, May 11, 1928, January 18, 1929, and February 15, 1929.

66 *Historic and Architectural Resources of Jamestown, Rhode Island* (Rhode Island Historical Preservation & Heritage Commission, 1995), 100.

67 "City Directory," *Jamestown*, 1915, Ancestry.com; "Obituary," *Newport Mercury*, October 15, 1937, 3.

68 US Census, South Kingstown, RI, 1870 and Jamestown, RI, 1880.

69 US Census, Jamestown, RI, 1880; US Agricultural Census, Jamestown, RI, 1880; RI Census, Jamestown, 1885.

70 "Lincoln University Biographical Catalogue," *New Era Printing*, 1918, accessed 1/10/2025, https://www.lincoln.edu/_files/langston-hughes-memorial-library/Library%20Alumni%20Directories/1918.pdf.

71 Rowena Stewart, *A Heritage Discovered: Blacks in Rhode Island* (Rhode Island Black Heritage Society, 1975), 30; Kimberly Dumpson, "Olivia Johns Rice in Stories In Stone," *Jamestown Historical Society Archive* (#A2021.132.002), Jamestown, RI, October 2021.

72 Frank H.C. Rice was listed as "Coachman" in the *Newport City Directory* of 1893, 1895, 1900, and 1910.

73 US Census, Newport, RI, 1900.

74 Myra Beth Young Armstead, *The History of Blacks in Resort Towns: Newport, Rhode Island and Saratoga Springs, New York, 1870–1930*, Doctoral Dissertation, University of Chicago, Chicago, IL, 1987, 113–14, 118–19; US Census 1910.

75 US Census, Jamestown, RI, 1920; RI Census, Jamestown, RI, 1935.

76 "Jamestown," *Newport Mercury*, April 22, 1922, 4, May 4, 1928, 7, and May 2, 1930, 4.

77 "Obituary," *Newport Daily News*, October 9, 1937.

78 "1920 and 1921 List of the Names of Voters in Jamestown, Rhode Island," *Town of Jamestown, Real Estate Voters, Personal Property Voters and Registry Voters*, certified October 28, 1920, Lewis W. Hull. Passed by Congress June 1919 and ratified August 1920, the 19th Amendment to the US Constitution granted women the right to vote in every state. See "19th Amendment to the U.S. Constitution: Women's Right to Vote (1920)," *National Archives*, accessed 11/25/2024, https://www.archives.gov/milestone-documents/19th-amendment.

79 Stewart, *A Heritage Discovered*, 30; Jamestown Land Evidence, 25:314 and 29:236.

80 "Oral History—Mattie R. Southern," *Southern Family Archives*, Jamestown, RI, August 24, 2020.

81 "Newport, 1750: Slaves Imported," *Newport Mercury*, February 4, 1977, 5.

82 "US Naval Enlistment Rendezvous," *Ancestry.com*, NARA No. M1953, Roll 18, Philadelphia, February 1, 1862; Dyer, *Annual Report*, 1178.

83 US Agricultural Census, Jamestown, RI, 1880.

84 US Census, South Kingstown, RI, 1870 and Jamestown, RI, 1880; US Agricultural Census, Jamestown, RI, 1880; RI Census, Jamestown, 1885.

85 Death Registry, City of Newport, RI, 1902, 572.

86 Author communications with Kimberly Conway Dumpson, descendant of Isaac Rice, 10/10/2020. Isaac Rice is buried in Rural Cemetery, New Bedford, MA. See "Isaac Rice," *FindaGrave.com*, accessed 5/27/21, https://www.findagrave.com/memorial/172107114/isaac-rice.

87 "Compromise of 1850," *Library of Congress*, accessed 5/21/2021, https://guides.loc.gov/compromise-1850. See also, Chapter 3—Historical Context for more discussion on the Compromise of 1850.

88 Mary Ellen Snodgrass, *The Underground Railroad: An Encyclopedia of People, Places, and Operations* (Routledge, 2015), 446. Also, Author communications with Kimberly Conway Dumpson, 10/10/2020.

89 Kimberly Dumpson, "The Power of the Story," *Rhode Island College*, accessed 5/27/2021, https://www.ric.edu/news-events/news/power-story.

90 "The New England Convention," *Weekly Anglo-African*, July 23, 1859, 1; Charles A. Battle, "Negroes on the Island of Rhode Island," 1932; "Coming to America: Harry Rice," *Providence Journal*, July 20, 1986, A-01. When Isaac Rice Sr. served as vice president of the New England Convention of Colored Citizens in 1859, George T. Downing, also of Newport and likely a colleague, served as president of the organization.

91 "Notice," *Newport Daily News*, January 20, 1855, 4; Richard C. Youngken, *African Americans in Newport. An introduction to the Heritage of African Americans in Newport, Rhode Island, 1700–1945* (Rhode Island Historical Preservation and Heritage Commission and Rhode Island Black Heritage Society, 2nd Printing, 1998), 55.

92 Henry N. Jeter, *Pastor Henry N. Jeter's Twenty-five Years Experience with the Shiloh Baptist Church and Her History, Corner School and Mary Streets, Newport, RI* (Remington Printing Co., 1901), 20; "For Colored Baptists," *Newport Mercury*, June 5, 1914, 5; "Local Briefs," *Newport Mercury*, August 24, 1914, 2; and "Local Briefs," *Newport Mercury*, June 15, 1917, 5.

93 "Shiloh Baptist Church," *Newport Mercury*, July 13, 1895, 1.

94 "For Colored Baptists," *Newport Daily News*, June 5, 1914, 5.

95 "Central Baptist Church Records," *Jamestown Historical Society*, A2021-304-003.

96 "Jamestown," *Newport Mercury*, May 3, 1902, 1; "The Mission at Jamestown," *Newport Mercury*, June 15, 1917, 5; Jamestown Town Council Letters, Jamestown Historical Society, A2014.600.001, for years 1901, 1906, 1907.

97 *Minutes of the Rhode Island Baptist Anniversaries, 1906* (Remington Printing Co, 1906), 11.

98 Sanborn Map Co., *Atlas of Newport, Jamestown, Middletown and Portsmouth, RI from Actual Surveys and City Records* (Sanborn Map Company, 1921), 29. Map also online at Brown Digital Repository, Brown University Library, Providence, RI, https://repository.library.brown.edu/studio/item/bdr:384505/.

99 *Newport City Directory*, 1922.

100 "Baptist Young People," *Newport Mercury*, April 20, 1945, 5.

101 Certificate of Incorporation, July 30, 1898. See State of Rhode Island, *Acts and Resolves Passed by the General Assembly of the State of Rhode Island and Providence Plantations, May Session 1897* (Providence: E.L. Freeman & Sons, 1897), 84–5.

102 Jamestown RI Land Evidence, 12:444. William Holliday was a laborer in
     Providence and married Harriet in 1889 (see RI Census, Providence, RI, 1885);
     Marriages Registered in the City of Providence, 1889, 390 (source at Rhode Island
     State Archives).

103 "Visiting Clergymen," *Providence Journal*, August 19, 1895, 3.

104 Richard R. Wright Jr., *Centennial Encyclopedia of the African Methodist Episcopal
     Church* (Book Concern of the A.M.E. Church, 1916), 225.

105 "Mr. J. E. Harper," *Newport Daily News,* August 1, 1896, 5.

106 "Harriet Tubman's Life," *Providence Journal*, November 28, 1886, 6.

107 Nancy Caswell Bailey Mason, "A Brief Historical Survey of Central Baptist
     Church," *Central Baptist Church of Jamestown*, R.I., accessed 7/30/20, http://www
     .cbcjamestown.com/ABriefHistoricalSurveyofCentralBaptistChurch.pdf.

108 *Historic and Architectural Resources*, 41.

109 "Newport Concerts," *New York Age*, July 20, 1905, 8.

110 "Hardship of Jenkins Orphans," *New York Age*, August 24, 1905, 7.

111 "Jamestown Notes," *New York Age*, July 13, 1905, 8.

112 "Rhode Island," *New York Age*, September 6, 1906.

113 "Death Certificate, Benjamin F. Morrell, February 8, 1930," *State of Rhode Island*.

114 Town of Jamestown, R.I., Probate Records, 1937, Estate No. 28695.

115 US Census, Slave Schedule, Dist. 1, Madison, KY, 1860; "Mt. Vernon
     Department," *Interior Journal*, Stanford, KY, May 27, 1881, 2.

116 "Paint Lick," *Interior Journal*, March 19, 1880, 3; US Census, Madison, KY, 1870.

117 "US Army, Register of Enlistments, 1798-1914," National Archives Microfilm
     Publication M233, 246; "Records of the Adjutant General's Office, 1780's–1917,"
     Record Group 94, National Archives, Washington, DC.

118 Jeter, *Pastor Henry N. Jeter's*, 91–7, accessed 6/19/20, https://docsouth.unc.edu/
     neh/jeter/jeter.html#p91.

119 "25th Infantry Scrapbook, I:145," Records of US Regular Army Mobile Units,
     1821–1942, Record Group 391, National Archives; Frank N. Schubert, *On the
     Trail of the Buffalo Soldier: Biographies of African Americas in the US Army 1866-
     1917* (Scarecrow Press, 1995), 302, 508.

120 US Census, Fort McKarett, Menard County, Texas, 1870.

121 Jeter, *Pastor Henry N. Jeter's*, 90.

122 Jeter, *Pastor Henry N. Jeter's*, 91; US Army, Register of Enlistments, 1885, image
     42.

123 "Emancipation Day," *Daily Deadwood Pioneer-Times*, Deadwood, South Dakota, August 2, 1882, 4.

124 "Fort Leavenworth," *Kansas City Times*, January 1, 1888, 3; RI Census, Jamestown, 1905; "Shiloh Church Anniversary," *Newport Mercury*, August 20, 1892, 1.

125 "Jamestown," *Providence Journal*, August 7, 1889, 13.

126 *Historic and Architectural Resources*, 52.

127 "Caught in the Ice—Dutch Island Garrison Held in an Open Boat Three Hours in Freezing Water," *Providence Daily Journal*, January 14, 1893.

128 "Jamestown," *Providence Daily Journal*, Providence, RI, December 6, 1888; "Sergeant Morrell's Cottage," *Newport Daily News*, February 22, 1899, 5; "Dutch Island," *Providence Daily Journal*, September 1, 1889, 12; "Frederick G.M. White, age 7," *US Federal Census*, Jamestown, RI, 1900.

129 "Marriage Record, Benjamin Morrell and Lucie Giles," *Town of Jamestown*, RI, 1906.

130 "Rhode Island Women's Clubs," *New York Age*, March 1, 1906, 4.

131 "Tax Assessment of the City of Newport, 1915," Mercury Publishing Co., Newport, RI, 1915, 229. For 3 Elm St. and 66 John St., see City of Newport Tax Assessor's Database, 2024.

132 "Rentals at 66 John Street," *Newport Mercury*, October 1, 1904, 8 and March 6, 1909, 8; "To let," *Newport Daily News*, September 30, 1914, 17; "Rental at 3 Elm Street, Real Estate," *Newport Mercury*, August 26, 1905, 1.

133 Lucie Johnson Giles had been a maid to Newport millionaire Frances Hoyt for years. The elderly woman later died and left Ms. Giles $2,000 in her will: "Newport," *Fall River Daily Evening News*, November 13, 1905, 5; "Mrs. Hoyt defends her maid," *New York Times*, April 10, 1903, 7; "Newport," *Fall River Daily Evening News*, November 13, 1905, 5.

134 Sanborn Map Co., *Atlas of Newport*; Town of Jamestown, *Tax List of the Town of Jamestown, RI* (Gladding Print, 1921), 28. For 3 Elm St. and 66–8 John St., see City of Newport, *Tax Assessment of the City of Newport for 1915* (Mercury Publishing Co., 1915), 229.

135 "2024 Property Assessment–60 Clarke Street, Jamestown, RI, 2020," *Town of Jamestown Tax Assessor Database*.

136 "Advertisements West View Cottage," *New York Age*, July 18, 1907, 8; July 16, 1908, 5; June 10, 1909; June 16, 1910; May 29, 1913, 2; June 10, 1915, 7; and September 7, 1916, 5.

137 "Jamestown," *Newport Daily News*, August 21, 1896, 4: "One of the most enjoyable hops of the season was given at the Champlin House . . . the Pioneer colored quartet gave a concert at the Bay View last evening"; *Newport Daily News*, August 10, 1899, 5: "There was a pleasant hop at Hotel Thorndike . . . This evening the Colored waiters at the Gardner House will give a burlesque cake walk . . . will doubtless attract a large number of people."

138 For *New York Age* article on the Morrells, see "Jamestown, RI, Notes," July 2, 1908, 7; "Bostonians Safe and Sound," September 3, 1908, 1; "West View Cottage," June 10, 1909, 8; "Mr. and Mrs. Harry Plato," August 5, 1909, 8; "Mrs. And Mrs. A.V. Jones," August 24, 1911, 3; "What is Doing Socially Among Boston People," July 16, 1908, 1. "Bostonians Safe and Sound," September 3, 1908, 1. For W. H. Lewis, see Adelaide Cromwell, *The Other Brahmins: Boston's Black Upper Class 1750-1950* (University of Arkansas Press, 1994), 55–7. For S.E. Courtney, see *The Southern Workman and Hampton School Record* Vol. 28 (Hampton, VA: Hampton Normal and Agricultural Institute, 1899), 185. Booker T. Washington may have been related to Lucy (Johnson) Morrell through his sister, Amanda Johnson. See *Historic and Architectural Resources*, 92 and Booker T. Washington, *The Story of My Life and Work* (J. L. Nichols & Company, 1901), 22; "Lucy and Amanda Johnson," *US Census*, West Virginia, Kanawha County, Malden, 054, 1880.

139 "Republican Caucus Harmonious," *Newport Daily News*, October 13, 1914, 7; "Jamestown," *Newport Daily News*, October 27, 1914, 7.

140 Jamestown Historical Society Archives, T2015.200.079 (May 22, 1905), T2015.200.081 (May 23, 1904), T2015.200.090 (May 25, 1903), 2010.001.048 (April 8, 1905), T2017.400.686 (July 24, 1906); "Jamestown," *Newport Daily News*, December 27, 1899, 5.

141 "Jamestown," *Newport Mercury*, September 27, 1929, 7.

142 "Slavery Days in Rhode Island," *Bulletin of the Jamestown Historical Society, No. 2*, November 1921, Jamestown Historical Society.

143 "A Ringing Letter," *Richmond Planet*, Richmond, VA, September 7, 1885; "A soldier speaks," *Richmond Planet*, Richmond, VA, July 25, 1886, 3.

144 "Lunenburg Case," *Richmond Planet*, September 28, 1895.

145 "Congratulations to Winning Candidates," *New York Age*, New York, September 29, 1929, 10; Shannon King, *Whose Harlem is This, Anyway?* (New York University Press, 2017), 110–18. In 1905, Frederick Moore was a journalist for the *New York Age*. He purchased the paper in 1907, increasing its circulation

from 5,000 to 14,000 per week by 1910, making it the most widely read African American newspaper in its time. Through the newspaper, Moore promoted black capitalism, Republican politics, and reported on cultural achievements. He won election to New York City alderman in 1927 and 1929. Source: Caroline Kreiger, "Frederick Randolph Moore, 1857–1943," *Black Past*, June 14, 2009, accessed 12/8/23, https://www.blackpast.org/african-american-history/moore -frederick-randolph-1857-1943/.

146 "Letter from B.F. Morrell to *The Crisis*, February 4, 1929" and "Letter from W.E.B. Du Bois to B.F. Morrell, February 9, 1928," W.E.B. Du Bois Papers (MS 312), Special Collections and University Archives, University of Massachusetts Amherst Libraries, accessed 11/26/2024, https://credo.library.umass.edu/ view/full/mums312-b179-i497 and https://credo.library.umass.edu/view/full/ mums312-b179-i498.

147 "Van Horne, Mathias Alonzo, December 9, 1871–February 4, 1932," *Charles Rosenberg, Oxford African American Studies Center*, accessed 6/19/2020, https:// oxfordaasc.com/browse?illus=true&t=AASC_Occupations%3A449.

148 "Morrell," *Boston Globe*, February 10, 1932, 26.

149 "Sergeant Morrell Dies Suddenly and Local Briefs," *Newport Mercury*, February 14, 1930, 5; "Sergt. Morrell Dead," *New York Age*, March 1, 1930, 10.

150 *The Newport City Directory* (A.J. Ward, 1876), 98. For place of birth, see William H. Netter, US Census, Jamestown, RI, 1910.

151 Armstead, *The History of Blacks*, 172–6; Kevin Gaines and Beth Parkhurst, *African-Americans in Newport, 1660-1960: Report to the Rhode Island Black Heritage Society*, Providence, 1992, 22 and Appendix, 9. Over half of Blacks living in Newport in 1890–1900 were from Virginia and Maryland, many brought by labor recruiting businesses owned by persons of color such as that of Lindsay Walker, native of Rappahannock, VA.

152 "Hayward's Livery and Boarding Stables," *Newport Daily News*, April 7, 1874, 4.

153 "Henry and Maria Reaster (Reister)," *US Census*, Baltimore, Maryland, 1870.

154 RI Census, Newport, RI, 1875; "Henry Reister," *Baltimore Directory*, 1863, 1870, *Newport Directory*, 1886; "Maria Reister," *Baltimore Directory*, 1870; RI Census, 1875.

155 "Another Disgraceful Outrage," *Baltimore Clipper*, February 9, 182, 2; "Another Rioter Caught," *Baltimore Sun*, February 9, 182, 2; "The Watch Returns," *Baltimore Sun*, November 1, 1842, 2. For jail records, see "Legacy of Slavery in Maryland," *Maryland State Archives, Accommodation Docket*, April 19, 1842,

accessed 4/28/21, http://slavery2.msa.maryland.gov/pages/Search.aspx. For 1804 slave law, see Jeffrey R. Brackett, *The Negro in Maryland: A Study of Slavery* (Baltimore: Johns Hopkins University, 1889), 101, 201.

156　US Census, Rhode Island 1910; Jamestown Directory, 1912.

157　"Police Station Report," *Newport Daily News*, August 12, 1910, 2.

158　US Census, Jamestown, 1910; Jamestown Directory, 1912.

159　"Special Officer," *Newport Daily News*, October 28, 1914, 12; "Jamestown," *Newport Mercury*, May 4, 1928, 7; Garage and stable: *Jamestown Directory*, 1924; Expressman and driver license: US Census, Jamestown, 1910; "Jamestown," *Newport Mercury*, June 28, 1918, 4; "Taxi Driver," *US Census*, Jamestown, 1930; *Jamestown Directory*, 1930.

160　"Laundress in Home," *US Census*, Jamestown, 1900, 1910; RI Census, Jamestown, 1915; Laundress, Caswell Block, *Jamestown Directory*, 1912, 1915, 1918, 1922.

161　Jamestown Directory, 1905, 1915, 1918, 1920, 1922.

162　US Census, Jamestown, 1920; *Jamestown Directory* 1922, 1926.

163　Jamestown Historical Society, Archive #P1972.194.

164　Jamestown Land Evidence, 24:336, November 8, 1923.

165　Jamestown, *Tax List*; Jamestown Land Evidence, 28:485, March 21, 1931.

166　"Mary Netter, Deaths," *Newport Mercury*, January 21, 1928, 4; US Index to Death Certificates, 1862–1948, Ancestry.com; "William Netter, Jamestown," *Newport Mercury*, January 7, 1938, 7.

167　US Census, District 178, New York, NY, 1880; New Jersey State Census, Newark, NJ, 1885, 142; *City Directory*, Newark, NJ, 1887, 1889, Ancestry.com.

168　*City Directory*, Newark, NJ, 1891, Ancestry.com.

169　*City Directory*, Newport, RI, 1894, 1896 and 1898, Ancestry.com.

170　"In Honor of Mr. Van Horne," *Newport Daily News*, November 16, 1899, 5.

171　"Former Steward Andrew W. Lodkey," *Fall River Daily Evening News*, May 3, 1900, 5; "Steward Andrew W. Lodkey," *Fall River Daily Herald*, May 14, 1900, 8; "D.M. Anthony's Sloop," *Fall River Daily Evening News*, May 28, 1900, 2; "Farewell Dinner," *Newport Mercury*, May 26, 1906, 1.

172　US Census, Newport, RI, 1900; *Newport Directory*, 1907, 20, 26; "Election of Officers," *Newport Daily News*, January 5, 1907, 5.

173　"Farewell Dinner," *Newport Mercury*, May 26, 1906, 1.

174　"An Outrage," *Newport Mercury*, July 21, 1888, 1. Occupying a carriage was a sign of high status and uncommon for African Americans, except as drivers for whites.

175 *City Directory*, Newport, RI, 1906, Ancestry.com; "Real Estate," *Newport Mercury*, May 4, 1907, 1; *City Directory*, Newport, RI, 1912.

176 *City Directory*, Newport, RI, 1912; *Jamestown, RI Directory*, 1914 and 1918.

177 *Jamestown, RI Directory*, 1921.

178 Sanborn Map Co., *Atlas of Newport*; Jamestown, *Tax List*, 25; RI Census, Jamestown, RI, 1915. $1,688 in 1921 equals almost $23,000 today (see "CPI Inflation Calculator," *US Bureau of Labor Statistics*, accessed 7/29/20, https://www.bls.gov/data/inflation_calculator.htm. For current assessment, see Town of Jamestown Tax Assessor Database.)

179 "Election of Officers," *Newport Mercury*, September 20, 1917, 1.

180 "Andrew W. Lodkey," *Newport Mercury*, May 1, 1936, 3; "Mrs. Andrew Lodkey," *Newport Mercury*, August 14, 1936, 3.

3

Historical Context

For insight into the lives of Blacks in Jamestown one must consider the context of the times in which they lived. From 1850 to 1920, profound societal changes influenced the future direction of all Americans, particularly those of color. The period was turbulent and fraught with upheavals defined in large measure by race. There were courageous acts, notable gains, and great accomplishments. There were also heightened fears and acts of passion that grievously altered or cut short the lives of many.

This chapter offers a glimpse into the lives of those who lived in the United States, the state of Rhode Island, and the town of Jamestown in this period. It is an accounting of the defining moments in American history before and during the Civil War and its aftermath.

1850–60: March to War

In the United States (1850–60)

Cataclysmic events roiled the country. All persons of color, many enslaved, were subject to some form of racial repression. In 1851, the US Congress passed the Indian Appropriations Act creating the Indian reservation system. The act seized tribal lands and confined Indigenous peoples to remote outreaches west of the Mississippi River.[1] In 1852, Harriet Beecher Stowe's *Uncle Tom's Cabin* portrayed the horrors of slavery in America. It became the best-selling book of the nineteenth century, second only to the Bible.[2]

Under increasing pressure to define where and when slavery could be legally accommodated, the US Congress enacted the Compromise of 1850 and the Kansas-Nebraska Act of 1854. Rather than enlighten the nation, these laws and the 1857 Supreme Court *Dred Scott Decision* deepened the chasm between antislavery and proslavery forces.[3] The turmoil caused by the Kansas-Nebraska Act upended the weakened Whig Party and created a new political entity—the Republican Party—in 1854. A composite of antislavery interests, the party sought to end the spread of slavery into the Kansas and Nebraska territories.[4] Emblematic of the rancor, in 1856, northern Republican senator Charles Sumner was beaten bloody and unconscious with a metal-capped cane on the floor of the US Senate by Representative Preston Brooks, a southern Democrat. The attack was in retaliation for Sumner's antislavery speech.[5] That year the California Supreme Court issued its *People v. Hall* ruling, forbidding testimony by Asians against whites in court, "virtually guaranteeing unpunished crimes against the race."[6] Two years later a California law made it illegal for any Chinese to enter the state.[7] Though struck down in 1862, the law affirmed the country's growing acceptance of racist dicta.

The Underground Railroad operated with increasing intensity in this period with Blacks central to its formation.[8] Mistakenly imagined as a mechanical device, the railroad according to historian Cheryl LaRoche represented a growing conviction that began in the 1830s "to aid those escaping slavery."[9] Clandestinely and at great risk to its conductors and passengers, the railroad's sophisticated ribbon of safe houses and escape routes robbed the South of its most valuable assets. It transported an estimated 100,000 freedom seekers to free states, Black townships, and into Canada.[10] The most prominent railroad conductors were William Still and Harriet Tubman.

William Still, the acting chairman of the Philadelphia Vigilance Committee, is credited with organizing the railroad, delivering 700 fugitives to safe havens, and keeping detailed records. His 780-page journal, published in 1886, held ledgers, illustrations, and original correspondence as well as passenger names and escape methods. The journal confirmed the existence of the railroad and aided in the reunification of fragmented families.[11]

Proclaiming "I never lost a passenger," formerly enslaved Harriet Tubman single-handedly led seventy fugitives in small gatherings at a time through Maryland marshes and woodlands to freedom, including her elderly parents. A "Moses" to many and enlisted by the US government as a scout, spy, soldier, and nurse, Ms. Tubman later became the first woman to direct an armed US military operation.[12]

Not all flights to freedom ended well, due in large part to the Fugitive Slave Act of 1850, a federal law that granted common citizens and local police unlimited authority to seize and arrest anyone they believed to be a fugitive in both free and slave states. Those that aided fugitives were fined; some were imprisoned.[13] According to *The 1619 Project: A New Origin Story*:

> September 18, 1850: Congress passes the Fugitive Slave Act, which requires that fugitives from slavery residing in free states be forcibly returned to their enslavers. This leads to the kidnapping of many Black people in Northern states, regardless of their status, driving some to migrate further north, into Canada. The new law is resisted by many abolitionists, including Harriet Hayden, herself a fugitive from slavery, who operates the Underground Railroad in Boston and helps hundreds of enslaved people escape.[14]

The Act angered many, including famed orator Frederick Douglass, who, disguised as a sailor, commandeered his own heart-stopping escape to freedom from Maryland to New York in 1838. Mr. Douglass condemned the Fugitive Slave Act for bringing "the most repugnant features of slavery into the heart of Northern cities and towns."[15] The law was divisive yet effective. Between 1850 and 1860, of the 343 freedom seekers apprehended and brought to trial, 97 percent were returned to bondage.[16]

Such was the case of Anthony Burns who fled Virginia for sanctuary in Boston, Massachusetts in 1854. When his enslaver Charles F. Suttle petitioned for his return, Mr. Burns was apprehended and brought before a federal rendition court which ruled in favor of the slave owner. Upon hearing this, frenzied white and Black abolitionists, in a failed attempt to free Mr. Burns, stormed the Boston courthouse and killed a federal marshal. Agitated spectators lined State Street as 2,000 federal troops escorted Mr. Burns to a waiting ship in Boston Harbor, returning him to bondage.[17] The events galvanized the Black church, strengthened the bonds between abolitionists, and fomented a Black militia movement with calls for preparedness.[18]

This was a time in America when the Civil War was imminent but not yet waged. Impatient and no longer able to bear the chafe of servitude, an increasing number took flight. The freedom seekers lived clandestine and circumspect lives in the North and forged alliances at the Colored Conventions. These were formal political gatherings of Black interests that began in 1830 and continued for sixty-nine years to 1899. More than 200 Colored Conventions were held in auditoriums, churches, and halls throughout the nation and Canada. The average attendance was 2,000. According to the Colored Conventions Project, they were "hubs of Black political thought and organizing":

> From 1830 until well after the Civil War, African Americans gathered across the United States and Canada to participate in political meetings held at the state and national levels. A cornerstone of Black organizing in the nineteenth century, these "Colored Conventions" brought Black men and women together in a decades-long campaign for civil and human rights.[19]

At the national level, the delegates convened mostly in Pennsylvania with meetings in Philadelphia, Harrisburg, and Pittsburgh. Other cities included Albany, Detroit, Geneva, New York, Rochester, and the District of Columbia. There were also regional meetings such as the 1859 New England Colored Citizens' Convention in Boston which appointed George T. Downing of Newport as its president. At every session, delegates were elected, concerns voiced, minutes recorded, and resolutions passed. The Colored Conventions Project estimates "tens of thousands" participated from every race and represented abolitionists, business owners, church leaders, community organizers, educators, freedom seekers, lawyers, newspaper editors and writers, politicians, scholars, suffragettes, and workers of every profession and trade. The meetings were energized with high-octane addresses by luminaries of the day such as George T. Downing, Henry Highland Garnet, James McCune Smith, Charles B. Ray, and Frederick Douglass.

Women held demure yet influential roles. They owned or managed the well-appointed boarding and rooming houses where conventioneers stayed. They provided the catered meals, refreshments, and entertainment often complimented in convention minutes. Others participated as writers, unofficial committee members, fundraisers, and supporters. None, however, served as delegates until activist Mary Ann Shadd Cary turned heads with her warning, "we have made . . . little progress considering our resolves."[20]

Her nomination as a delegate at the 1855 national convention in Philadelphia caused "spirited discussion" on the appropriateness and merits of women as delegates. Her nomination was approved with thirty-eight of the delegates in support and twenty-three opposed. Though not recorded in the convention minutes, Ms. Cary's acceptance speech was reported by William J. Wilson in the *Frederick Douglass Papers:*

> She at first had ten minutes granted her. At their expiration ten more were granted . . . but so interested was the House, that it granted additional time to her to finish . . . [T]he House was moved and breathless in its attention to her masterly exposition.[21]

Mary Ann Shadd Cary was born free in 1823 in the slave state of Delaware. She relocated with her parents and twelve siblings at age ten to Pennsylvania where she received a Quaker education and trained as a teacher. Her family home was a stop on the Underground Railroad at a time of great risk. In adulthood, she moved with a growing number of Blacks to Canada, married, and had two children. She became the first Black female newspaper editor in North America, publishing the antislavery newspaper, *The Provincial Freeman,* in Canada in 1853. In 1858, she attended a secret convention organized by abolitionist John Brown and published, after his death, *Voice from Harper's Ferry* in 1861.

Ms. Cary recruited men of color for the Union Army and when the war ended, she enrolled in the Howard University Law School, becoming one of the first women of color to complete a law degree in 1883. She established colored schools in Delaware, Pennsylvania, New York, New Jersey, and Canada and proselytized on the importance of Black migration to Canada, writing *A Plea for Emigration—Notes of Canada West (1852).* A devotee of women's suffrage, Ms. Cary founded the Colored Women's Progressive Franchise Association and addressed the National Woman Suffrage Association convention as a member in 1878. She died from stomach cancer in 1893 at age seventy in Washington, DC.[22]

The turbulent decade ended with the state execution of white abolitionist John Brown in Virginia in 1859. Mr. Brown's antislavery beliefs were shaped a decade earlier in 1849 with his purchase of a 244-acre farm abutting a settlement of free Blacks in upstate New York. He raised eleven of his twenty children there and bonded with the community. In 1854, he was named "Captain of the Liberty Guards" as he, with his son and son-in-law, engaged in fractious battles with proslavery forces in the territory of Kansas. He is purported to have "hacked five men to death" in a raid at Pottawatomie Creek.[23]

In 1858, John Brown crisscrossed the North, raising money to establish a free Black province in Canada. A year later, possibly impatient with the pace of change, with sixteen whites and five Blacks, he seized a federal armory in Harper's Ferry, Virginia on October 16, 1859. The intent was to distribute armory weapons to enslaved Blacks on nearby plantations and lead an insurrection against plantation owners. Quickly surrounded by federal troops, several of the raiders were instantly killed. A few escaped but most, including John Brown, were captured. Charged with "murder, conspiring with enslaved people to rebel, and treason against the state," he stood trial for five days. After forty-five minutes of deliberation, the jury found him guilty. John Brown was hung on December 2, 1859.[24] According to historians James and Lois Horton, news of an insurrection led by a white abolitionist thundered throughout the South:

> The Harpers Ferry raid shocked southerners and confirmed their belief that abolitionists were planning a war . . . that would incite slave revolts.[25]

Their concerns were justified. Nearly thirty years earlier, a similar revolt led by Nat Turner in Southampton County, Virginia, resulted in the deaths of at least fifty-five whites. Turner, an enslaved Baptist pastor believing he was directed by God, rallied seventy-five enslaved workers in the slaughter of plantation owners, their families, and overseers as they marched to an armory in the county seat, Jerusalem, for weapons. Three thousand local whites and state militia quelled the uprising. Nat Turner was captured, tried, and hung on November 11, 1831. According to historical accounts, the revolt "shocked the white south and, in retaliation, white southerners tightened laws restricting enslaved people's lives." [26]

For abolitionists in 1859, the John Brown epoch was a harbinger of things to come. Poet Henry Wadsworth Longfellow wrote, "This will be a great day in our history . . . the date of a new revolution . . . sowing the wind to reap the whirlwind."[27] John Brown's death inspired Julia Ward Howe's lyrics for the *Battle Hymn of the Republic*.[28]

In Rhode Island (1850–60)

In 1850, nearly 3,700 Blacks comprised 2.5 percent of the Rhode Island population. The state had abolished slavery in 1843, making all persons of color free citizens, though most were already free by this time. As with its past, Rhode Island stayed its ties to the institution of slavery. Its textile mills, concentrated on its southern flank, manufactured "Negro cloth" as clothing for the enslaved in the South. By mid-century " . . . more than 80 families in 22 towns and cities owned part of a 'Negro cloth' mill."[29] Local textile magnate Isaac P. Hazard avowed at the time, "It is our intention to make cheap goods for Southern planters."[30] According to historian Seth Rockman:

> Entering what contemporaries called the 'Southern market' . . . Hazard . . . cultivated customers among the largest slaveholders in South Carolina, Georgia, Alabama, Mississippi, and Louisiana. An 1845 report on American woolen manufacturing attested to [his] success in catapulting Rhode Island to preeminence in cloth for the coerced: nearly half of [its] woolen enterprises specialized in 'negro kerseys.' [The state's] entrepreneurs, hand-weavers, and seamstresses were inextricably linked to . . . the planters and slaves who constituted the dual consumers of their 'negro cloth.'[31]

Though a boon for the Rhode Island textile industry, Negro cloth and other clothing for the enslaved populations provided meager coverage or protection. According to an eyewitness account by formerly enslaved Frederick Douglass:

> The [enslaved] children . . . had neither shoes, stockings, jackets, nor trousers, given to them; their clothing consisted of two coarse linen shirts per year. When these failed them, they went naked until the next allowance-day. Children from seven to 10 years old . . . almost naked, might be seen at all seasons of the year.[32]

At this time Rhode Island's cosmopolitan coastal city, Newport, once a leading slave trading port, was a maritime economy aspiring to become a seasonal resort

George T. Downing, Newport, RI [1819–1903]. Civil rights advocate, equal education activist, and entrepreneur extraordinaire. Courtesy: New York Public Library Digital Collections. Accessed January 14, 2025. https://digitalcollections.nypl.org/items /78997472-cbb8-516f-e040-e00a180643ee.

for the affluent. A critical mass of free and mostly gainfully employed Blacks numbering over 600 lived in the city of 9,563. Newport Black businesses defied racial stereotypes and accomplished remarkable feats of entrepreneurship.

One of the city's preeminent businessmen was George T. Downing, an African American born in New York City in 1819. He was mentored early in life by his father Thomas Downing, one of the city's wealthiest men and proprietor of the acclaimed New York Oyster House restaurant. His childhood home at Broadway and Wall Street was a stop on the Underground Railroad.[33] George Downing moved to Rhode Island in the 1840s where he established successful businesses in Newport and Providence. In 1841, he married Serena Leanora de Grasse, the daughter of a prosperous landowner from Calcutta, India.[34] They had three daughters and three sons. In 1854, he built and operated the widely praised and "sumptuously furnished" Sea Girt Hotel on Newport's toney Bellevue Avenue.[35] Mysteriously, the structure was destroyed by fire after only six years of service. According to author John M. Rice:

It burned to the ground on December 15,1860 . . . The *Chicago Tribune* reported . . . the fire as possibly the work of an arsonist and Downing's daughter Serena Washington wrote . . . 'an incendiary's torch was placed to the structure.' The origins . . . were never discovered, although some thought [it] was in retaliation for Downing's advocacy for civil rights.[36]

The rumored torching was emblematic of the clashing political forces in Newport at the time. According to Rice:

Newport was on a front line of the antislavery movement. On the proslavery side was a coalition of wealthy slave plantation owners who stayed . . . in the summer to escape the hot and humid South . . . along [with] wealthy Rhode Island merchants, and politicians. On the antislavery side . . . [there was] a coalition of White and Black folks including Quakers, Congregationalists, and many Black organizations.[37]

Undeterred by setbacks and mindful of the challenges faced by the race, in 1857 George Downing spearheaded a nine-year campaign to integrate the state's public schools. He circulated pamphlets, held public forums, and penned editorials denouncing inequities in education. That year he established and chaired an Integration Committee and, with other activists, petitioned the General Assembly to ban school segregation. The debate and agitation continued through the years of the Civil War to 1866, when the practice was finally condemned and banned.[38] Mr. Downing was elected president of the New England Colored Citizens' Convention in 1859, a pivotal position befitting his leadership.[39] In 1865, he managed the US House of Representatives café dining room in Washington, DC, a position with considerable political access and influence.[40] Following a remarkable life of entrepreneurship and advocacy, Mr. Downing died at the age of eighty-three in his Newport home on July 21, 1903.

Newport's third school for colored children was established in 1859. In this period, five Underground Railroad safe houses operated in Rhode Island. One was the Newport home of Isaac Rice Sr.[41] [*Grandfather of Frank H.C. Rice of Jamestown, profiled in Chapter 2.*] The community's Black church—the Union Colored Congregational Church—was already in place, established by the Free African Benevolent Society in 1824.[42]

In Jamestown (1850–60)

On the island there were forty-five farms covering 5,500 acres. Many of the landowners in the 358-member community were once enslavers, having owned Africans as chattel, routinely working them in their fields and homes without compensation. Slavery was an accepted practice.[43] Now in 1850, the few Blacks that remained on the island walked free. While slavery was abolished in Rhode Island, it thrived in other states and Jamestown whites were attentive to the discourse it engendered. Six topics of the island's debate society centered on slavery and race.[44] It is certain that most of the island Blacks were also attentive. They totaled fourteen, eight females and seven males between the ages of fourteen and ninety-four. All were born in Rhode Island except two. They were ostensibly free but lacked financial independence and worked in most cases as laborers and domestics for the families that once enslaved them. Three were of school age but not enrolled. The community included formerly enslaved James Howland who, at age ninety-four, continued to work and live in the home of the Howlands, his former enslavers. He died one year before the Civil War and is reputed to be one of the last survivors of slavery in Rhode Island. [*James Howland is profiled in Chapter 2*].

1860–70: War and Reconstruction

In the United States (1860–70)

In 1860, 4.5 million persons of African descent lived in the United States. Eighty-nine percent were enslaved. Their value was estimated to be $1,000 per person or $4 billion total ($152 billion in 2024[45]). The slave market "held greater value than all of the nation's banks, railroads, and factories combined."[46] Moreover, from 1839 to 1859, uncompensated slave labor spiked the country's commodity output per capita by nearly 25 percent.[47]

Most of the nation's 46,300 slave enterprises were concentrated in the South, producing and selling cotton. Forty-five percent held twenty to thirty enslaved persons. Five percent held 100 to 500 enslaved persons. Each of the remaining 23,000 plantations enslaved as many as 1,000 men, women, and children.[48]

On the eve of the Civil War, raw cotton from these enterprises represented 61 percent of all US exports.[49]

While America's economy and wealth depended largely on slave labor, the enslaved population itself suffered stunningly high mortality rates. With insufficient diets devoid of essential proteins and nutrients, "half of its infants died during the first year of life, twice the rate of white babies. [Their] average life expectancy was 21 to 22 years compared to 40 to 43 years for antebellum whites. Relatively few lived into old age." [50]

Having won the presidency and a majority of the seats in the US Congress, the still relatively new Republican Party was victorious in the 1860 national election.[51] According to the Library of Congress, the mood of the country changed dramatically after the votes were cast. Political and economic tensions between the northern industrialized states and the southern agrarian states had "reached a fever pitch."[52] Unwilling to accept northern dictates, the state of South Carolina complaining of "an increasing hostility on the part of the non-slaveholding States" issued a *Declaration of Succession* and separated from the United States in December 1860.[53] South Carolina averred:

> Those [Union] States have assumed the right of deciding upon the propriety of our domestic institutions; . . . they have denounced as sinful the institution of slavery; they have permitted . . . societies, whose avowed object is to disturb the peace and to eloign the property of the citizens of other States.[54]

In rapid succession, southern states with similar grievances—Alabama, Arkansas, Florida, Georgia, Louisiana, Mississippi, North Carolina, Tennessee, Texas, and Virginia—also severed and joined with South Carolina. They established a confederacy with the institution of slavery as its ballast. Abraham Lincoln, a Republican, was inaugurated the sixteenth US president on March 4, 1861. A month later soldiers from the new Confederate States of America attacked Fort Sumter, a Union stronghold in Charleston, South Carolina. The action sparked the four-year Civil War between the North and the South, declared on April 15, 1861.

Northerners initially believed the war would be "brief, almost bloodless; some predicting its end in 60 days."[55] This prospect faded in 1862 as Union losses multiplied and Confederate victories increased. With its troops dwindling, the US Congress enacted the Confiscation Act of 1862[56] which freed enslaved Blacks in areas under Union control and authorized their assistance in minor military roles. Bolder action was taken in 1863 with President Lincoln signing the landmark Emancipation Proclamation which promised freedom to every enslaved person in the rebel states. It defined the war as a crusade for the preservation of the Republic and hastened the enlistment of Blacks into Union ranks.[57] Nearly 180,000 men of color comprised 10 percent of the Union Army. Nineteen thousand served in the Union Navy.

The promise of the proclamation inspired one of the few recognized women artists of the period, African American and Native American sculptress Edmonia Lewis, to sculpt the masterpiece *Morning of Liberty*.[58]

As the Civil War intensified, the US government waged a separate war against Indigenous peoples in the west, confiscating their already downsized lands for westward expansion. Beginning in 1861, federal troops clashed with Chief Cochise and the Chiricahua Apache nation for control of tribal lands in Arizona and New Mexico.[59] In southern Minnesota, the largest mass execution in US history was reported in 1862 with the hanging of thirty-eight Dakota tribal fighters by federal troops in the Sioux Uprising and Dakota War.[60] Two years later, 230 Cheyenne and Arapaho men, women, and children were slain by federal troops in the Sand Creek Massacre.[61]

Meanwhile Harriet Tubman in 1863, with her self-appointed band of scouts and soldiers from the 3rd Rhode Island Heavy Artillery Regiment and the 2nd South Carolina Volunteer Infantry Regiment (Colored), led incursions through plantations along the Combahee River in South Carolina. Her frenzied forays routed the Confederates and enabled the escape of 750 enslaved men, women, and children to freedom. That same year she witnessed the Morris Island, South Carolina battle fought by the Black 54th Massachusetts Volunteer Infantry Regiment against Confederate forces. As depicted in the 1989 award-winning film *Glory*, 42 percent of the regiment were killed, a sacrifice that heightened respect for all Black fighting men.[62] One of the injured soldiers, Lewis Douglass, son of abolitionist Frederick Douglass, wrote:

> Saturday night we made the most desperate charge of the war on Fort Wagner, losing in killed, wounded and missing in the assault, three hundred

of our men. The splendid 54th is cut to pieces . . . If I die tonight, I will not die a coward.[63]

As the tide of war slowly turned in the North's favor, President Lincoln won reelection in 1864. Frederick Douglass and civil rights activist Sojourner Truth attended the March 1865 inauguration on the US Capitol steps where the president eloquently counseled, "With malice toward none; with charity for all . . . let us strive on to finish the work we are in; to bind up the nation's wounds."[64] Mr. Douglass recalled, "I felt then that there was murder in the air, and I kept close . . . for felt that I might see him fall that day."[65]

The Civil War ended one month later in April 1865 with the Union as victor. The four-year conflagration claimed 623,000 lives, the greatest number of US casualties in any war before or since. Of the total losses, nearly 40,000 soldiers of color died, 75 percent from infection and disease.[66] Six days after victory on April 14, 1865, President Lincoln was assassinated by a hardened Confederate at Ford's Theatre in Washington, DC.

The US Congress enacted its first Freedmen's Bureau Act that year with plans to transfer 40-acre tracts of confiscated southern plantation land to freed Blacks. This would follow Union General William Tecumseh Sherman's Special Field Order #15 which granted each formerly enslaved Black family 40 acres in the coastal region of Georgia.[67] It was envisioned that a similar policy could be decreed throughout the South as reparation for the centuries of forced servitude borne by Blacks. This hope was dashed by Lincoln's vice president and now the 17th US president, Andrew Johnson. In late 1865, he ordered all lands under federal control be returned to the previous owners.[68]

That same year the US Congress, led by Representative Thaddeus Stevens of Pennsylvania, ratified the landmark 13th Amendment which abolished the institution of slavery.[69] Millions fled the plantations. Families torn asunder by slavery placed advertisements in search of lost relatives.[70] On June 19, 1865, in Galveston Bay, Texas, a quarter of a million Blacks were the last to be informed of their freedom. Today, the date termed "Juneteenth" is a federal holiday and an official state holiday in twenty-four states and the District of Columbia.[71]

One year after the 13th Amendment, the US Congress passed the landmark 14th Amendment in 1866 which granted citizenship to every formerly enslaved person. The amendment guarantees equal protection under the law and citizenship to all people born or naturalized in the United States.[72]

This postwar period, with its extraordinary efforts to accommodate Blacks and reform the South, is defined as the Reconstruction Era (1865–77). The Confederate states, except for Tennessee, were patrolled by federal troops and divided into five military districts. They were required to ratify the 13th and 14th Amendments and write new state constitutions approved by their white and new Black voters.[73]

The 1867 Reconstruction Act that followed set the terms for the orderly reentry of the rebel states into the Union.[74] It also granted freed Blacks (termed freedmen) equal access and protection under the law. To aid their transition, the US War Department established the Freedman's Bureau, which opened offices in the former rebel states, the border states (Maryland, Kentucky, West Virginia), and in Washington, DC. Nearly 100 freedman hospitals and medical clinics were established throughout the South, as well as educational and training facilities. The Freedman Bureau was tasked with enormous responsibilities but was also "chronically underfunded and understaffed with just 900 agents at its peak."[75]

The nation's first impeachment of a US president occurred in this period. President Johnson, a southern Democrat, and the Republican-led Congress were at loggerheads. The Tenure of Office Act, passed by the US Congress in 1867, forbade the president from replacing Edwin Stanton as secretary of war. Johnson defiantly fired Stanton the following year, which led to his impeachment by the House of Representatives. The Senate, however, fell one vote short of the two-thirds needed to convict Johnson, and he retained his presidency.[76] Despite these lingering postwar political feuds, the spirit of the polity was high. Most were relieved that the war was over and eager to assist with reconciliation. As recorded in the National Archives:

> During the years after the war, black and white teachers from the North and South, missionary organizations, churches and schools worked tirelessly to give the emancipated population the opportunity to learn. Former slaves of every age took advantage of the opportunity . . . Grandfathers and their grandchildren sat together in classrooms.[77]

Whites in the military-monitored rebel states grew increasingly uneasy, however, with the changing order.[78] In 1866, a three-day uprising in Tennessee resulted in the deaths of forty-six Blacks and two whites and the burning of ninety-one homes, four churches, and eight schools. A US Congressional report concluded the violence was perpetuated by white policemen, firemen, and businessmen.[79] Another outbreak, three days later in Louisiana, resulted in the murder of 34 Blacks and 199 wounded. Union Army General Phil Sheridan reported Blacks were:

> attacked with fire-arms, clubs, and knives, in a manner so unnecessary and atrocious as to compel me to say that it was . . . an absolute massacre . . . which the Mayor and police . . . perpetrated without the shadow of a necessity.[80]

In 1869, the former Union Commanding General, Ulysses S. Grant, won election as the eighteenth US president. He served two terms to 1877. With Reconstruction as his focus, President Grant signed the *Force Acts* (also termed the *Ku Klux Klan Acts*) which "prohibited groups from banding together or to go in disguise with the intention of violating the constitutional rights of citizens."[81] The legislation also federalized national elections, authorized federal judges and US marshals to supervise local polling places, and approved the suspension of habeas corpus if necessary to protect civil liberties.[82] Though Grant unequivocally supported civil rights, First Lady Julia Dent Grant had enslaved Blacks most of her life. Together they benefited from slave labor while living in Missouri from 1854 to 1860, making Grant the last US president to have owned an enslaved person.[83]

Signaling its transition from an agricultural to an industrialized economy, America opened its first transcontinental railroad in 1869. The railroad cut a vast trade corridor from coast to coast with portions running through usurped Indigenous lands.[84] Its most dangerous and unsafe construction was assigned to marginalized Chinese laborers. Many venerable Black universities were established in this period including Fisk (1866), Lincoln (1866), Howard (1867), and Hampton (1868). Their graduates represented the next wave of leadership and promise for the race.

In Rhode Island (1860–70)

In 1861, the number of Blacks in Rhode Island increased from 3,760 to 3,952 and represented 2.3 percent of the population. With the Civil War looming, palpable anxiety was felt by every citizen. The 2nd Rhode Island Infantry was assigned that year to the First Battle of Bull Run in Virginia. After a devastating defeat, state officials, including Rhode Island governor William Sprague, traveled to the battlefield to "return the fallen sons to native soil."[85] With its military thinning, Rhode Island's new governor, James Youngs Smith, petitioned the US War Department for permission to enlist Blacks, one of the first northern states to make the request. The Rhode Island 14th Heavy Artillery Regiment [Colored] was mustered in 1863. Men of color from throughout the country enlisted as the regiment grew to over 1,700. They were stationed within sight of the Jamestown shoreline on Dutch Island in Narragansett Bay. [*Profiles of the soldiers of the Rhode Island 14th Heavy Artillery Regiment (Colored) are provided in Chapter 2.*]

In Newport, Blacks numbered 691, about 7 percent of the city population. Likely due to the Underground Railroad, one-fifth hailed from the slave states of Maryland and Virginia. The community's stability and growth made way for two new churches, the Mt. Zion AME in 1845 and the Shiloh Baptist in 1869.[86] In sharp contrast to the educational inequities in the southern states, all of Rhode Island's public schools were now integrated and open to colored children in 1866, the result of fierce Black activism.

In Jamestown (1860–70)

In this period, the number of whites in Jamestown increased slightly by 10 percent to 387. The Black population was static at thirteen. They were ten males and three females ranging in age from two to sixty. They worked as laborers and domestics. Though six were children, none attended school. When the Civil War ended in 1865, the number of island Blacks increased to seventeen. Most were Rhode Island-born farm laborers such as Henry Johnson, age sixty, and William Warmsley, age twenty-five. The new arrivals included teenager Anna Colbert, a servant from New Jersey, and Mary Williams, a domestic from the former slave state of Virginia. James Howland had since passed away and the Champlins—a nuclear family with a father, four sons, and one daughter, all born in Jamestown—continued to live on the island, eventually purchasing land for a farm. [*The Champlin family is featured in Chapter 2.*]

It is likely that the tiny microcosm of island Blacks conversed on the news of the decade—the daring fugitive flights to freedom, the tempo and toll of the war, the Union victories and defeats, the signing of the emancipation proclamation, the shocking assassination of the president, the John Brown insurrection, and the dizzying changes wrought by Reconstruction. They likely witnessed the building of two Civil War encampments: Camp Meade in the center of town and Camp Bailey on nearby Dutch Island, home of the 14th Heavy Artillery Regiment (Colored). While two islanders died in uniform in the war,[87] there is no record of island Blacks enlisting or serving.[88]

1870–80: Reconstruction Aftermath

In the United States (1870–80)

The US Congress ratified the 15th Amendment to the US Constitution in 1870. Believed impossible just ten years prior, the amendment granted Black males the right to vote. It accompanied a growing list of legislative reforms to redress racial grievances such as the Civil Rights Act of 1875, which affirmed the "equality of all men before the law" and prohibited discrimination in public places "on the basis of color, race, or previous condition of servitude."[89] While these gains were notable and hard-won, unimaginable violence pervaded the South. The 1875 Clinton, Mississippi, Riot, led by whites, resulted in the annihilation of a Black settlement.[90] Despite this, by 1877 when the Reconstruction Era officially ended, "2,000 citizens of color were actively engaged in local, state, and federal government, many as elected or appointed US Senators, state Supreme Court judges, lieutenant governors, and mayors." [91]

One such citizen of color was Hiram Rhodes Revels of Mississippi, the first Black US senator in US history.[92] The son of a Baptist preacher, he was born free in North Carolina. First studying at a private school for Blacks, he completed his education in the North, attending seminaries in Indiana and Ohio. He became an ordained AME minister in 1845 and studied theology at Knox College in Illinois. In the 1850s, he ministered to free and enslaved communities in various states and aided freedom seekers. In 1861, Reverend Revels, now a pastor in Baltimore, assisted in the recruitment of Black soldiers in Maryland. Returning to Mississippi at war's end, he served as a Union Army chaplain and presided at the Natchez AME Church. He was elected town alderman in 1868 and then state senator in 1869, one of thirty-five Blacks elected or appointed to the Mississippi legislature that year. Needing to fill its vacancies in the US Senate, the state legislature was urged to consider a Black Republican. Reverend Revels recalled:

> An opportunity of electing a Republican to the United States Senate, to fill an unexpired term occurred, and the colored members after consulting together on the subject, agreed to give their influence and votes for one of their own race . . . as it would in their judgement be a weakening blow against color line prejudice.[93]

When Mississippi was readmitted into the US Senate in 1870, Reverend Revel's credentials were presented but immediately challenged with charges that he had not been a voting US citizen for nine years as required by the US Constitution. Supporters dismissed the objections advising that before 1866 he was a voting citizen in Ohio. The US Senate approved the appointment, forty-eight to eight. The Mississippi senator was sworn into office on February 25, 1870. Though his term was brief, he championed education for Blacks, fought for civil rights, and spoke against racial segregation. When his appointment ended in 1871, he returned to Mississippi and served two separate terms as president of Alcorn College, a Black land grant college now Alcorn State University. Notable graduates from the school include Senator Revel, Alex Haley, Medgar Evers, Myrlie Evers-Williams, and Steve McNair.[94] In his final years, Reverend Revel remained active in the church and politics until his death from a paralytic stroke at age seventy-three on January 16, 1901.[95]

Senator Revel's historic appointment was followed by twenty appointed or elected US Representatives of color, "all Republicans from southern states, some just out of slavery."[96] The second and last Black US senator of the nineteenth century, Mississippian Blanche K. Bruce, was appointed in 1874. Sixty-three former Confederates also served as US senators in this period.[97]

In 1877, the nineteenth US president, Rutherford B. Hayes, withdrew federal peacekeeping troops from three southern states, relinquishing control to state and local governments.[98] The number of troops patrolling the South "declined from 17,657 in 1868 to less than 5,000 that year."[99] With their departure, progress toward racial justice abruptly ended. According to Crispus Attucks Wright, a surviving child of enslaved parents:

> It was an interesting period. My father wrote that we had a number of legislators, a number of congressmen . . . There was a vast advancement and then it all stopped.[100]

Black scholar W.E.B. Du Bois mused, "the slave went free; stood a brief moment in the sun; then moved back again toward slavery."[101]

There are several explanations for the largely unfulfilled promise of the Reconstruction Era. One is the agreement between President Hayes and his political opponents to relax the federal military presence in the South, thus sanctioning local rule and unleashing pent-up rage over the advancement of Blacks.[102] Other factors include the inability of the US Congress to devise a strategic reconstruction plan with a timeframe, quantifiable goals, and objectives. Without this, southern terrorists such as the emerging Red Shirts and the Knights of the White Camelia forged their own agendas.[103] The US Commission on Civil Rights cites the suppression of the Black vote as another contributing factor:

> Candidates were systematically scratched off ballots. Negroes were harassed by election officials asking questions not pertinent . . . votes were stolen from the boxes; polls were not opened at all; . . . the door to the voting place was blocked by police . . . who allowed in only those who would vote Democratic.[104]

Perhaps the most poignant factor was the rock-solid belief held by Southerners that, though the war was lost, their culture and values would live on. This spirit is captured in the southern manifesto, *The Lost Cause*, published in 1867 by Edward A. Pollard. According to the author:

> The war has not swallowed up everything. . . . [T]he war did not decide negro equality; it did not decide negro suffrage; it did not decide States Rights . . . it did not decide the right of a people to show dignity in misfortune; and to maintain self-respect in the face of adversity. And these things which the war did not decide, the Southern people will still cling to, still claim; and still assert.[105]

Eager to rebuild their ravaged homeland and stricken by the loss of free Black labor, re-empowered southerners found a loophole in the 13th Amendment which banned involuntary servitude except for the punishment of a crime. They devised a peonage or "convict leasing" system.[106] Southern Blacks without labor or employment papers in their possession, involved in minor crimes, or for no justifiable reason were aggressively confiscated by local police, incarcerated as criminals or vagrants, leased as prisoners to private industries, and assigned interminable sentences in punishing work conditions.[107] Their children were often claimed by whites as abandoned and worked as "apprentices." Over an eighty-year period, before peonage was outlawed in 1941:

> As many as 200,000 black Americans were forced into back-breaking labor in coal mines, turpentine factories and lumber camps. They lived in squalid conditions, chained, starved, beaten, flogged and sexually violated. They died by the thousands from injury, disease and torture.[108]

As the federal government grappled with the gravitas of the changing South, its relations with other races were equally challenging. The Naturalization Act, enacted by the US Congress in 1870, barred Chinese immigrants from obtaining US citizenship. This led to uprisings, such as the California Chinese Massacre of 1871 that ended with the lynching of eighteen Chinese.[109] That year, changes to the Indian Appropriations Act by the US Congress no longer recognized tribal communities as viable entities. It ended tribal treaty-making and designated Native Americans as "legal wards."[110] The rescission of once inviolable government treaties opened old wounds and triggered over 650 battles.

One enduring example is the 1868 *Fort Laramie Treaty* in which the government ceded the Black Hills in the Dakota Territory to the Lakota Sioux tribes and prohibited whites from entering without authorization. US Army Lt. Col. George Armstrong Custer led an exploratory expedition of 1,000 troops into the Hills to establish a military outpost and to investigate claims of gold. When the claims were confirmed, thousands of miners rushed in, sparking the Black Hills War (1876–7). One notable battle of the war—the Battle of Little Bighorn—is forever memorialized in American history as the crushing defeat and slaughter of Lt. Col. Custer and his 210 men by tribal forces.[111] US troops ultimately vanquished the tribes and reclaimed the Black Hills. Over a century later, their actions were ruled illegal by the Supreme Court.[112]

Roughly 12,500 men of color served in the Indian Wars between 1866 and 1891. Their military orders were to protect settlers and open the frontier for westward expansion. One in every five cavalry men and eight to 10 percent of infantry soldiers were men of color.[113] Known as Buffalo Soldiers, they served in the 9th and 10th Cavalry and the 24th and 25th Infantry. They faced discrimination in the military and within the communities they protected, but their feats of bravery and valor are legendary. Eighteen Buffalo Soldiers earned Medals of Honor between 1870 and 1890.[114] Their regiments were led mainly by whites, with the exception of three Black officers, all West Point graduates: Henry O. Flipper, John Hanks Alexander, and Charles Young.

Charles Young was born to formerly enslaved parents in 1864. According to the National Park Service, he attended the US Military Academy at West Point and in 1889 became the third Black cadet to graduate as a commissioned officer. As a Buffalo Soldier, he served first with the 25th Infantry as a second lieutenant in Montana and later with the 9th Cavalry in Nebraska and Utah. During and after the Philippine War, he served as captain and company commander with the 9th Cavalry and later as a major with the 10th.[115] At the end of his career, Charles Young rose to the rank of full colonel, the highest rank held by an African American at that time.[116]

Dignified work, a regular paycheck, food, and clothing were appealing to many who only months or years earlier were enslaved or living in poverty. Despite a prohibition against women serving, the work of the Buffalo Soldier and its benefits attracted Cathay Williams. Born to an enslaved mother and free father in Missouri in 1844, she enlisted in the US Army under the name of "William Cathay" in 1866.[117] She was the first and only known female to serve as a Buffalo Soldier in the Indian Wars. After three years of engagement, her ruse was discovered. She was honorably discharged in 1868.

Jamestown resident Sergeant Major Benjamin Morrell served as a Buffalo Soldier in Texas and later in the Dakota Territory from 1867 to 1886. [*His story is told in Chapter 2.*] The last surviving Buffalo Soldier, Reverend Robert Walker Dixon Sr., died in 2024 at the age of 103 in Albany, New York.[118]

In Rhode Island (1870–80)

In 1870, the number of Blacks in Rhode Island increased by 80 percent to 4,980, comprising 2.3 percent of the state population. In Newport, the community was described as insular, strong, and distinct.[119] Sixty-eight percent lived in next-door dwellings or in multiple family units with other Black households concentrated in the Bellevue Avenue, Historic Hill, and Point neighborhoods.[120] A nuclear family headed by a father and/or mother and children was typical for 28 percent of the community.

The Gilded Age commenced in America in this period, from the late 1870s to the late 1890s. It was an era of prosperity and wealth for the barons of railroads, shipping, and steel and a period of poverty, discontent, and labor strikes for the poor and working class. The Gilded Age is credited with modernizing America with the introduction of popular technologies such as the telephone and the automobile:

> The late 19th century saw the advent of new communication technologies, including the phonograph, the telephone, and radio; the rise of mass-circulation newspapers and magazines; the growth of commercialized entertainment, as well as new sports, including basketball, bicycling, and football, and . . . new transportation technologies, such as the automobile, electric trains and trolleys.[121]

According to the Preservation Society of Newport County, local Blacks thrived in the period: "Newport's earliest African heritage doctors, dentists, teachers, hospitality entrepreneurs and elected officials appeared during the Gilded

Age."[122] Reverend Mahlon Van Horne became the first person of color elected to a Rhode Island public school board in 1872.[123] That year, local resident Mary Dickerson opened a dressmaking shop on fashionable Bellevue Avenue. She later established the Women's Newport League and became a founding member of the National Association of Colored Women's Clubs (NACWC) in 1896.[124] These organizations enabled women of color to collectively combat racism, empower their communities, and secure women's suffrage. The NACWC still exists.[125]

Also, sadly in the period, 14 miles southwest of Newport, native Narragansett families suffered searing pain with the unlawful confiscation of their children by the US government in 1879, a practice sanctioned by state governments and occurring unchecked across the nation. The abducted children were transported to distant government facilities termed Indian boarding schools to "cleanse" them of their Indigenous identities.[126]

In Jamestown (1870–80)

The island of Jamestown held eighty-three dwellings and forty-two farms in 1870. Its population was shrinking. The number of whites fell by 5.5 percent to 378. The number of Black residents fell by 39 percent to eight. Dominated by the five-member Champlin family, the colored community comprised seven males and one female from fourteen to fifty-six years of age. All were farm laborers, domestics, and Rhode Island-born except two.

Suddenly and sharply, the island economy lurched to life in 1873 with the launch of steam ferry service across Narragansett Bay from Jamestown to Newport. This signified the Jamestown Resort Era; a historic period of growth and transformation that commenced in 1875.[127] Land surrounding the steam ferry service, within and near the town center, quickly transitioned to commercial and retail properties. A former slaveholding family, the Howlands, and the former owners of James Howland, were the first to convert their farmland of twenty acres to platted streets, profiting handsomely.[128] Taxable property on the island was now valued at $1 million, up from $300,000 three years earlier.[129]

Jamestown East Ferry wharf looking east across Narragansett Bay to Newport. Beginning in 1873, largely due to ferry service, the island population and economy grew and diversified. Courtesy: Jamestown Historical Society Collections, P2013.115.048.

By 1875, the number of colored Jamestown residents increased by 113 percent to seventeen, comprising ten males and seven females. They ranged in age from nine to eighty-two with occupations as laborer, housekeeper, and servant. Most were native Rhode Islanders (10) but reflective of the times, seven arrived from former slave states. Annie and Washington Moor, both age forty and servants, hailed from the former slave state of Maryland as did Josephine Talbot, a housekeeper, age thirty. A pubescent sixteen-year-old laborer, James Williams, arrived from the former slave state of Virginia. The community was now dominated by two Black families: the Champlins [*profiled in Chapter 2*] and the Talbots with a mother and father originally from Maryland and their five children, all but one born in Rhode Island. Two of the children—James, age nine and William, age ten—attended school.

1880–90: "A Stupendous Fraud"

In the United States (1880–90)

The Reconstruction Era was now over and momentum toward social equality and civil rights stalled. Life was precarious for persons of color. The US

Congress enacted the Chinese Exclusion Act in 1882, which banned Chinese immigration for ten years. One year later, the Supreme Court declared the Civil Rights Act of 1875—the Reconstruction law that promised equal rights and equitable access to public services and facilities—unconstitutional.[130] This presaged a growing urgency by whites, primarily in the South but also in other areas of the country, to separate the races.[131] In 1887, the Dawes Act granted presidential authority to divide and allot Native lands to white speculators, further decimating weakened tribal communities.[132]

In the South, sharecropping was a common practice. Poor families rented plots of land or shares from landowners, many of whom were former plantation and slave owners.[133] Often the sharecroppers borrowed heavily for food and supplies and carried crippling debts. For many, this was an ironclad form of debt servitude.[134] In 1888, civil rights champion Frederick Douglass visited South Carolina and Georgia to assess post-Reconstruction conditions. He observed that one-third of the sharecroppers were Black and destitute.[135] According to accounts in a subsequent speech:

> His voice quivered [as] he told the nation, 'I here and now denounce his [the slave's] so-called emancipation as a stupendous fraud—a fraud upon him, a fraud upon the world.'[136]

Ironically, two years earlier in 1886, the Statue of Liberty, an enduring symbol of American freedom, was installed in New York City Harbor, inspiring the words, "Give me your tired, your poor, your huddled masses yearning to breathe free."[137] The *Cleveland Gazette,* a Black newspaper mindful of the rapidly deteriorating freedoms of African Americans, requested the statue torch not be lit until conditions improved.[138]

The decade ended with the 1890 massacre by federal troops of over 350 men, women, and children of the Minneconjou Sioux Tribe at Wounded Knee Creek in South Dakota. Twenty soldiers of the US Army 7th Cavalry were awarded US Congressional Medals of Honor for their involvement. A century later, in 1990, the 101st US Congress issued a resolution expressing "deep regret" for the massacre.[139]

In Rhode Island (1880–90)

In 1880, the Black population in Rhode Island increased by 77 percent to 6,488, but remained 2.3 percent of the total population. The increase was likely due to the growing number of southern Blacks migrating north. The State General Assembly, in 1881, repealed a colonial era act which prohibited interracial marriages. Achievements in Black entrepreneurship continued with the opening of the successful Daisy Tonsorial Parlor barbershop on Bellevue Avenue in Newport in 1882.

Newport's Reverend Mahlon van Horne rose again to prominence in 1885, becoming the first Black elected to the State General Assembly which in 1890 banned racial discrimination in public accommodations and established the Bannister House for the care of aged colored women.[140] Despite these milestones, the state of Rhode Island brusquely repudiated its Indigenous population. According to the Narragansett, from 1880 to 1884, the General Assembly officially "detribalized" its community and refused to recognize its government and officers.[141]

In Jamestown (1880–90)

There were eighteen colored residents on the island in 1880, twelve males and six females. Three were from former slave states. Francis Bauldin, a launderer aged forty-one, and Emily Tasker, a cook aged sixty-four, hailed from the former slave state of Maryland. Thomas Artist, a farm laborer aged thirty, arrived from the former slave state of Virginia. The Talbot family had since moved on, but in addition to the Champlins, the Rice family had arrived. They were a nuclear family with father Isaac Jr., a carpenter; mother Hannah, a Narragansett; and three sons and two daughters. [*Members of the Rice family are profiled in Chapter 2.*]

The island economy thrived in the Resort Era. The decline in the number of whites ended with a 21 percent jump to 459 in 1880. By 1883 two hotels—the Gardner House and the Bay View Hotel—were constructed near the steam ferry wharf, the latter built by the former slaveholding Knowles family.

Jamestown Day Parade west and south of the East Ferry wharf, looking south along Walcott Avenue. The Thorndike Hotel is on the right. The yacht club and pier are in center distance. Blacks on the island were likely aware of and observed the celebration. Circa 1890s. Courtesy: Jamestown Historical Society Collections, GN1979.146.

Just north, 85 acres were subdivided. Ornate summer cottages dotted the shoreline.

According to town records, property owners and brothers George, William, and Alexander of the Black Champlin family registered and voted in local town elections in 1883. George and Alexander Champlin also voted in 1885.[142] These are the first known Black votes cast in Jamestown.

Growth continued in 1889 with the construction of the Champlin House and, to the curiosity of many, a fully constructed hotel—the Bay Voyage— was floated across Narragansett Bay to the island. The nearby Bay View Hotel expanded and yet another hotel, the Thorndike, was erected to accommodate the growing influx of visitors and tourists.[143] The Champlin House later became part of the Dr. Bates Sanitarium, a resort for rest and recuperation, a medical center, and a nursing home for the chronically ill.[144] It and other businesses fueled by the strong economy offered steady work as well as business opportunities for settled Blacks and those migrating from the South.

1890–1900: Perseverance

In the United States (1890–1900)

Violent racial crimes dominated America's newspaper headlines from 1890 to 1900. The rising number of Black lynchings by whites in the South prompted journalist and civil rights advocate, Ida B. Wells, to publish *Southern Horrors: Lynch Law in All Its Phases* in 1892.[145] She reported:

> the butcheries of black men . . . have gone on; also, the flaying alive of a man in Kentucky, the burning of one in Arkansas, the hanging of a fifteen-year-old girl in Louisiana, a woman in Jackson, Tenn., and one in Hollandale, Miss., . . . the dark and bloody record of the South shows Afro-Americans lynched during the past eight years.[146]

The year *Southern Horrors* was published, the Ellis Island Immigration Station opened in New York City, eventually welcoming over twelve million immigrants and refugees to American freedom.[147] This welcome was in stark contrast to the arrival of chained Africans centuries earlier and the lynching of their descendants in 1892. Federal anti-lynching legislation would not be signed into law in the US until 2022.[148]

The oldest of eight children, Ida B. Wells was born into slavery in Mississippi in 1862 and educated during Reconstruction at Rust University, a freedmen school. She began teaching at age fourteen and continued the occupation to care for her siblings after the untimely deaths of her parents and brother from yellow fever. In 1881, she relocated with two sisters to Tennessee where she worked as an educator and attended summer sessions at Fisk University in Nashville. In 1884, she filed a lawsuit against the Chesapeake & Ohio Railroad for unfair treatment, having been roughly removed from a lady's rail car despite having a ticket. She won the case, but the ruling was overturned in federal court.

Under the pen name "Iola," she wrote newspaper articles criticizing conditions for Black children in Memphis schools in 1891. Her teaching contract was not renewed and at age twenty-seven, she turned to journalism. After purchasing a share in the *Memphis Free Speech and Headlight*, Ida Wells became a co-owner and editor of the Black newspaper.[149] Learning of the lynching death of a dear friend in 1892, she began documenting white mob violence and publishing her research in her newspaper and others such as the *New York Age* and the *Chicago Tribune*. Within months, she wrote *Southern Horrors*. This enraged locals who set fire to her newspaper office building. Forced to leave, she relocated to Chicago and married African American lawyer Ferdinand Barnett in 1895. They had four children.

From 1898 to 1902, Ida Wells-Barnett served as secretary of the National Afro-American Council. In 1909, she attended the founding meeting of the NAACP. In 1910, she established and served as president of the Negro Fellowship League which aided migrants from the South and, in 1913, she established the first Black women's suffrage group, the Alpha Suffrage Club of Chicago.[150] She recruited and organized suffragists of color for the historic 1913 suffrage parade in Washington, DC, and infamously refused when asked by organizer Alice Paul to march in the segregated section. Ms. Wells-Barnett continued her dedication to civil rights and freedom until her death at age sixty-eight from kidney disease in 1931.[151]

Dr. Daniel Hale Williams, an 1883 graduate of Chicago Medical School and the nation's first Black cardiologist, made groundbreaking advances in the field of medicine in this period. In 1891, he opened America's first Black hospital—the Provident Hospital in Chicago—at a time when colored physicians were denied hospital privileges and Blacks, equitable health care and services. In 1893, he performed the country's first successful open-heart surgery and, in 1895, he was an original founder of the National Medical Association, which opened professional membership to colored physicians.[152] Families of color were also successful in the period, purchasing property in increasing numbers. According to the *African American Encyclopedia*, the 1890 Census "gives . . . evidence of the improved condition of the Negro," noting 207,616 homes and farms were owned by Blacks.[153] The Champlin family farm and the Morrell properties in Jamestown were likely included in this number.[154]

The nation mourned the death of civil rights icon, Frederick Douglass, who died at the age of seventy-seven of a heart attack in his Washington, DC home in 1895. The revered statesman was eulogized as "among the last survivors of that band of Abolitionists . . . so potent in their influence."[155]

That same year, Tuskegee University president Booker T. Washington delivered his controversial Atlanta Compromise speech urging Blacks to not agitate but instead cooperate with whites. Delivered September 18, 1895, his message of racial accommodation and gradualism was supported by Black luminaries of the period, such as *New York Age* newspaper owner Frederick Randolph Moore, and opposed by others including W.E.B. Du Bois and Ida B. Wells-Barnett.[156] Mr. Washington implored:

> To those of my race who depend on bettering their condition . . . or who underestimate the importance of cultivating friendly relations with the southern white man who is their next-door neighbor, I would say, 'Cast down your bucket where you are. Cast it down in making friends in every manly way.'[157]

One year after the Atlanta Compromise speech, the Supreme Court in 1896 issued its *Plessy v. Ferguson* ruling, declaring racial segregation the law of the land. The "separate but equal" doctrine reinforced local and state "Jim Crow" laws that legalized stark inequities for Blacks in housing, transportation, education, and public services.[158] Tennessee became the first to segregate its railroad cars by race, followed by Florida (1887) and eleven other southern states from 1888 to 1904.

The Jim Crow system encapsulated the belief that whites were superior to Blacks in intelligence, morality, social standing, and every aspect of American life. It was defined by strict "etiquette norms" practiced and refined in the South but also honored in other regions of the country. According to the Jim Crow Museum, typical etiquette norms included:

- A black male could not offer his hand (to shake hands) with a white male because it implied being socially equal. [He] could not offer his hand . . . to a white woman, because he risked being accused of rape.
- Black and white people were not supposed to eat together. If they did . . . , white people were to be served first, and some sort of partition was to be placed between them.
- Under no circumstance was a black male to offer to light the cigarette of a white female.

- Black people were not allowed to show public affection toward one another, especially kissing, because it offended white people.
- Jim Crow etiquette prescribed that black people were introduced to white people, never white people to black people.
- White people did not use courtesy titles of respect when referring to black people, [such as] Mr., Mrs., Miss, Sir, or Ma'am. . . . black people were called by their first names.
- Black people had to use courtesy titles when referring to white people and were not allowed to call them by their first names.
- White motorists had the right-of-way at all intersections.[159]

Perhaps it was the permission granted by the *Plessy v. Ferguson* decision and the pervasiveness of Jim Crow laws coupled with a repugnance of the growing influence of Black elected officials and the Black press that caused whites in Wilmington, North Carolina, to stage a coup d'état. Weeks before local elections, armed Rough Riders and Red Shirts gathered in the city. On election day, November 8, 1898, they along with agitated local whites blocked Blacks from voting, seized ballot boxes, and replaced Republican ballots with Democratic ballots. The following day, 450 of the city's most influential citizens including clergy, led by US Congressman Alfred Moore Waddell, gathered at the courthouse to sign a "White Declaration of Independence." On November 10, 1898, they reassembled, gutted and set ablaze Love and Charity Hall, which housed the Black newspaper, *The Daily Record*. Threatening death, they banished the white Mayor and other elected whites and Blacks and assigned their vacated seats to white supremacists. The Wilmington police chief, a police officer, and a US Commissioner were forcibly expelled from the city. The mob then turned its attention to the city's colored quadrant. Bewildered Blacks were beaten and killed. Wild with fear, young and old fled their homes and hid unsheltered in cold swamps outside of the city for several days.

The attacking whites were members of the White Government Union, a growing network of clubs across the state of North Carolina. Their stated aim was to elevate the white race by voting for supremacists in the November election. Martial law was declared by Governor Daniel Russell Jr., but the militia was told in error that Blacks were responsible for the bedlam resulting in further unprovoked attacks and killings of colored residents. The troops conducted rapid-fire gun raids at the St. Stephen AME Church, where Black families sought refuge.

There is no official count of the number killed during the Wilmington conflagration. Estimates range from fourteen to several hundred. When the 1900 census was taken one year later, the number of Black city and county residents in the area was down by 800. The white population increased by more than 2,500.[160]

America's need in the South and in other corners of the country to systematically separate and subjugate people of color was on full display in this period and inspired authoritarian regimes abroad. In 1925, Adolf Hitler praised the US practice of alienating Native Americans in his political manifesto, *Mein Kampf.* According to research conducted by the US Holocaust Museum:

> Hitler was contemptuous of American democracy. However, he was impressed by the American notion of "Manifest Destiny." The United States used this concept to justify the brutal forced displacement of Native Americans. The Americans expanded westward and destroyed Native Americans to make room for white settlers. According to Hitler, this history served as a precedent for Germany.[161]

As it grew in authority and power, Hitler's government dispatched German researchers to America to document and observe the execution of its Jim Crow and race laws such as the *1924 Racial Integrity Act of Virginia*, which defined whites as "those who had no trace whatsoever of 'blood' other than Caucasian, or had one-sixteenth or less American Indian 'blood' and no other non-Caucasian blood."[162] In 1948, white South Africans similarly sought racial supremacy over Blacks through government apartheid laws and programs.[163]

Injecting a beacon of pride and hope into the darkening clouds of racism, Indiana-born Marshall "Major" Taylor swept into history as the fastest man in the world after winning the 1899 Track Cycling World Championship. He was hailed as the "Black Cyclone." Another flourishing figure of the time was US Deputy Marshal Bass Reeves. Born into slavery in Arkansas, he grew up in Texas then moved north into Indian Territory and lived with the Cherokee, Creek, and Seminole. He married Nellie Jennings in 1864, established a farm in Arkansas, and reared ten children. In 1875, along with 200 others, he responded to President Grant's call for law and order in the Wild West and was hired as a federal deputy marshal. He was of considerable stature (six feet, two inches), claimed to know the territories "like a cook knows her kitchen," and was a skilled marksman.

Bass Reeves was one of the first African Americans appointed US deputy marshal west of the Mississippi River and served in the position for thirty-two years. It is reported he arrested more than 3,000 men and women. In the opinion of friends and foes alike, he performed his federal duties fearlessly and fairly. He sometimes wore a mask, hired Indigenous friends to assist his work, and paid his debts with silver dollars. His life is purported to be the prototype for the Lone Ranger, a fictional white former Texas Ranger who fought outlaws with his Native friend Tonto. When Bass Reeves died in 1910 of Bright's disease at the age of seventy-two, the *Muskogee Phoenix* wrote:

> In the history of the early days . . . the name of Bass Reeves has a place in the front rank among those who cleansed out the old Indian Territory of outlaws and desperadoes. No story of the conflict . . . can be complete without mention of the Negro who died yesterday . . . sent to arrest some of the most desperate characters that ever infested Indian Territory.[164]

In sharp contrast to the derring-do of Bass Reeves, a benevolent dark-complexioned Nancy Green debuted at the 1893 Chicago World's Columbian Exposition. She eventually became the country's first living trademark—Aunt Jemima—an iconic pancake flour promoter whose visage on product boxes filled American kitchen pantries, Black and white, for a century. Rooted in vaudeville and blackface minstrels, popular at the time, the non-threatening persona of the bright-eyed Black brimming with Southern hospitality was concocted by white businessmen and soothed a race-conflicted nation. In real life Ms. Green rejected the derogatory mammy caricature. Born enslaved in Kentucky in 1834, she lived a dignified free life as a philanthropist and a founding member of the Chicago Olivet Baptist Church, once the largest African American church in the country. Purported to be wealthy, she "used her economic power to advocate against poverty and support organizations fighting for equal rights."[165] Tragically, in 1923 at age eighty-nine, Nancy Green was killed in an accident on a Chicago sidewalk. Reports of her death filled the front pages of national newspapers.[166]

As the decade ended, a contemplative America took stock of its race relations. According to historian Khalil Gibran Muhammad:

> Following the 1890 census, the first to gather statistical data on African Americans born after slavery, a damaging cautionary tale arose about the threat Black people posed.[167]

This "cautionary tale" was captured in a widely distributed report replete with eugenic theories and written in 1896 by insurance company statistician, Frederick L. Hoffman. His 329-page diatribe, *Race Traits and Tendencies of the American Negro*, became a runaway bestseller. Fueled by conjecture and unfounded suppositions, it warned of the danger of Blacks to white society, concluding:

> All the facts prove that a low standard of sexual morality is the . . . cause of the . . . anti-social condition of the [Black] race at the present time. All the facts prove that education, philanthropy, and religion have failed to develop a higher appreciation [by Blacks] of the . . . virtues of the Aryan race.[168]

Hoffman's theories were read by a postbellum society facing rising crime rates, an alarming smallpox epidemic, and an increasing demand for equity and inclusion by Blacks.[169] It is likely his writings reinforced, if not widened the racial divide in America.

In Rhode Island (1890–1900)

The number of Blacks in 1890 totaled 7,393 and comprised 2.14 percent of the Rhode Island population. This was a 14 percent increase from the previous decade in absolute numbers.

Newport hired its first Black police officer, James Ray, in 1890. The following year the first New England newspaper owned and operated by persons of color was published in Providence.[170] Named *Torchlight*, it was edited by Black journalist John Carter Minkins, newly arrived from the former slave state of

Virginia. For fifty years, Mr. Minkins excelled in Rhode Island as the first Black editor-in-chief of a white-owned newspaper, the *Providence News Democrat*, and later as a reporter and managing editor for several newspapers including the *Evening and Sunday Telegram*, the *Pawtucket Times*, and the *Pawtucket Free Press.*[171]

In Newport, Black businessmen and brothers J. T. and D. B. Allen opened the swank Hygeia Spa Café on Easton's Beach and a dining room in the Perry mansion on Touro Street in 1893. That year gifted classical artist and Providence resident, Sissieretta Jones, became one of the first Black sopranos to perform at Carnegie Hall. Reputed to be the highest-paid vocalist of color of her time, she performed at the White House, for British royalty, and at sold-out venues in Australia, India, southern Africa, South America, and the West Indies.[172]

In Newport the Black population swelled to 1,496 in 1895, representing 8.28 percent of city residents. In this, the Gilded Age, an appreciable number were members of the middle and professional classes. The iconic Vanderbilt Breakers was constructed just off Bellevue Avenue in 1895, the same year Howard University Medical School graduate, Dr. Marcus F. Wheatland, established a medical practice in the city. Nationally recognized as a radiology specialist and one of the first of any race to use the X-ray machine, Dr. Wheatland, an African American, also served as president of the National Medical Association. He was elected to the Newport City Council in 1910.[173] The city economy was red hot. Labor and services were in high demand. Mt. Olivet Baptist Church opened in 1897, shortly after the city's first dentist of color, Alonzo Van Horne, began scheduling patients.

In Jamestown (1890–1900)

The Jamestown economy also churned. The island hosted 900 visitors in the summer of 1890, nearly 200 more than its resident population of 707.[174] The number of Blacks was now fifteen, including three children. The adults worked as laborers, farm helpers, domestics, and cooks. Two of the children attended school, Elizabeth and Phoebe Davis, ages eight and ten. With this critical mass and the surge of seasonal workers and domestics brought by wealthy vacationing families, the Mt. Zion AME Church officially opened in Jamestown in 1896. For nearly 100 years it was a sacred place for the island's Black community. [*The Mt. Zion AME Church is featured in Chapter 2.*]

1900–10: Hope

In the United States (1900–10)

The national Black anthem, *Lift Every Voice and Sing,* was performed for the first time in 1900 in the former slave state of Florida at Stanton School, its first high school for Blacks.[175] The National Negro Business League also formed that year.[176] Theodore Roosevelt ascended to the presidency after the assassination of William McKinley in 1901. As the twenty-sixth US president, he began his tenure by inviting formerly enslaved and now renowned civil rights and education icon Booker T. Washington to dine at the White House, "creating a national sensation."[177] In 1902, Roosevelt appointed Black physician Dr. William D. Crum to the position of collector of customs in Charleston, South Carolina. The appointment "bestowed authority over whites and was considered scandalous" in the first state to secede from the Union and where the first shots of the Civil War had been fired.[178]

In 1903, a seminal collection of thought-provoking essays, *The Souls of Black Folk,* was published by Fisk University and Harvard College graduate W.E.B. Du Bois, one of the first scholars of color to contemplate the pathology of racism in America and in Black life.[179] In *The Souls* he writes:

> One ever feels his twoness,—an American, a Negro; two souls, two thoughts, two unreconciled strivings; two warring ideals in one dark body, whose strength alone keeps it from being torn asunder.[180]

William Edward Burghardt Du Bois was born February 23, 1868, in Great Barrington, Massachusetts. He lived in a one-parent household with his mother, Mary Silvina Burghardt, a domestic worker separated from his father, Alfred Du Bois, a barber and laborer. In 1884, he graduated with honors as the first Black graduate from the town high school. Du Bois was accepted into Fisk University in 1885, six months after his mother's untimely death.

W.E.B. Du Bois (1868—1963). American sociologist, author, scholar, and founder of the Niagara Movement and the NAACP. Courtesy: Library of Congress, https://www .loc.gov/item/95517789/.

Given his loss, he preferred to stay in-state and attend Harvard University, but the less expensive alternative and the tuition support offered by four local churches influenced his decision to travel to Nashville, Tennessee. He excelled academically at the historically Black university, studied German as a second language, pursued public speaking, and edited the school newspaper, the *Fisk Herald*.[181]

He graduated in 1888 then transferred to Harvard University where he earned a bachelor's degree cum laude in 1890, a master's degree in 1891, and a doctorate degree in 1895. Eager to test his German fluency and travel abroad, he applied and was accepted into Friedrich-Wilhelm III Universität (Humboldt University) in Berlin, Germany in 1892.[182] The young Du Bois observed the machinations of the German political system while at the university and touring the country. According to biographer Hamilton Beck:

> Du Bois was interested in the Social Democrats, not because he agreed . . . with their Politics, but because they were a political movement for the disenfranchised and underprivileged, and so he saw in them a possible model for what could happen someday for his own race in America.[183]

Returning to the states in 1894, he taught at Wilberforce University in Ohio where he met Nina Gomer, a student, whom he married in 1896. They had two children. While at Wilberforce he undertook a University of Pennsylvania-sponsored sociology study of the Seventh Ward in Philadelphia, requiring 2,500 door-to-door interviews. His work, *The Philadelphia Negro*, was published in 1899.

With journalist William Monroe Trotter, Dr. Du Bois established the Niagara Movement in 1904, a Black civil rights advocacy group. The effort, while timely, floundered due to lack of funds and sharp criticism from Black conservatives such as Booker T. Washington. Five years later in 1909, Dr. Du Bois founded the NAACP in response to escalating violence against Blacks. To this day, the NAACP stands as the nation's premier civil rights organization. In 1910, Dr. Du Bois served on the organization's board and as editor of its magazine, *The Crisis*. According to the NAACP:

> Under [his] guidance, the journal attracted a wide readership, reaching 100,000 in 1920 . . . With Du Bois as its mouthpiece, [we] came to be known as the leading protest organization for Black Americans.[184]

During the First World War, Dr. Du Bois advocated for more Black officers and the fair treatment of Black troops in Europe. He led a "silent protest" march in New York City against racism in 1917, the first of its kind. He visited Liberia in 1923 and the Soviet Union in 1926, which heightened his interest in Marxism. The NAACP reports his intellectual interests broadened over time:

> Throughout his life, Du Bois was active in the Pan-Africanism movement, attending the First Pan-African Conference in London in 1900. He later

organized a series of Pan-African Congress meetings around the world in 1919, 1921, 1923, and 1927, bringing together intellectuals from Africa, the West Indies, and the United States.[185]

He left the NAACP in 1934 after an internal rift "over his controversial stance on segregation with his viewing the "separate but equal" status as an acceptable position for Blacks."[186] He chaired the Atlanta University Sociology Department from 1940 to 1944 then, after a ten-year absence at the age of seventy-six, he returned to the NAACP as director of special research from 1944 to 1948. According to the organization, he now viewed the world through the prism of a global citizen:

> ... he attended the founding convention for the United Nations ... lobbying the global body to acknowledge the suffering of Black Americans. He wrote the famous NAACP publication, "An Appeal to the World," a precursor to a report charging the United States with genocide for its ugly history of state-sanctioned lynchings. Du Bois also turned a spotlight onto the injustices of colonialism, urging the United Nations to use its influence to take a stand against such exploitative regimes.[187]

Leaving the NAACP for the final time, he joined the Council on African Affairs and chaired the Advisory Council of the Peace Information Center in 1950. He received the distinguished International Peace Prize from the World Council of Peace in 1953.

According to the *Boston Review,* a darkness enveloped Dr. Du Bois and his second wife, Shirley Du Bois, from 1951 to 1958:

> In 1951, at the age of 83, Dr. Du Bois was indicted, arrested, and arraigned in federal court as an agent of the Soviet Union because he had circulated a petition protesting nuclear weapons. The Justice Department saw Du Bois's petition as a threat to national security ... They put Du Bois on trial in order to brand him as "un-American" ... A federal judge acquitted him because prosecutors failed to present any evidence ... In 1952 the State Department illegally revoked Du Bois's passport to stop him from traveling to a peace conference in Canada. ... The Supreme Court restored passport rights for suspected communists in 1958.[188]

With the passport restriction finally lifted, he traveled to eastern Europe, China, and Russia and received the Lenin Peace Prize in Moscow in 1960. In his final years, he was invited by President Kwame Nkrumah and the Ghana Academy of Sciences to live in their country and write an *Encyclopedia Africanas*. He accepted but, before leaving the States, joined the American Communist Party. He resided in Accra from 1961 to 1963 with a colony of African American expatriates.

Dr. Du Bois died August 27, 1963, at the age of ninety-five, the day before the historic March for Jobs and Freedom led by Dr. Martin Luther King in Washington, DC. His gravestone sits at the western wall of Osu Castle in Accra where Africans were held captive before being transported into slavery in the seventeenth and eighteenth centuries.[189]

In line with Dr. Du Bois' presence and influence at the time, the decade from 1900 to 1910 marked the emergence of the Black intellectual, activist, educator, and entrepreneur. The Nashville Streetcar Boycott, from 1905 to 1907, set the stage for repudiation of Jim Crow laws. Protests began with the passage of a Tennessee law stipulating "conspicuous signs" be posted on streetcars with seating designated by skin color. Local Blacks boycotted the transit company which removed the signs after suffering revenue losses for two years.[190] The boycott was the precursor of the 1955 Montgomery Bus Boycott which captivated the nation a half-century later.

Also in this period, an estimated fifty all-Black townships were incorporating in the western states, twenty in Oklahoma alone.[191] Such was the case of the Greenwood township in 1906. Black entrepreneur O.W. Gurley relocated from Arkansas to Oklahoma during the land rush in 1889 and eventually purchased forty acres in Tulsa. In partnership with other enterprising freedmen, Mr. Gurley founded the Greenwood township. It comprised thirty-five city blocks, attracted a population of 10,000, and became known as the *Black Wall Street*.[192] According to the *Oklahoma Economist,* the township spawned Black-owned:

> luxury shops, restaurants, grocery stores, hotels, theaters, barbershops, nightclubs, funeral homes, and professional offices for [its growing roster of] doctors, lawyers, and dentists. [It administered] its own schools, post office, bank, hospital, and jitney service.[193]

Greenwood flourished for fifteen years until ransacked and burned to ashes by an enraged mob of whites in 1921. In its final hours, "an estimated 150 to 300 [residents] were killed, 1,000 houses were burned and another 400 looted . . . the entire business district was destroyed."[194]

Accomplishments in the decade, particularly for women of color, included Maggie Lena Walker's 1903 opening of the Penny Savings Bank in Richmond, Virginia. Ms. Walker became the first American woman of any race to be a bank president.[195] In 1904, renowned educator and civil rights activist Mary McLeod Bethune opened the Daytona Literary and Industrial Training School for Negro Girls (renamed Bethune-Cookman College in 1931). Ms. Bethune was honored posthumously in 2022 by the US Congress with a US Capitol statue that replaced the statue of a confederate.[196]

In 1905, *The Chicago Defender* was the nation's most influential Black weekly newspaper and likely reported on Dr. Du Bois social and civil rights activities.[197] In 1906, Cornell University hosted the nation's first Black fraternity, Alpha Phi Alpha. That year Madam C. J. Walker, a Denver washerwoman, established a hair and cosmetic cream business and became the first known Black female millionaire.[198]

Philosopher Alain Locke was the first Rhodes Scholar of color in 1907. He later became an architect of the Harlem Renaissance, also known as the New Negro Movement.[199] Also that year, Charles Curtis was elected the first US senator of Native American descent in US history. A member of the Kaw Nation, he went on to serve as US Senate Majority Leader (1924–9) and as the thirty-first vice president of the United States (1929–33).[200] The nation's first Black sorority, Alpha Kappa Alpha, was incorporated at Howard University in 1908.

The decade was also hauntingly marred by racial violence. In 1906, the Brownsville Affray race riot involved questionable accusations against Black infantry soldiers at Fort Brown, Texas. President Theodore Roosevelt summarily dismissed without honor 170 of the accused men.[201] That same year, colored citizens were attacked by armed whites in Atlanta, Georgia. As reported worldwide, during the conflagration Blacks were shot, beaten, and stabbed to death.[202] Two years later the 1908 Springfield, Illinois, race riot erupted, caused by hasty reactions to rape allegations. Unable to confront the accused whom the police had sequestered, vigilantes raided just the city's Black district, destroying homes and businesses, and killing six.[203] These disturbing events prompted Dr. Du Bois to establish the NAACP.[204]

In Rhode Island (1900–10)

In Providence, Brown University admitted its first Black female student in 1901, Ethel Tremaine Robinson. She graduated with honors in 1905 with a Bachelor of Philosophy.[205] By 1906, "intelligence offices" operated by Blacks opened in Newport. These played a central role in enticing an increasing number of freed men and women to the North through job notices and sophisticated word-of-mouth. According to researcher Myra Armstead:

> Recent migrants to the city ran eleven of Newport's intelligence offices. With the exception of [one], the officers were natives of the South . . . [their offices] may have been part of the documented national pattern in which such employment bureaus were instrumental in bringing southern blacks North after the Civil War.[206]

Newport elected its first city councilor of color in 1908. Six percent of its Black residents owned property, up from 5 percent in 1879.

In Jamestown (1900–10)

By 1903, there were now nine hotels on the tiny island, most tightly concentrated in the town center near the steam ferry. The number of island Blacks reached a high of eighty-two, a 356 percent increase since 1880. The community comprised forty-five males and thirty-seven females, ranging in age from one to sixty. While only one member of the Champlin family remained, a substantial number of new Black families, married couples, widowers, and singles inhabited the island along with the Rice family. While the majority (23) originated from Rhode Island, twenty-one were from the former slave state of Virginia. Others hailed from Delaware, Florida, Georgia, Kentucky, Louisiana,

Couple strolling on Union Street. The male is believed to be Samuel Snowden, a Gardner House Hotel dishwasher, 25. Born in Maryland in 1875, he is listed as an island resident in the 1900 US Census. Courtesy: Jamestown Historical Society Collections, P1982.075.

Maryland, North Carolina, Pennsylvania, and the District of Columbia. Most were laborers, service workers, and domestics, but for the first time, they also included skilled workers such as Isaac Jones, stone mason; Robert Johnson, salesman; and Mary A. B. Jones, dressmaker.

By 1905, the Jamestown Black population reached an all-time high of 116 for the period. In addition to farm laborers and domestics, they worked and entertained in the Resort Era hotels and provided support services throughout the island as chauffeur, express man, coach man, teamster, cook, waiter, grocery salesman, nurse, maid, and steward. In step with the entrepreneurial spirit of the Resort Era, they established businesses offering laundry, hostler, and shoeshine services. For most, however, their time on-island was brief. In an effort to attract and keep them, hotel owners provided segregated rooming houses with rent-free accommodations for Black employees.[207]

The table below is a sample of the Black residents in Jamestown in 1900. A full census from 1850 to 1920 is provided in the appendix.

Town of Jamestown, Rhode Island, Black Community—1900 Census (Sample)

Married

- Benjamin F. Morrell and wife Nannie A, married 25 years from Kentucky and North Carolina; one adopted child, Frederick G. M. White from Montana, age 8.
- George L. Payne and wife Sarah, ages 26 and 25; married five years with two children; from RI and Virginia.
- Isaac Johnson, stone mason, and wife Eliza, ages 48 and 44; married 22 years with six children.
- James Scott, hotel waiter and wife Diana K., cook; ages 38 and 34; married 13 years.
- Mary F. Netter, age 58, head of household with six children, three in school (Lila, Edith, and Sherwood) married 30 years; and daughter Florence Holly with husband Charles, ages 22 and 26; married three years.
- Thomas Davis and wife Melissa; ages 41 and 60; married 21 years with three children.
- Walter Jordan, grocery salesman, and wife Rebecca, ages 44 and 30; married 11 years.
- Walter Thomas, farm laborer, and wife Quintina, ages 35 and 25, married three years with one child; from Maryland.
- William H. Jones and wife Mary A.B., ages 45 and 34, married 15 years; from Maryland/Virginia; and mother-in-law Evalina Coates, age 50, from Virginia.

Single

From Jamestown and Rhode Island:

- Hannah E. Champlin, age 43
- Willard F. Clarke, age 16

From former slave state of Virginia

- Jane Tanner, age 14
- John Colvert, age 20
- John Robinson, age 24
- Marshall Carter, age 20
- Minerva Washington, age 26
- Monnie Grant, age 39
- Mollie Andrews, age 37
- Powtan Parker, 17
- Washington Campbell, age 32
- Wilfred Lawson, age 22
- William S. Rose, age 34

From former slave state of Georgia

- Henrietta Dosia, age 21
- James Berriman, age 25

From former slave state of Maryland

- Alfred Clifford, age 26
- Henrietta Mahony, age 39
- Samuel Snowden, age 25

From West Indies

- Irene Davis, age 47

1910–20: The Great Migration

In the United States (1910–20)

The migration and spread of six million Blacks from the South to every conceivable corner of America continued for sixty years.[208] According to author Isabel Wilkerson, this mass movement:

> . . . would reshape the social and political geography of every city they fled to. When the migration began, 90 percent of all African Americans were living in the South. By the time it was over . . . 47 percent . . . were living in the North and West. A rural people had become urban, and a Southern people had spread themselves all over the nation.[209]

The migration challenged and changed the social order and served as a catalyst for organizations with missions similar to the NAACP. The National Urban League was founded in 1910 to aid African Americans with employment, housing, civil rights, and social justice.[210] The United Negro Improvement Association, promoting self-reliance and Black independence, was established in Harlem in 1914 by Marcus Garvey and gained popularity.[211]

The nation paused in 1913 to mourn the passing of Harriet Tubman, one of the first progenitors of Black migration.[212] Born in Maryland in 1822, Ms. Tubman died on March 10, 1913, of pneumonia in Auburn, New York at the age of ninety-one.

In 1915, the blockbuster film *Birth of a Nation*, which glorified white terrorists and demonized Blacks, was screened in the White House by the twenty-eighth US president, Woodrow Wilson. The president's quotes in the film acknowledge and respect the rise of the Ku Klux Klan.[213] The US Department of Labor confirmed in 2000 that the Wilson administration promulgated anti-Black policies in federal hiring and employment. According to the Equal Justice Initiative:

> By the end of 1913, Black employees . . . had been relegated to separate or screened-off work areas and segregated lavatories and lunchrooms . . . [and] appointed to menial positions or reassigned to divisions slated for elimination.[214]

The First World War was waged in the Wilson years from 1914 to 1918, with over 100,000 American troops killed on foreign soil. Despite their relegation to second-class citizenship, more than 350,000 Blacks enlisted and served overseas in segregated units. Most of the recruits were male, but a small number of African American women also aided the war effort. Called the "Golden Fourteen," fourteen worked in the Washington, DC Navy Department, tracking Navy ship assignments. Others worked as Motor Corps drivers, transporting soldiers to stateside military facilities for the Red Cross and the National League for Women's Service. Eighteen Black nurses served stateside in the US Army Nurse Corps and overseas, a small number provided aid and meals to Black soldiers in France.[215]

The Immigration Act of 1917 was enacted at this time and again restricted Asian immigration but, in recognition of their patriotism, Asian veterans of the war received the right of naturalization in 1918. That same year, Choctaw Native American soldiers were heralded as war heroes for their skill in transmitting secret messages in their native language, giving Allied forces a critical edge.

In 1917, a race riot in East St. Louis motivated the NAACP to mobilize its first national protest against racial violence. Nearly 10,000 marched in silent protest in New York City.[216] That year, the Camp Logan Riot resulted in the hanging of thirteen Buffalo Soldiers from the 3rd battalion of the 24th Infantry Regiment. This was sparked by smoldering tensions after the unit was assigned to guard a war training facility—Camp Logan—on the outskirts of Houston. The city held to stringent Jim Crow practices which caused the soldiers to be harassed and jeered.[217] A minor conflict ignited into a riot, leaving sixteen whites and four Black soldiers dead.

In court proceedings that lasted twenty-two days, the federal government charged sixty-three Black soldiers for their involvement. With just one lawyer among them, they pleaded not guilty. Forty-five received prison sentences. Five were acquitted. Thirteen were sentenced to death and hung on December 11, 1917. The gallows, constructed by the US military, were hastily dismantled by the time the public received the news.[218]

The Camp Logan incident was followed by a noticeable rise in race violence in what is called the *Red Summer of 1919*.[219] W.E.B. Du Bois observed:

During that year seventy-seven Negroes were lynched, of whom one was a woman and eleven were soldiers; of these, fourteen were publicly burned, eleven of them being burned alive. That year there were race riots large and small in twenty-six American cities including thirty-eight killed in a Chicago riot of August; from twenty-five to fifty in Phillips County, Arkansas; and six killed in Washington.[220]

According to the Equal Justice Initiative:

During . . . the Red Summer, anti-Black riots erupted in . . . Houston, Texas; East St. Louis and Chicago, Illinois; Washington DC; Omaha, Nebraska; Elaine, Arkansas; . . . and Charleston, South Carolina. White mobs . . . protecting their economic and social dominance . . . attacked [Black] communities, destroyed property, and killed or injured hundreds.[221]

The violence extended as far north as New London, Connecticut, and Orono, Maine.[222] The outbreaks were attributed to whites angered by the return of tens of thousands of Black First World War veterans and fearful that their homeland jobs would be given to them. The increasing number of colored families migrating from the South and settling in or near areas once perceived as exclusive white enclaves, coupled with a deadly influenza pandemic afflicting 25 percent of the population, contributed to the growing panic and paranoia.

One of the most tragic red summer incidents, and the least reported until recently, was the Elaine, Arkansas, massacre. Over the course of twelve days in 1919, an estimated 100 Blacks (a precise number has never been determined) and five whites were killed. The cause was the indignation expressed by white landowners when colored sharecroppers requested fairer and higher prices for their cotton. The sharecroppers were attacked at a farmer's union meeting. Over the course of several days, members of the Elaine Black community were hunted as prey and killed by whites. Eerily similar to the 1898 Wilmington, North Carolina, insurrection, Arkansas governor Charles Brough, responding to false rumors of a Black uprising, called in US troops who, rather than aid the Black community, ravaged it. After the killings, more than sixty Blacks were charged with crimes and sentenced. Twelve were convicted of murder by an all-white jury and sentenced to death. No whites were arrested. The events were covered by journalist Ida B. Wells-Barnett and the news spread. Appeals for justice and cash donations flowed into Elaine from communities of color across the nation. The NAACP, with local African American lawyer Scipio Africanus Jones, represented the convicted men on appeal and won a reversal of their death sentences.[223] This marked the beginning of a nationwide response and resistance movement from the Black community that later galvanized the civil rights protests of the 1950s and 1960s.

The 19th Amendment was finally ratified in 1920 and guaranteed all American women the right to vote, a milestone following decades of agitation and protest.[224] The historic election day, however, November 2, 1920, was marred by what is known as the Ocoee Massacre, when 200 Blacks fled their Florida homes set ablaze by a mob of 250 whites. July Perry, a respected and beloved member of the community, was beaten, shot, dragged, and lynched as a warning to other Blacks wishing to vote. An estimated thirty to eighty Blacks were killed. Their homes, churches, and fraternal lodge were burned to the ground.[225]

In Rhode Island (1910–20)

By 1920, the absolute number of Blacks in Rhode Island had increased to 10,036 but their share of the state population had decreased to 1.7 percent. Despite, or perhaps because of, notable advancements in racial justice and Black entrepreneurship, tensions persisted in the state. The NAACP opened an office in the capital city of Providence in 1913, following a race riot in Newport. As reported, "a mob estimated at 5,000 men, women and children chased a 20-year-old [Black man] with cries of 'lynch him.'"[226] In 1917, a throng of 1,800 activists from the largest New England cities filled Providence streets for a Negro Silent Protest Parade.

In 1919, the NAACP led by Rev. James Lucas of the Mount Olivet Baptist Church, hurriedly opened a Newport branch office when the colored community gathered en masse to protest the slapping of a Black woman by a white employer. As reported:

> Fifty Newporters applied to . . . the national office of the NAACP for a local charter and paid the requisite one-dollar membership fee . . . a Sunday mass

meeting was held at Mount Zion AME Church to kick off a [membership] drive.[227]

The Newport branch was also opened to support returning Black First World War veterans, combating employment and housing discrimination.[228] The Newport economy faltered in this period. The downturn was attributed to the economic changes resulting from the war, the federal income tax introduced in 1913, and the federal estate tax introduced in 1916. These reportedly curtailed the spending of the wealthiest American families and, in some cases, led to their downfall.

In Jamestown (1910–20)

By 1910, the Resort Era continued to fill island hotels and spur the economy. The number of white residents increased 7.7 percent to 1,175. The Black population, however, declined dramatically to fifty-three with twenty-eight males and twenty-five females, ranging in age from newborn to eighty-two. In contrast to previous decades when the Black community was mostly Rhode

Caswell Block at East Ferry, Jamestown, the location of several Netter family businesses. Courtesy: Jamestown Historical Society Collections, GN1979-143.

Jamestown community gathering on its main street, Narragansett Avenue, with Black and white participants. Circa: early 1900s. Courtesy: Jamestown Historical Society Collections, P2016.101.061.

Island-born, most were now from the former slave state of Virginia (21). Seven were from North Carolina and Rhode Island, respectively. The remaining hailed from Delaware, Florida, Georgia, Kentucky, Louisiana, Maryland, Pennsylvania, and West Virginia. Supported by the island's steady demand for services, they were laborers, servants, hotel workers, drivers, laundresses, cooks, dressmakers, entrepreneurs, and ferry boat workers. The Black Netter family established downtown businesses in this period and purchased land and homes near the Mount Zion AME Church. [*The Netter family is featured in Chapter 2.*]

In 1915, the island Black population dipped again to forty-two with twenty males and twenty-two females. Six were children attending school, including three daughters of the Dunn family. In addition to laborer and servant, Blacks were trained professionals working as fireman, nurse, carpenter, painter, and dressmaker. There are no recorded incidents of race violence or intimidation or any other documented reason for the declining number of Jamestown Blacks. The remoteness of the rural island and the slumping Newport economy were likely factors, as well as the rise in jobs and opportunity in the nation's urban centers—Providence, Boston, New York, Chicago, Detroit, and Philadelphia—where Blacks were migrating in record numbers.[229]

By 1920, the Jamestown white population increased 39 percent to 1,633 while the number of colored residents fell to nineteen, representing nine males and ten females ranging in age from newborn to sixty-six. Most now hailed from five former slave states: Virginia (6), Maryland (4), Georgia (3), North Carolina (2), and Alabama (1). They included restaurant and property owners Andrew and Milissa Lodkey, former Georgians who opened the island's first known Black-owned restaurant. [*The Lodkeys are profiled in Chapter 2.*]

Exercising their new rights after ratification of the 19th Amendment, nine Jamestown women of color registered and voted in 1920 and 1921. They were Grace A. Butler, Evaline T. Coates, Mary Jones, Ella B. Lewellen, Milissa Lodkey, Ella Netter, Olivia Rice, Bertha L. Thomas, and Quintina Thomas.[230] These were the first women of color to vote in Jamestown history.

Notes

1 "1851 Indian Appropriations Act," *University of Maryland, University Libraries, Research Guide*, accessed 8/2/23, https://lib.guides.umd.edu/c.php?g=1261350&p =9246797.

2 Dorothy Wickenden, *The Agitators–Three Friends Who Fought for Abolition and Women's Rights* (Scriber, 2021), 100.

3 Compromise of 1850: The law required slavery be decided by popular sovereignty in the admission of new states, prohibited the trading of slaves in the District of Columbia, and settled a Texas boundary dispute. See "From Pre-Columbian to the New Millennium 30d—The Compromise of 1850," *US History*, https://www.ushistory.org/us/30d.asp. Fugitive Slave Act of 1850: A component of the Compromise of 1850, the law empowered police and local citizens in free and slave states to capture and detain suspected fugitives. It subjected those aiding and abetting runaways to criminal sanctions. See Library

of Congress, Pub.L. 31–60, 31st US Congress, Sept. 16, 1850, Ch. 60, https://www.loc.gov/item/llsl-v9/ and Eric Foner, "A Historian Explains the Significance of the Fugitive Slave Act," *American Social History Project*, https://shec.ashp.cuny.edu/items/show/1489. Dred Scott Decision: This Supreme Court decision ruled enslaved people were not citizens and not entitled to protection by the federal government or the courts. See "Dred Scott v. Sandford, 1857," *National Archives*, https://www.archives.gov/milestone-documents/dred-scott-v-sandford. Kansas-Nebraska Act: The law enabled settlers to decide if slavery should be permitted in their new territories. See "Kansas-Nebraska Act," *US Senate*, https://www.senate.gov/artandhistory/history/minute/Kansas_Nebraska_Act.htm.

4 "History and Society—Republican Party," *Britannica*, accessed 7/28/23, https://www.britannica.com/topic/Republican-Party. The Republican Party formed when antislavery interests comprising former members of the Democratic, Whig, and Free-Soil parties joined forces to oppose the extension of slavery into the Kansas and Nebraska territories.

5 "The Caning of Senator Charles Sumner, May 22, 1856," *US Senate*, https://www.senate.gov/artandhistory/history/minute/The_Caning_of_Senator_Charles_Sumner.htm.

6 "People v. Hall (1854)," *Immigration History*, https://immigrationhistory.org/item/people-v-hall/.

7 Anti-Chinese California Laws, US Hastings College of the Law Library, 1858, Cal. Stat. 295, accessed 7/24/23, http://libraryweb.uchastings.edu/library/research/special-collections/wong-kim-ark/laws3.htm.

8 James Oliver Horton and Lois E. Horton, *In Hope of Liberty, Culture, Community and Protest Among Northern Free Blacks, 1700–1860* (Oxford University Press, 1977), 229.

9 Cheryl Janifer LaRoche, *Free Black Communities and the Underground Railroad* (University of Illinois Press, 2014), xi–xii.

10 LaRoche, *Free Black Communities*, 19–71, 123. Blacks migrating to Canada established free settlements which were often Underground Railroad destinations.

11 William Still, *The Underground Railroad Records—The Hardships, Hairbreadth Escapes and Death Struggles of the Slaves in their Efforts for Freedom* (Philadelphia, 1886), https://www.google.com/books/edition/Still_s_Underground_Rail_Road_Records/KD9LAAAAYAAJ.

12 "Harriet Tubman and the Underground Railroad," *National Park Service*, https://www.nps.gov/articles/harriet-tubman-and-the-underground-railroad.htm; "The Combahee Ferry Raid," *Smithsonian National Museum of African American History and Culture*, 2016, https://nmaahc.si.edu/explore/stories/combahee-ferry-raid; "After the Underground Railroad, Harriet Tubman Led a Brazen Civil War Raid," *History.com*, https://www.history.com/news/harriet-tubman-combahee-ferry-raid-civil-war; Wickenden, *The Agitators–Three Friends who Fought for Abolition*, 220–4.

13 "Convicts of Alabama State Penitentiary, 1846," https://alabamagenealogy.org/covington2/jail.htm. The first inmate entered into the Alabama Wetumpka State Penitentiary in 1842 received a 20-year sentence for harboring a runaway slave.

14 Nikole Hannah-Jones, *The 1619 Project: A New Origin Story* (New York Times Company, 2021), 214–17.

15 LaRoche, *Free Black Communities*, 2–3; "Frederick Douglass Project," *University of Rochester*, The Frederick Douglass Institute and Department of Rare Books and Special Collections, accessed 12/26/23, https://rbscp.lib.rochester.edu/2509; "Frederick Douglass," *National Park Service*, accessed 2/17/22, https://www.nps.gov/frdo/learn/historyculture/frederickdouglass.htm. Mr. Douglass traveled to Britain in 1845 for 19 months, leaving the US to escape "slave catchers" and kidnappers. When abolitionists purchased his freedom, he returned to the United States legally free.

16 Catherine A. Paul, "Fugitive Slave Act of 1850," *Virginia Commonwealth University, Social Welfare History Project*, accessed 8/2/23, https://socialwelfare.library.vcu.edu/federal/fugitive-slave-act-of-1850.

17 "Anthony Burns (1834–1862)," *Encyclopedia Virginia, Virginia Humanities*, accessed 7/28/23, https://encyclopediavirginia.org/entries/burns-anthony-1834-1862/; "1854 Anthony Burns and the Fugitive Slave Act," *The African American Experience in Massachusetts Courts*, accessed 7/28/23, http://www.longroadtojustice.org/topics/slavery/anthony-burns.php. Boston abolitionists later purchased Anthony Burns' freedom. He attended Oberlin College in Ohio, lectured on his life experiences, and died in Canada in 1862 from health problems related to his post-trial confinement.

18 Horton and Horton, *In Hope of Liberty, Culture, Community*, 263.

19 Colored Conventions Project, Center for Black Digital Research, Pennsylvania State University, 2021, accessed 12/20/23, https://coloredconventions.org/.

20 Megan Specia, "Overlooked No More: How Mary Ann Shadd Cary Shook
    Up the Abolitionist Movement," *New York Times*, June 6, 2018, accessed
    12/22/23, https://www.nytimes.com/2018/06/06/obituaries/mary-ann-shadd
    -cary-abolitionist-overlooked.html; "Mary Ann Shadd Cary—Herstory in the
    Colored Conventions—1855 National Convention of Colored People held in
    Philadelphia, PA," *Colored Conventions Project*, accessed 12/20/23, https://
    coloredconventions.org/mary-ann-shadd-cary/.

21 "Mary Ann Shadd Cary," *Colored Conventions Project*, accessed 12/20/23, https://
    coloredconventions.org/mary-ann-shadd-cary/shadd-cary-and-the-conventions
    /1855-national-convention/.

22 "Aboard the Underground Railroad—Mary Ann Shadd Cary," *National Park
    Service*, accessed 12/22/23, https://www.nps.gov/nr/travel/underground/
    dc2.htm; "Mary Ann Shadd Cary," *National Women's Hall of Fame*, accessed
    12/21/23, https://www.womenofthehall.org/inductee/mary-ann-shadd-cary/;
    "Mary Ann Shadd—American Educator, Publisher, and Abolitionist," *Britannica*,
    accessed 12/22/23, https://www.britannica.com/biography/Mary-Ann-Shadd
    -Cary.

23 "John Brown American Abolitionist," *Britannica*, accessed 8/5/23, https://www
    .britannica.com/biography/John-Brown-American-abolitionist.

24 "John Brown's Raid," *National Park Service*, https://www.nps.gov/articles/john
    -browns-raid.htm.

25 Horton and Horton, *In Hope of Liberty, Culture, Community*, 243, 258, 264–5.

26 "Nat Turner's Rebellion," *National Museum of African American History and
    Culture, Smithsonian*, https://nmaahc.si.edu/explore/stories/nat-turners
    -rebellion. Before Turner's revolt, other slave rebellions included Gabriel's
    Rebellion in Richmond, Virginia in 1800, the German Coast Uprising in
    Louisiana in 1811, the Fort Blount Revolt in Florida in 1816, and Denmark
    Versey's Rebellion in Charleston, South Carolina in 1822. See "Slave Rebellions
    and Uprisings," *American Battlefield Trust*, June 10, 2024, https://www
    .battlefields.org/learn/articles/slave-rebellions-and-uprisings.

27 Wickenden, *The Agitators–Three Friends who Fought for Abolition*, 154; J.J.
    Gould, "Longfellow's Anti-Slavery Poem 'Paul Revere's Ride' Turns 150," *The
    Atlantic*, December 20, 2021, https://www.theatlantic.com/entertainment/
    archive/2010/12/longfellows-anti-slavery-poem-paul-reveres-ride-turns-150
    /68279/; Library of America, *Reader's Almanac*, http://blog.loa.org/2010/12/
    henry-wadsworth-longfellow-frederick.html.

28 Wickenden, *The Agitators–Three Friends who Fought for Abolition*, 203.

29 Christy Clark-Pujara, *Dark Work. The Business of Slavery in Rhode Island* (New York University Press, 2016), 85, 90.

30 Seth Rockman, "Negro Cloth: Mastering the Market of Slave Clothing in Antebellum America" in *American Capitalism: New Histories (Columbia University Press, 2018)*, https://www.degruyter.com/document/doi/10.7312/beck18524-008/html?lang=en.

31 Rockman, "Negro Cloth," Chapter 6.

32 "Image 28 of Narrative of the Life of Frederick Douglass, an American Slave," *Library of Congress*, https://www.loc.gov/resource/lhbcb.25385/?sp=28&st=text.

33 "New England Colored Citizens' Convention, August 1, 1859," *Colored Conventions Project*, Ref Note 4, accessed 12/22/23, https://omeka .coloredconventions.org/items/show/269; Briona Lambeck, "The Double Life of New York's Black Oyster King," *Atlas Obscura*, September 28, 2022, accessed 12/21/23, https://www.atlasobscura.com/articles/new-york-oyster-history; Sarah Malinowski, "Thomas Downing—NYC Oyster King & Abolitionist," *Fishers Island Oyster Farm*, accessed 12/21/23, https://www.fishersislandoysters.com/ blog/2021/2/22/thomas-downing.

34 "George T. Downing, 1819–1903: Entrepreneur, Caterer, Civil Rights Activist," *Encyclopedia.com*, https://www.encyclopedia.com/african-american-focus/news -wires-white-papers-and-books/downing-george-t.

35 Myra Beth Young Armstead, *The History of Blacks in Resort Towns: Newport, Rhode Island and Saratoga Springs, New York, 1870–1930*, Doctoral Dissertation, University of Chicago, Chicago, IL, 1987, 61; May Wijaya, "The World was his Oyster—George T. Downing," *Rhode Tour*, https://rhodetour.org/items/show/41.

36 John M. Rice, "Frederick Douglass and His Abolitionist Friends in Newport and New Bedford," *Newport History*, 97, 286, Article 2, 25, https://digitalcommons .salve.edu/newporthistory/vol97/iss286/2; Patrick T. Conley, "George T. Downing: Rhode Island's Most Prominent African American Leader," *Small State—Big History: Online Review of Rhode Island History*, accessed 11/18/23, https://smallstatebighistory.com/george-t-downing-rhode-islands-most -prominent-african-american-leader/. Downing recovered $40,000 from insurance proceeds to build a larger structure on the site called the Downing Block. During the Civil War, he rented its upper floor to the US Naval Academy as an infirmary.

37 Rice, "Frederick Douglass," 10.

38 Clark-Pujara, *Dark Work,* 138—43.

39 Colored Conventions Project.

40 Colin McBride, "George T. Downing," *Black Past,* 2017, accessed 12/2/23, https://www.blackpast.org/african-american-history/downing-george-t-1819-1903/.

41 "Underground Railroad in Coventry, RI," *The Western Rhode Island Civic Historical Society, Pawtuxet Valley Preservation and Historical Society*, accessed 8/6/23, http://www.westernrihistory.org/underground-railroad-in-coventry-ri-by-pawtuxet-valley-preservation-and-historical-society. The society identifies five Underground Railroad stations in Rhode Island: (1) Moses Brown House, Providence, (2) Isaac Rice Homestead, Newport, (3) Elizabeth Buffam Chace House, Central Falls, (4) Pidge Farm, Pawtucket, and (5) Charles Perry House, Westerly where fugitives hid in sod huts in nearby woods.

42 "Black History Month Newport: Places of Worship—The Center of the African Heritage Community then and Today is the Church," *What's Up Newport,* February 16, 2024, https://whatsupnewp.com/2024/02/black-history-month-newport-places-of-worship/.

43 Evarts Greene and Virginia Harrington, *American Population Before the Federal Census of 1790* (Columbia University Press, 1932), 61–9.

44 Rosemary Enright and Susan Maden, "Societies Offered up Lively Debates," *Jamestown Press*, May 13, 2021.

45 CPI Inflator Calculator, https://www.in2013dollars.com/us/inflation/1860?amount=4000000000.

46 Catarina Saraiva, "Four Numbers That Show the Cost of Slavery on Black Wealth Today," *Bloomberg Equality*, March 18, 2021, https://www.bloomberg.com/news/articles/2021-03-18/pay-check-podcast-episode-2-how-much-did-slavery-in-u-s-cost-black-wealth.

47 Mark Stelzer and Sven Beckert, *The Contribution of Enslaved Workers to Output and Growth in the Antebellum United States*, Harvard University, Cambridge, https://equitablegrowth.org/working-papers/the-contribution-of-enslaved-workers-to-output-and-growth-in-the-antebellum-united-states/; Kathryn Zickuhr, "New Research Shows Slavery's Central Role in U.S. Economic Growth Leading up to the Civil War," *Washington Center for Equitable Growth*, June 24, 2021, https://equitablegrowth.org/new-research-shows-slaverys-central-role-in-u-s-economic-growth-leading-up-to-the-civil-war/.

48 Colin A. Palmer, *Passageways: An Interpretive History of Black America, Volume I, 1619–1963* (Wadsworth Group, 2002), http://nationalhumanitiescenter.org/pds/maai/enslavement/text3/text3read.htm.

49 Sven Beckert, "Empire of Cotton," *The Atlantic,* December 12, 2014, https://www
.theatlantic.com/business/archive/2014/12/empire-of-cotton/383660/.

50 "What was Life Like Under Slavery," *Digital History*, ID #3040, 2021, https://
www.digitalhistory.uh.edu/disp_textbook.cfm?smtid=2&psid=3040; "Historical
Context: Facts about the Slave Trade and Slavery," accessed 7/28/23, https://www
.gilderlehrman.org/history-resources/teacher-resources/historical-context-facts
-about-slave-trade-and-slavery.

51 Notation to author from Dr. Marcus Nevius, associate professor of history,
Kinder Institute on Constitutional Democracy, University of Missouri,
Columbia, Missouri, 6/24/23, "The apportion of seats the [Republican] party
claimed in Congress was due in large part to the secession of the southern states
from the Union, beginning with South Carolina in December 1860, just weeks
after the election."

52 "Succession, States," *Library of Congress*, accessed 11/27/23, https://www.loc
.gov/rr/geogmap/placesinhistory/archive/2011/20110314_secession.htm; "War
Declared: States Secede from the Union!" *National Park Service*, https://www.nps
.gov/kemo/learn/historyculture/wardeclared.htm.

53 "South Carolina Declaration of Succession (1860)," *National Constitution Center*,
accessed 12/27/23, https://constitutioncenter.org/the-constitution/historic
-document-library/detail/south-carolina-declaration-of-secession-1860.

54 John Pierce, "The Reasons for Secession: A Documentary Study," *American
Battlefield Trust*, October 3, 2023, accessed 12/27/23, https://www.battlefields.org
/learn/articles/reasons-secession.

55 Wickenden, *The Agitators–Three Friends who Fought for Abolition*, 183.

56 "Confiscation Acts—United States History [1861–1864]," *Britannica*, https://
www.britannica.com/event/Confiscation-Acts.

57 "The Emancipation Proclamation," *National Archives*, https://www.archives.gov
/exhibits/featured-documents/emancipation-proclamation. The proclamation
declared "all persons held as slaves . . . within the rebellious states are, and
henceforward shall be free."

58 "Edmonia Lewis, African and Native American Sculptor," *The Art Story*,
https://www.theartstory.org/artist/lewis-edmonia. Ms. Lewis reported racial
discrimination in America forced her to relocate to Rome, Italy. Today she
is featured in the US Postal Service Black History stamp collection, accessed
1/13/2025, https://about.usps.com/newsroom/national-releases/2022/0126-usps
-salutes-legendary-sculptor-edmonia-lewis.htm.

59 "Cochise," *History.com*, June 30, 2020, https://www.history.com/topics/native
-american-history/cochise; "Cochise," *New World Encyclopedia*, https://www
.newworldencyclopedia.org/entry/Cochise.

60 Eric Niderost, "The Dakota War of 1862: What Caused the Great Sioux
Uprising," 2014, https://warfarehistorynetwork.com/article/dakota-war-of-1862
-what-caused-the-great-sioux-uprising/.

61 "How the West was Won," *Britannica*, https://www.britannica.com/topic/
American-frontier/How-the-West-was-won#ref1262441.

62 "The 54th Massachusetts Regiment," *National Park Service*, https://www.nps.gov
/articles/54th-massachusetts-regiment.htm; Wickenden, *The Agitators–Three
Friends who Fought for Abolition*, 227–9; Kevin M. Levin, "Why 'Glory' Still
Resonates More Than Three Decades Later," *Smithsonian Magazine*, September
14, 2020, https://www.smithsonianmag.com/history/why-glory-still-resonates
-more-three-decades-later-180975794/.

63 "The 54th Massachusetts and the Second Battle of Fort Wagner," *National Park
Service*, https://www.nps.gov/articles/the- -massachusetts-and-the-second-battle
-of-fort-wagner.htm.

64 Debra Michals, "Sojourner Truth, 1797–1883," *National Women's History
Museum*, 2015, accessed 2/27/22, https://www.womenshistory.org/education
-resources/biographies/sojourner-truth; "Primary Documents in American
History—Abraham Lincoln's Second Inaugural Address," *Library of Congress*,
https://www.loc.gov/rr/program/bib/ourdocs/lincoln2nd.html.

65 Wickenden, *The Agitators–Three Friends who Fought for Abolition*, 266.

66 "Black Soldiers in the U.S. Military During the Civil War," *National Archives,
Educator Resources*, accessed 3/2/23, https://www.archives.gov/education/lessons
/blacks-civil-war.

67 "Sherman's Field Order No. 15," *New Georgia Encyclopedia*, https://www
.georgiaencyclopedia.org/articles/history-archaeology/shermans-field-order-no
-15/.

68 Nadra Kareem Nittle, "The Short-Lived Promise of '40 Acres and a Mule,'"
History.com, November 9, 2022, https://www.history.com/news/40-acres-mule
-promise.

69 "The African American Odyssey: A Quest for Full Citizenship Reconstruction
and Its Aftermath," *Library of Congress*, https://www.loc.gov/exhibits/african
-american-odyssey/reconstruction.html. The Reconstruction Era from 1865 to

1877 aimed to readmit the southern states into the Union and define the terms by which the races could co-exist.

70 "After Slavery, Searching for Loved Ones in Wanted Ads," *National Public Radio*, 2017, https://www.npr.org/sections/codeswitch/2017/02/22/516651689/after -slavery-searching-for-loved-ones-in-wanted-ads.

71 "The Historical Legacy of Juneteenth," *The Smithsonian, National Museum of African American History and Culture*, June 19, 2019, https://nmaahc.si.edu/explore /stories/historical-legacy-juneteenth; Katherine Schaeffer, "More than half of States will recognize Juneteenth as an official public holiday, 2023." Pew Research Center, June 9, 2023. https://www.pewresearch.org/short-reads/2023/06/09/more-than- half-of-states-now-recognize-juneteenth-as-an-official-holiday/.

72 14th Amendment to the US Constitution, National Archives, https://www .archives.gov/milestone-documents/14th-amendment. A companion to the 13th Amendment, the 14th Amendment was ratified in 1868. It granted the former enslaved full citizenship and protection under law.

73 "The Civil War: The Senate's Story," *US Senate*, https://www.senate.gov/ artandhistory/history/common/civil_war/VictoryTragedyReconstruction.htm.

74 "The Civil War: The Senate's Story. Landmark Legislation—The Reconstruction Act of 1867," *US Senate*, https://www.senate.gov/artandhistory/history/common /generic/Civil_War_AdmissionReadmission.htm; "Legacy of Thaddeus Stevens," *Thaddeus Stevens College of Technology*, https://stevenscollege.edu/legacy-of -thaddeus-stevens/; "Thaddeus Stevens—American Politician," *Britannica*, https://www.britannica.com/biography/Thaddeus-Stevens.

75 Jennifer M. Smith, "The Color of Pain: Blacks and the US Health Care System, Part III, Section B," *National Lawyers Guild Review*, accessed 7/14/23, https:// www.nlg.org/nlg-review/article/the-color-of-pain-blacks-and-the-u-s-health -care-system-can-the-affordable-care-act-help-to-heal-a-history-of-injustice -part-i/; National Archives, "The Freedmen's Bureau," https://www.archives.gov /research/african-americans/freedmens-bureau; "Creation of the Freedmen's Bureau," *History.com*, https://www.history.com/topics/black-history/freedmens -bureau. The Bureau of Refugees, Freedmen, and Abandoned Lands was created by the US Congress in 1865 to address the needs of freedmen and to oversee lands abandoned or seized in the Civil War.

76 "The Impeachment of Andrew Johnson. Why was Andrew Johnson impeached?" *National Park Service*, accessed 11/29/23, https://www.nps.gov/anjo/learn/ historyculture/impeachment.htm.

77 "The Freedmen's Bureau," *National Archives*.

78 "The Origins of Modern-Day Policing," *National Association for the Advancement of Colored People*, https://naacp.org/find-resources/history -explained/origins-modern-day-policing.

79 Bobby L. Lovett, "Memphis Race Riot of 1866," *Tennessee Encyclopedia*, 2018, https://tennesseeencyclopedia.net/entries/memphis-race-riot-of-1866/.

80 "An Absolute Massacre—The New Orleans Slaughter of July 30, 1866," *National Park Service*, https://www.nps.gov/articles/000/neworleansmassacre.htm; Ferrell Evans, "The 1868 Louisiana Massacre That Reversed Reconstruction-Era Gains," *History.com*, 2020, https://www.history.com/news/voter-suppression-history -opelousas-massacre.

81 "Ulysses S. Grant, The 18th President of the United States," *The White House*, https://www.whitehouse.gov/about-the-white-house/presidents/ulysses-s-grant.

82 "The Enforcement Acts of 1870 and 1871," *US Senate*, https://www.senate.gov/ artandhistory/history/common/generic/EnforcementActs.htm.

83 Sarah Fling, "The Formerly Enslaved Household of the Grant Family," *The White House Historical Association*, April 17, 2020, https://www.whitehousehistory.org/ the-formerly-enslaved-household-of-the-grant-family.

84 "Transcontinental Railroad," *History.com*, https://www.history.com/topics/ inventions/transcontinental-railroad.

85 "Governor William Sprague IV of Rhode Island," *Library of Congress*, accessed 12/3/23, https://www.loc.gov/item/2021669488/. Sprague (1830–1915) was a wealthy textile manufacturer and politician who served as RI governor from 1860 to 1863 and as US senator from 1863 to 1875. When governor, he organized troops for the Civil War and accompanied the RI infantry regiment in the First Battle of Bull Run, in which his horse was shot dead from under him; "My Very Dear Wife—The Last Letter of Major Sullivan Ballou," *National Park Service*, https://www.nps.gov/articles/-my-very-dear-wife-the-last-letter -of-major-sullivan-ballou.htm. RI infantryman Ballou's letter is preserved in its archives according to the NPS because "Of the tens of thousands of letters written in the days leading up to the First Battle of Manassas, certainly none is more famous than the last letter of Major . . . Ballou. As poignant as it is prescient, [the] epistle captures . . . the spirit of patriotic righteousness that led many men to the enlistment office."

86 Keith Stokes, "Black History Month Newport: Places of Worship," *What's Up Newport*, February 9, 2022, accessed 7/26/23, https://whatsupnewp.com/2023/02 /black-history-month-newport-places-of-worship/.

87 Rosemary Enright and Sue Maden, "JHS 100 Years: Jamestowners in the Civil War," *Jamestown Press,* July 12, 2012, https://www.jamestownpress.com/articles/jhs-100-years-jamestowners-in-the-civil-war/.

88 Rosemary Enright and Sue Maden, "Jamestown Historical Society 100 Years: The Civil War at Home," *Jamestown Press,* July 26, 2012, https://www.jamestownpress.com/articles/jamestown-historical-society-100-years-the-civil-war-at-home/.

89 "Civil Rights Act of 1875," *Britannica*, https://www.britannica.com/topic/Civil-Rights-Act-United-States-1875.

90 Melissa Janczewski Jones, "The Clinton Riot of 1875: From Riot to Massacre," *Mississippi History Now,* 2021, https://www.mshistorynow.mdah.ms.gov/issue/the-clinton-riot-of-1875-from-riot-to-massacre; "On this day Sep 04, 1875— Massacre by White Mob in Clinton, Mississippi, Leaves Dozens of Black People Dead," *Equal Justice Initiative,* https://calendar.eji.org/racial-injustice/sep/04.

91 Sana Butler, *Sugar of the Crop—My Journey to Find the Children of Slaves* (The Lyons Press, 2009), 14–15; Eric Foner and Olivia Mahoney, *America's Reconstruction: People and Politics after the Civil War* (Harper Collins, 1995); Eric Foner, *A Short History of Reconstruction, 1863–1877* (Harper, 2015).

92 "Hiram Revels: First African American Senator," *US Senate, Senate Historical Office,* 2020, accessed 8/4/23, https://www.senate.gov/artandhistory/senate-stories/First-African-American-Senator.htm.

93 "Hiram Revels: First African American Senator," *US Senate.*

94 "Notable Alcornites," *Alcorn State University,* https://www.alcorn.edu/discover-alcorn/notable-alcornites/.

95 "Hiram Rhodes Revel," *National Park Service, US Office of the Historian,* https://www.nps.gov/people/hiram-rhodes-revels.htm.

96 "The Civil War: The Senate's Story," *US Senate,* https://www.senate.gov/artandhistory/history/common/civil_war/VictoryTragedyReconstruction.htm.

97 "The Civil War: The Senate's Story," *US Senate.*

98 Called the Compromise of 1877, this was an unwritten political agreement that settled lingering disputes over the 1876 presidential election. Republican Rutherford B. Hayes's presidential win would no longer be contested with the proviso that federal troops would be removed from South Carolina, Florida, and Louisiana.

99 Daniel Byman, "White Supremacy, Terrorism, and the Failure of Reconstruction in the United States," *International Security* 46, no. 1 (Summer 2021): 53–103, https://doi.org/10.1162/isec_a_00410.

100 Butler, *Sugar of the Crop,* 16.

101 "Black History Month: Apprenticeship and Slavery," *Women's History Network,* https://womenshistorynetwork.org/black-history-month-apprenticeship-and -slavery/.

102 Butler, *Sugar of the Crop.*

103 Byman, "White Supremacy, Terrorism"; "Knights of the White Camelia Rituals, 1868," *Briscoe Center for American History,* University of Texas at Austin, Archival Resources On-Line, https://txarchives.org/utcah/finding_aids/04518 .xml; James M. Beeby, "Red Shirt Violence, Election Fraud, and the Demise of the Populist Party in North Carolina's Third Congressional District, 1900," *North Carolina Office of Archives and History, The North Carolina Historical Review* 84, no. 1 (2008): 1–28, https://www.jstor.org/stable/23523367.

104 "Report of the Joint Select Committee to Inquire into the Condition of Affairs in the Late Insurrectionary States, Part I: History of Negro Political Participation," *US Commission on Civil Rights, Thurgood Marshall Library, University of Maryland School of Law,* 1968, 1–5 [Rep. No. 41, 42d Cong., 2d Sess., Washington, DC].

105 Edward A. Pollard, *The Lost Cause* (E. B. Treat and Co., 1867), 752, https://www .google.com/books/edition/The_Lost_Cause/v2wFAAAAQAAJ?hl=en&gbpv=1 &printsec=frontcover.

106 "Reconstruction: The Black Codes," *PBS Learning Media,* https://mass .pbslearningmedia.org/resource/reconstruction-black-codes/reconstruction-the -black-codes/.

107 "Reconstruction in America: Racial Violence after the Civil War, 1865–1876," *Equal Justice Initiative,* 39, https://eji.org/report/reconstruction-in-america/; Safiya Charles, "2,000 more Lynching Victims Brought to Light in EJI's New Reconstruction Era Report," *Montgomery Advertiser,* June 15, 2020, https://www .montgomeryadvertiser.com/story/news/2020/06/16/equal-justice-initiative -reconstruction-era-reports-2000-more-lynching-victims-found-emancipation /3196140001/ .

108 "Peonage Explained: The System of Convict Labor was Slavery by Another Name," *The Milwaukee Independent,* July 3, 2020, http://www.milwaukeein dependent.com/syndicated/peonage-explained-system-convict-labor-slavery -another-name/; Ashley Mott, "Fact Check: Southern States Used Convict Leasing to Force Black People into Unpaid Labor," *USA Today,* July 7, 2020, https://www.usatoday.com/story/news/factcheck/2020/07/07/fact-check-convict -leasing-forced-black-people-into-unpaid-labor/5368307002/; "Prison Labor in

America: US Steel's Use of Alabama Convicts Shrouded in Mystery," *Associated Press,* September 19, 2022, https://www.al.com/business/2022/09/prison-labor-in -america-us-steels-use-of-alabama-convicts-shrouded-in-mystery.html.

109 Frank Shyong, "History forgot the 1871 Los Angeles Chinese Massacre, but we've All been Shaped by its Violence," *Los Angeles Times,* October 24, 2021, https:// www.latimes.com/california/story/2021-10-24/150th-anniversary-los-angeles -chinese-massacre.

110 Tara Kibler, "A Columbus Day Exploration of Indigenous American History," October 14, 2019, https://home.heinonline.org/blog/2019/10/a-columbus-day -exploration-of-indigenous-american-history/.

111 "Sioux Wars," *Encyclopedia of the Great Plains, University of Nebraska,* 2011, accessed 7/25/23, http://plainshumanities.unl.edu/encyclopedia/doc/egp.war .044; "How the West Was Won," *Britannica,* https://www.britannica.com/topic/ American-frontier/How-the-West-was-won#ref1262441.

112 "Supreme Court: United States, Petitioner, v. Sioux Nation of Indians et al., No. 79–639," *Cornell Law School, Legal Information Institute,* https://www.law.cornell .edu/supremecourt/text/448/371.

113 "A Segregated Military: Indian Wars, Spanish-American War and World War I," *Smithsonian, National Museum of African American History and Culture,* May 25, 2020, https://nmaahc.si.edu/explore/stories/segregated-military-indian-wars -spanish-american-war-and-world-war-i.

114 Trevor K. Plante, "Researching African Americans in the U.S. Army, 1866–1890, Buffalo Soldiers and Black Infantrymen," *Prologue Magazine, National Archives,* 33, 1, Spring 2001, https://www.archives.gov/publications/prologue/2001/spring/ buffalo-soldiers.html.

115 "The Philippine War—A Conflict of Conscience for African Americans," *National Park Service,* accessed 12/3/23, https://www.nps.gov/articles/the- philippine-war-a-conflict-of-conscience.htm. For an accounting that erases Buffalo Soldier participation, see "The Philippine-American War, 1899–1902," *US Department of State, Office of the Historian,* accessed 12/3/23, https://history .state.gov/milestones/1899-1913/war.

116 "Charles Young—Buffalo Soldier," *National Park Service,* accessed 9/7/23, https:// www.nps.gov/prsf/learn/historyculture/charles-young-buffalo-soldier.htm; "Buffalo Soldiers—Legend and Legacy," *Smithsonian Institute, National Museum of African American History and Culture,* accessed 9/7/23, https://nmaahc.si.edu/ explore/stories/buffalo-soldiers.

117 "Cathay Williams," *National Park Service*, accessed 9/6/23, https://www.nps.gov
    /people/cwilliams.htm; "Cathay Williams, The First African-American Woman
    To Enlist In The Army and the only female member of the Buffalo Soldiers,"
    National Association of Black Military Women, accessed 9/7/23, https://www
    .nabmw.org/cathay-williams.

118 "Last Buffalo Soldier Laid to Rest in Albany," *Spectrum News,* November 25,
    2024, https://spectrumlocalnews.com/nys/capital-region/news/2024/11/25/last
    -buffalo-soldier-laid-to-rest-in-albany

119 Armstead, *The History of Blacks in Resort Towns*, 51.

120 Armstead, *The History of Blacks in Resort Towns*, 107, 116.

121 "Overview of the Gilded Age," *Digital History*, ID 2916, https://www
    .digitalhistory.uh.edu/era.cfm?eraid=9&smtid=1.

122 "The Gilded Age Newport in Color," *Newport Mansions, The Preservation Society
    of Newport County*, https://www.newportmansions.org/events/gilded-age
    -newport-in-color/.

123 "African Heritage and Historical Sites in Rhode Island," *Preservation Rhode
    Island*, https://www.preserveri.org/african-heritage-sites; Nate Christensen,
    "Mahlon Van Horne, 1840–1910," *BlackPast*, https://www.blackpast.org/african
    -american-history/van-horne-mahlon-1840-1910/.

124 "Mary Dickerson, Businesswoman, and Club Woman," *African American
    Registry*, https://aaregistry.org/story/mary-dickerson-business-and-club-woman
    -born/; "Gilded Age of Newport in Color," *Newport Mansions*.

125 Nicholas Som, "4 African American Women's Clubs That Helped Write
    History," *National Trust for Historic Preservation*, 2019, accessed 8/7/23, https://
    savingplaces.org/stories/4-african-american-womens-clubs-that-helped-write
    -history.

126 G. Wayne Miller, "'Away From Home' Exhibit Tells the Story of Native Children
    Stripped of their Identity," *Providence Journal,* November 10, 2021, https://
    www.providencejournal.com/story/news/local/2021/11/10/away-from-home
    -exhibit-tells-of-native-children-forcibly-removed-to-american-indian-boarding
    -schools/6353102001/. According to Loren Spears, director of the Narragansett
    Tomaquag Museum, "The Most Famous [Indian Boarding School] is Probably
    Carlisle Boarding School, and we have Documentation of Narragansett Children
    at Carlisle," which operated from 1879 through 1918 in Carlisle, Pennsylvania.

127 "Jamestown in the Resort Era, 1875–1930," *Jamestown Historical Society*, https://
    jamestownhistoricalsociety.org/exhibits/jamestown-in-the-resort-era-1875-1930/.

128 Notation to author from Rosemary Enright, Jamestown Historical Society, 6/24/23: "In 1872, Howland exchanged his waterfront property for about five percent of the stock in the newly formed Jamestown & Newport Ferry Company. The wharf for the new steam ferry was built there. He then sold the land just west of the ferry wharf to a consortium of Jamestown men who thought cottages close to the ferry landing would attract summer visitors. They laid out Union, Lincoln, Friendship, and Brook streets, platted 70 lots along them, and called the development 'Ferry Meadows.'"

129 Rosemary Enright and Susan Maden, "Ferry Traffic Used to Develop Conanicus-Bryer Neighborhood," *Jamestown Press,* March 11, 2021; "Town's Black Population has Ebbed, Flowed," *Jamestown Press,* February 8, 2018.

130 "Landmark Legislation: Civil Rights Act of 1875," *US Senate,* https://www.senate.gov/artandhistory/history/common/generic/CivilRightsAct1875.htm.

131 David Pilgrim, "What Was Jim Crow?" *Jim Crow Museum, Ferris State University,* 2012, accessed 11/9/23, https://jimcrowmuseum.ferris.edu/what.htm. Jim Crow is defined by Pilgrim as a racial caste system within primarily, but not exclusively, southern and border states between 1877 and the mid-1960s. He advises Jim Crow was more than a series of rigid anti-Black laws. It was a way of life.

132 "The Dawes Act," *National Park Service,* https://www.nps.gov/articles/000/dawes-act.htm.

133 "Sharecropping," *History.com,* June 7, 2019, https://www.history.com/topics/black-history/sharecropping.

134 "Slavery by Another Name: The Economy of Sharecropping," *Signature Theatre,* https://www.sigtheatre.org/events/201920/gp/slavery-by-another-name-the-economy-of-sharecropping/.

135 "Sharecropping," *Public Broadcasting Service,* https://www.pbs.org/tpt/slavery-by-another-name/themes/sharecropping.

136 "I Denounce the So-Called Emancipation as a Stupendous Fraud by Frederick Douglass (1888)," *History Is A Weapon,* https://www.historyisaweapon.com/defcon1/douglassfraud.html; Gilder Lehrman Institute of American History, "Frederick Douglass on the disfranchisement of Black Voters, 1880." https://www.gilderlehrman.org/history-resources/spotlight-primary-source/frederick-douglass-disfranchisement-black-voters-1888.

137 "Together We Tell The Story," *Statue of Liberty—Ellis Island Foundation, Inc.,* https://www.statueofliberty.org/ellis-island/.

138 "Postponing Bartholdi's Statue until there is Liberty for Colored as Well," *The Cleveland Gazette,* November 27, 1886, 2.

139 Congress.gov, *S.Con.Res.153—101st Congress (1989–1990),* https://www.congress .gov/bill/101st-congress/senate-concurrent-resolution/153; "Wounded Knee Massacre United States History [1890]," *Britannica,* https://www.britannica.com /event/Wounded-Knee-Massacre; Stephen Groves, "State senate urges inquiry into Wounded Knee Medals of Honor," *Associated Press,* February 22, 2021. https://apnews.com/general-neews-1ffb1c5fe6dd8a33af7bcb94d3c9095d.

140 Keith W. Stokes, "Don't Forget the Role in Civil Rights Newport's Rev. Mahlon Van Horne Played," *Opinion Letter, Newport Daily News,* January 17, 2022, https://www.newportri.com/story/opinion/letters/2022/01/17/letter-newports -rev-mahlon-van-horne-civil-rights-leader/6526645001/; Nate Christensen, "Mahlon Van Horne (1840–1910)," *Black Past,* June 3, 2011, https://www .blackpast.org/african-american-history/van-horne-mahlon-1840-1910/; Nellie M. Gorbea, "Trailblazing Women in Rhode Island History—Christiana Carteaux Bannister," https://www.goprovidence.com/blog/post/trailblazing-women-in -rhode-island-history/.

141 Narragansett Indian Tribe, https://narragansettindiannation.org/history/ perseverance/.

142 See the profile of the Champlin family in Chapter 2 which includes documentation from the town of Jamestown voting records.

143 Rosemary Enright and Susan Maden, "Ferry Traffic Used to Develop Conanicus-Bryer Neighborhood," *Jamestown Press,* May 11, 2021.

144 Rosemary Enright and Susan Maden, "The Dr. Bates Sanitarium in Jamestown, 1900–1944," *Journal of the Newport Historical Society* 78, no. 260: 2, accessed 11/9/23, https://digitalcommons.salve.edu/newporthistory/vol78/iss260/2/.

145 Arlisha R. Norwood, "Ida B. Wells-Barnett, 1862–1931," *National Women's History Museum,* 2017, accessed 8/5/23, https://www.womenshistory.org/ education-resources/biographies/ida-b-wells-barnett; "Ida B. Wells-Barnett: American Journalist and Social Reformer, 2023," *Britannica,* accessed 8/7/23, https://www.britannica.com/biography/Ida-B-Wells-Barnett.

146 Ida B. Wells-Barnett, "Southern Horrors: Lynch Law in All Its Phases, 1892," *The Project Gutenberg Literary Archive Foundation,* https://www.gutenberg.org/files /14975/14975-h/14975-h.htm#PREFACE.

147 "Together We Tell The Story," *Statue of Liberty—Ellis Island Foundation, Inc.,* https://www.statueofliberty.org/ellis-island/.

148 "Antilynching Act Signed into Law, 03.29.22," *Equal Justice Initiative*, https://eji.org/news/antilynching-act-signed-into-law/; "H.R.55—Emmett Till Antilynching Act, 2022," *Congress.gov*, https://www.congress.gov/bill/117th-congress/house-bill/55.

149 "Ida B. Wells-Barnett," *PBS, Biographies*, https://www.pbs.org/blackpress/news_bios/wells.html.

150 "Ida B. Wells-Barnett: American Journalist and Social Reformer," *Britannica*, 2023, accessed 8/7/23, https://www.britannica.com/biography/Ida-B-Wells-Barnett; "Life Story: Ida B. Wells-Barnett (1862–1931)," *Women and the American Story*, accessed 8/5/23, https://wams.nyhistory.org/modernizing-america/fighting-for-social-reform/ida-b-wells/.

151 Ida B. Wells, *National Park Service*, https://www.nps.gov/people/idabwells.htm.

152 Jennifer M. Smith, "The Color of Pain: Blacks and the US Health Care System," accessed 7/14/23, https://www.nlg.org/nlg-review/article/the-color-of-pain-blacks-and-the-u-s-health-care-system-can-the-affordable-care-act-help-to-heal-a-history-of-injustice-part-i/; "Daniel Hale Williams, American Physician," Britannica, https://www.britannica.com/biography/Daniel-Hale-Williams.

153 James T. Haley, "The Low Percentage of Mortgaged Property in the South and Its Relationship to the Negro Population," *African American Encyclopedia*, 368 (1895), https://books.google.com/books?id=G-c9AQAAMAAJ&pg=PA134#v=onepage&q&f=false.

154 See Chapter 2 for discussion on the Champlin family farm and the Morrell properties.

155 "The Unexpected and Sudden Death of Mr. Douglass," *African American Encyclopedia, The American Missionary*, 405, https://books.google.com/books?id=G-c9AQAAMAAJ&pg=PA134#v=onepage&q&f=false; "Frederick Douglass," *National Park Service*, https://www.nps.gov/frdo/learn/historyculture/frederickdouglass.htm.

156 W.E.B. Du Bois's rebuttal to the Atlanta Compromise Speech is published in "The Souls of Black Folk; Essays and Sketches (full text)," Documenting the American South, https://docsouth.unc.edu/church/duboissouls/dubois.html.

157 "The Civil Rights Act of 1964: A Long Struggle for Freedom—Booker T. Washington's Atlanta Compromise Speech," *Library of Congress*, accessed 8/18/23, https://www.loc.gov/exhibits/civil-rights-act/multimedia/booker-t-washington.html.

158 "Plessy v. Ferguson law case [1896]," *Britannica*, https://www.britannica.com/event/Plessy-v-Ferguson-1896.

159 "What Was Jim Crow," *Jim Crow Museum*, https://jimcrowmuseum.ferris.edu/what.htm.

160 LeRae Umfleet, "1989 Wilmington Race Riot Report," *1898 Wilmington Race Riot Commission*, May 31, 2006, accessed 11/18/24, https://digital.ncdcr.gov/Documents/Detail/1898-wilmington-race-riot-report/2257408?item=2277536.

161 "What were Some Similarities Between Racism in Nazi Germany and in the United States, 1920s-1940s?" *The United States Holocaust Museum*, https://encyclopedia.ushmm.org/content/en/question/what-were-some-similarities-between-racism-in-nazi-germany-and-in-the-united-states-1920s-1940s.

162 The United States Holocaust Museum; "Racial Integrity Law (1924—1930)," *Encyclopedia Virginia*, https://encyclopediavirginia.org/entries/racial-integrity-laws-1924-1930/.

163 Benjamin Zinkel, "Apartheid and Jim Crow: Drawing Lessons from South Africa's Truth and Reconciliation," *Law Journals at University of Missouri School of Law Scholarship Repository*, J. Disp. Resol., 2019, https://scholarship.law.missouri.edu/jdr/vol2019/iss1/16; "Apartheid," *History.com*, March 3, 2020, https://www.history.com/topics/africa/apartheid; Elizabeth Esch, "White Rights: What Apartheid South Africa Learned from the United States," *Barnard College, Center for Research on Woman, Lunchtime Lecture*, February 11, 2010, https://bcrw.barnard.edu/event/white-rights-what-apartheid-south-africa-learned-from-the-united-states/.

164 Art T. Burton, "Bass Reeves, 1838–1920," *The Encyclopedia of Oklahoma History and Culture, Oklahoma Historical Society*, accessed 11/13/23, https://www.okhistory.org/publications/enc/entry.php?entry=RE020; Clay Coppedge, "Bass Reeves, Lawman Extraordinaire—Could the West's first African American Deputy Marshal have inspired the Lone Ranger?" *Texas Coop Power*, October 2018, accessed 11/13/23, https://texascooppower.com/bass-reeves-lawman-extraordinaire/.

165 "Nancy Green—Women in History," *Kentucky Center for African American Heritage*, accessed 11/13/23, https://kcaah.org/women-in-history/nancy-green/.

166 Sam Roberts, "Overlooked No More: Nancy Green, the 'Real Aunt Jemima'," *New York Times*, July 17, 2020, accessed 11/13/23, https://www.nytimes.com/2020/07/17/obituaries/nancy-green-aunt-jemima-overlooked.html; Miriam Fauzie, "Fact Check: Aunt Jemima Model Nancy Green didn't Create the Brand," *USA*

Today, June 30, 2020, accessed 11/13/23, https://www.usatoday.com/story/news/factcheck/2020/06/30/fact-check-aunt-jemima-model-didnt-create-brand-wasnt-millionaire/3241656001/.

167 Khalil Gibran Muhammad, "The Condemnation of Blackness: Race, Crime, and the Making of Modern Urban America," from "Racism in America—A Reader," (Harvard University Press, 2020), 56, accessed 12/18/23, https://doi.org/10.4159/9780674251656.

168 Frederick L. Hoffman, "The Race Traits and Tendencies of the American Negro," *Publications of the American Economic Association* 11, no. 1/3 (1896): 1–329, accessed 12/20/23, https://www.jstor.org/stable/2560438?searchText=&searchUri=&ab_segments=&searchKey=&refreqid=fastly-default%3A3d91a5601189ea77e0eaa45e88855d04. Hoffman's statistical findings on the incarceration and disease rates for Blacks were rebutted by Eastern State Penitentiary physician Dr. M.V. Ball, citing the physical, emotional, and psychological toll of racial oppression as contributing factors. See Proceedings of the Annual Congress of the National Prison Association of the United States, Dr. M.V. Ball, *Tuberculosis in Prisons* (Brothers Printers, 1894), 244–8, accessed 12/18/23, https://play.google.com/books/reader?id=D1s9AAAAYAAJ&pg=GBS.PA242&hl=en. Hoffman's work was also rebutted and rebuked by scholar W.E.B. Du Bois, stating "no amount of counting will justify a departure from the severe rules of correct reasoning," accessed 12/20/23, https://www.jstor.org/stable/1009520?searchText=&searchUri=&ab_segments=&searchKey=&refreqid=fastly-default%3A40869433a798d9638477b7be972bb237%3FsearchText%3D&searchUri=&ab_segments=&refreqid=fastly-default%3A3d91a5601189ea77e0eaa45e88855d04&searchKey=.

169 When the Hoffman study released, a smallpox epidemic plagued urban centers. See Charles V. Chapin, "Variation in Type of Infectious Disease as shown by the History of Small Pox in the United States, 1895–1912," *Journal of Infectious Diseases* 13, no. 2 (1913): 2, accessed 12/20/23, https://www.jstor.org/stable/30073361?seq=1.

170 "Newspapers," *African American Encyclopedia*, 134, https://books.google.com/books?id=G-c9AQAAMAAJ&pg=PA134#v=onepage&q&f=false.

171 J. Stanley Lemons and Diane Lambert, "John Carter Minkins: Pioneering African-American Newspaperman," *The New England Quarterly* 76, no. 3 (2003), 413–38, https://www.jstor.org/stable/1559809.

172 Michael Cooper, "Overlooked No More: Sissieretta Jones, a Soprano Who Shattered Racial Barriers," *New York Times,* August 18, 2018, https://www .nytimes.com/2018/08/15/obituaries/sissieretta-jones-overlooked.html.

173 Lauren Clem, "Beyond the Mansions: For Newport's African Heritage Families, the Gilded Age Gave Rise to a Thriving Entrepreneur Community," *Rhode Island Monthly,* June 1, 2023, https://www.rimonthly.com/beyond-the-mansions/; "New Timeline," *Newport Daily News,* June 2, 2014, https://www.newportri.com/ story/news/2014/06/02/timeline/12757887007/.

174 Rosemary Enright and Susan Maden, "Ferry Traffic Used to Develop Conanicus-Bryer Neighborhood," *Jamestown Press,* March 11, 2021.

175 "The History of Stanton High School," *Florida Memory, State Library and Archives of Florida,* February 2, 2017, https://www.floridamemory.com/items/ show/326636; Adelle Banks, "Christian Hymn, Anthem of Civil Rights and Black Churches, Marks 125 Years," *The Roys Report,* June 24, 2025, https://julieroys. com/christian-hymn-anthem-civil-rights-black-churches-marks-125-years/.

176 "National Business League, Nation's First Black Business Organization Turns 120 Years Old," *Cision PR News Service,* September 3, 2020, https://www.prnewswire .com/news-releases/national-business-league-nations-first-black-business -organization-turns-120-years-old-301123502.html.

177 "Teddy Roosevelt's 'Shocking' Dinner With Washington, 2012," *National Public Radio,* https://www.npr.org/2012/05/14/152684575/teddy-roosevelts-shocking -dinner-with-washington.

178 Jae Jones, "William Demosthenes Crum: Caused An Uproar when Appointed Collector of Customs in Charleston, SC," *BlackThen,* 2019, https://blackthen.com /william-demosthenes-crum-renowned-physician-appointed-collector-customs -charleston-sc/.

179 William Edward Burghardt Du Bois, "The Souls of Black Folk; Essays and Sketches (full text)," *Documenting the American South,* https://docsouth.unc.edu/ church/duboissouls/dubois.html.

180 Du Bois, "The Souls of Black Folk."

181 Caroline Mimbs Nyce, "W.E.B. Du Bois at Fisk University," *The Atlantic,* 2016, https://www.theatlantic.com/education/archive/2016/02/web-du-bois-at-fisk -university/624867/.

182 Hamilton Beck, "W.E.B. Du Bois as a Student Abroad in Germany 1892–1894," *Frontiers—The Interdisciplinary Journal of Study Abroad* 2, no. 1: 45–63, https:// doi.org/10.36366/frontiers.v2i1.25.

183 Beck, "WEB Du Bois.

184 "W.E.B. Du Bois," *NAACP*, https://naacp.org/find-resources/history-explained/
civil-rights-leaders/web-du-bois.

185 "W.E.B. Du Bois," *NAACP*.

186 "W.E.B. Du Bois," *NAACP*.

187 "W.E.B. Du Bois," *NAACP*.

188 Andrew Lanham, "When W.E.B. Du Bois Was 'Un-American'," *Boston Review,*
January 13, 2017, https://www.bostonreview.net/articles/when-civil-rights-were
-un-american/.

189 Dr. Henry Louis Gates, Jr. and Evelyn Brooks Higginbotham, "W.E.B. Du Bois,"
Hutchins Center for African and African American Research (Harvard University,
2008), accessed 8/5/23, https://hutchinscenter.fas.harvard.edu/web-dubois.

190 Samuel Momodue, "Nashville Streetcar Boycott 1905–1907," *Blackpast*,
November 2016, https://www.blackpast.org/african-american-history/nashville
-s-streetcar-boycott-1905-1907; Nina Cardona, "50 Years Before Rosa Parks,
A Bold Nashville Streetcar Protest Defied Segregation," September 22, 2015.
https://wpln.org/post/50-years-before-rosa-parks-a-bold-nashville-streetcar-
protest-defied-segregation/.

191 Dell Gines and Chad Wilkerson, "The Past, Present and Future of Black Wall
Street," *Federal Reserve Bank of Kansas City,* 2021, https://www.kansascityfed.org
/oklahomacity/oklahoma-economist/oklahoma-economist-the-past-present-and
-future-of-black-wall-street.

192 "1889—April 22—The Oklahoma Land Rush Begins," *History.com*, https://www
.history.com/this-day-in-history/the-oklahoma-land-rush-begins.

193 Alexis Clark, "Nine Entrepreneurs Who Helped Build Tulsa's 'Black Wall Street',"
History.com, accessed 5/14/21, https://www.history.com/news/black-wall-street
-tulsa-visionaries; Alexis Clark, "Tulsa's 'Black Wall Street' Flourished as a Self-
Contained Hub in Early 1900s," *History.com*, 2021, https://www.history.com/
news/black-wall-street-tulsa-race-massacre.

194 "The Past, Present, and Future of Black Wall Street," *Oklahoma Economist,* May
26, 2021, https://www.kansascityfed.org/oklahomacity/oklahoma-economist/
oklahoma-economist-the-past-present-and-future-of-black-wall-street/.

195 Arlisha R. Norwood, "Maggie Lena Walker 1864–1934," *National Women's
History Museum*, 2017, https://www.womenshistory.org/education-resources/
biographies/maggie-lena-walker.

196 "A Statue Honoring Mary McLeod Bethune is Unveiled at the U.S. Capitol," *National Public Radio*, July 14, 2022, https://www.npr.org/2022/07/14 /1111473859/a-statue-honoring-mary-mcleod-bethune-is-unveiled-at-the-u-s -capitol.

197 "Niagara Movement—American Civil Rights Organization," *Britannica*, https:// www.britannica.com/topic/Niagara-Movement; "Survey Report—African American Struggle for Civil Rights in Rhode Island: The Twentieth Century Phase 2: Statewide Survey and National Register Evaluation," *Public Archeology Laboratory*, 2019, 6, https://www.rihs.org/wp-content/uploads/2019/10/20th -Century-African-American-Sites-in-RI-PAL-report-and-survey.pdf.

198 Madam C.J. Walker website, https://madamcjwalker.com/.

199 "Alain LeRoy Locke," *Stanford Encyclopedia of Philosophy*, March 23, 2012, https://plato.stanford.edu/entries/alain-locke/.

200 "Charles Curtis of Kansas becomes the First Native American Elected to the U.S. Senate," *History.com*, https://www.history.com/this-day-in-history/charles-curtis -of-kansas-becomes-first-native-american-senator.

201 Adam Augustyn, "Brownsville Affair," *Encyclopedia Britannica*, https://www .britannica.com/event/Brownsville-Affair; Garna Christian, "Brownsville Raid of 1906," *Handbook of Texas, Texas State Historical Association*, https://www .tshaonline.org/handbook/entries/brownsville-raid-of-1906; "1906: Image 1 of Roosevelt's Hostility to the Colored People of the United States. The Record of the Discharge of the Colored Soldiers at Brownsville," *Library of Congress*, https://www.loc.gov/resource/rbpe.24001000/?sp=1&st=text.

202 Clifford Kuhn and Gregory Mason, "Atlanta Race Riot of 1906," *New Georgia Encyclopedia*, 2020, https://www.georgiaencyclopedia.org/articles/history -archaeology/atlanta-race-riot-of-1906/.

203 Roberta Senechal, "The Springfield Race Riot of 1908," *Illinois Periodicals Online*, https://www.lib.niu.edu/1996/iht329622.html.

204 "W.E.B. Du Bois," *NAACP*, https://naacp.org/find-resources/history-explained/ civil-rights-leaders/web-du-bois.

205 Caelyn Pender, "Brown's First Black Female Graduate: Ethel Robinson's Legacy on College Hill," *The Brown Daily Herald*, February 2021, accessed 12/4/23, https://www.browndailyherald.com/article/2021/02/brown-s-first-black-female -graduate-ethel-robinson-s-legacy-on-college-hill.

206 Myra Beth Young Armstead, *The History of Blacks in Resort Towns*, 175—6.

207 John Doty interview by Valerie J. Southern, Jamestown, RI, July 30, 2023, Recollections of family and island history.

208 "The Great Migration—1910–1970," *National Archives, African American Heritage*, https://www.archives.gov/research/african-americans/migrations/great -migration.

209 Isabel Wilkerson, "The Long-Lasting Legacy of the Great Migration—When millions of African-Americans fled the South in Search of a Better Life, they Remade the Nation in Ways that are Still Being Felt," *Smithsonian*, 2016, accessed 8/20/23, https://www.smithsonianmag.com/history/long-lasting-legacy-great -migration-180960118/.

210 National Urban League, accessed 8/20/23, https://nul.org/quick-facts.

211 "Universal Negro Improvement Association," *Encyclopedia of Cleveland History, Case Western Reserve University*, https://case.edu/ech/articles/u/universal-negro -improvement-assn-unia; "Marcus Garvey (1887–1940)," *Biography.com*, https:// www.biography.com/activist/marcus-garvey.

212 Chasity Moreno, "Harriet Tubman: Death or Liberty," *New York Public Library*, 2018, https://www.nypl.org/blog/2018/04/18/harriet-tubman-history.

213 "File: Wilson-quote-in-birth-of-a-nation.jpg," *Wikimedia Commons*, https:// commons.wikimedia.org/wiki/File:Wilson-quote-in-birth-of-a-nation.jpg; Benbow, Mark E. "Birth of a Quotation: Woodrow Wilson and 'Like Writing History with Lightning," *The Journal of the Gilded Age and Progressive Era* 9, no. 4 (2010): 509–33. https://doi.org/10.1017/S1537781400004242.

214 Judson MacLaury, "The Federal Government and Negro Workers Under President Woodrow Wilson, 2000," *US Department of Labor*, https://www .dol.gov/general/aboutdol/history/shfgpr00; "A History of Racial Injustice— President Wilson Authorizes Segregation Within Federal Government," *Equal Justice Initiative*, https://calendar.eji.org/racial-injustice/apr/11.

215 "African-American Women and WWI," *The National World War I Museum and Memorial*, https://www.theworldwar.org/learn/about-wwi/african-american -women-and-wwi.

216 "Survey Report—African American Struggle for Civil Rights in Rhode Island: The Twentieth Century Phase 2: Statewide Survey and National Register Evaluation," https://www.rihs.org/wp-content/uploads/2019/10/20th-Century -African-American-Sites-in-RI-PAL-report-and-survey.pdf.

217 Lila Rakoczy and Andy Rhodes, "Camp Logan Mutiny Revised," *Texas Historical Commission*, June 2017, accessed 11/14/23, https://www.thc.texas.gov/blog/camp-logan-mutiny-revisited.

218 "Dec. 11, 1917: Black Soldiers Executed for Houston Riot," *Zinn Education Project*, accessed 11/26/23, https://www.zinnedproject.org/news/tdih/black-soldiers-executed/.

219 "Red Summer—The Race Riots of 1919," *The National WWI Museum and Memorial*, accessed 8/23/23, https://www.theworldwar.org/learn/about-wwi/red-summer; Cameron McWhirter, *Red Summer—The Summer of 1919 and the Awakening of Black America* (St. Martin's Griffin, 2012).

220 "What Was Jim Crow," *Jim Crow Museum*, https://jimcrowmuseum.ferris.edu/what.htm.

221 "Red Summer of 1919," *Equal Justice Initiative*, October 28, 2019, accessed 8/23/23, https://eji.org/news/history-racial-injustice-red-summer-of-1919/.

222 "The New London Race Riots of 1919 Follow a Pandemic," *New England Historical Society*, https://newenglandhistoricalsociety.com/the-new-london-race-riots-of-1919-follow-a-pandemic/.

223 "Hundreds of Black People Killed in Elaine, Arkansas, Massacre," *Equal Justice Initiative*, accessed 8/23/23, https://calendar.eji.org/racial-injustice/sep/30; Jessica Yamane, "Healing the Land: Elaine," *Anderson Institute on Race and Ethnicity, University of Arkansas-Little Rock*, accessed 8/23/23, https://ualr.edu/race-ethnicity/healing-the-land-elaine/.

224 "19th Amendment to the U.S. Constitution: Women's Right to Vote," *National Archives*, https://www.archives.gov/historical-docs/19th-amendment.

225 Robert Stephens, "The Truth Laid Bare," *Pegasus, The University of Southern Florida*, 2020, accessed 8/19/23,https://www.ucf.edu/pegasus/the-truth-laid-bare/; Isis Davis-Marks, "The Little-Known Story of America's Deadliest Election Day Massacre," *Smithsonian Magazine,* 2020, accessed 8/18/23, https://www.smithsonianmag.com/smart-news/new-exhibition-florida-honors-victims-bloodiest-election-massacre-american-history-180976283/.

226 Keith Stokes, "No Strange Fruit for Newport," *1696 Heritage Group*, https://www.1696heritage.com/no-strange-fruit-for-newport/; Armstead, *The History of Blacks in Resort Towns*, 224.

227 Armstead, *The History of Blacks in Resort Towns*, 226.

228 Keith Stokes, "A Place for All," *Newport Daily News,* June 2, 2014, https://www.newportri.com/story/news/2014/06/02/a-place-for-all/12744751007/.

229 "The Great Migration, 1910–1970," *National Archives, African American Heritage*, accessed 8/20/23, https://www.archives.gov/research/african-americans/migrations/great-migration.

230 1920 and 1921 List of the Names of Voters in Jamestown, Rhode Island—Real Estate Voters, Personal Property Voters, and Registry Voters, Certified October 28, 1920, Lewis W. Hull, Town Hall, Town of Jamestown, RI, accessed 4/1/22.

4

Conclusion

The growth of the Black community in Jamestown from a handful of freed individuals in 1850 to an established enclave of proud and productive citizens by 1920 is a noteworthy American story of resilience and perseverance.

The community's history stands in profound contrast to the turbulence and instability that plagued America in this period. The nation convulsed with slavery, the Civil War, the collapse of Reconstruction, and the rise of Jim Crow, witnessing race riots, lynchings, and the denial of fundamental human rights. Citizens in Rhode Island, reliant on slavery for generations, grappled with their complicity in the institution, uneven racial progress, and segregated and unequal education for Blacks. In Jamestown, meanwhile, Blacks carved out a space of quiet peace, dignity, stability, and growth; their community emerged as an unexpected haven.

The roots of this resilience lay in the opportunities of a growing economy and in timing. By 1850, slavery had ended in Rhode Island and Jamestown's dwindling Black population—descendants of enslaved Africans—regenerated into a community of free laborers, domestics, and farmers. Early figures like James Howland, born into slavery and living a long life, personified this profound transition from bondage to freedom. Later, eight-year-old Hannah Champlin watched the transformation of Dutch Island, visible from Jamestown shores, into a training ground for the 14th Rhode Island Heavy Artillery (Colored) after the start of the Civil War in 1861. The community witnessed the promise of Black military service and a fledgling acceptance of equal rights.

In the late nineteenth century, during the Gilded Age, Jamestown's Resort Era proved transformative. Its ferry-driven tourist economy opened opportunities that attracted Black migrants, from former slave states such as Georgia, Maryland, and Virginia, seeking refuge from racial violence and repression, and what Frederick Douglass called sharecropping's "stupendous fraud." In Jamestown, they found a peaceful rural environment with fewer strictures than in Providence or Newport. The island's size, remote location, and seasonal economy enabled many to leave behind their grueling farmhand jobs for positions such as carpenter, chauffeur, coachman, cook, dressmaker, expressman, ferryboat fireman, laundress, nurse, salesman, and stone mason. Crucially, this era saw the first Black land ownership, such as the Champlin farm in 1872, and a growing agency, illustrated by the Champlin brothers voting in 1883—the first recorded Black votes in Jamestown history.

While there was considerable hope for equality and freedom in America, the national climate circumscribed racial freedom. The 1896 *Plessy v. Ferguson* Supreme Court decision reinforced "separate but equal" Jim Crow laws while white uprisings rolled back Black political power such as the Wilmington, North Carolina insurrection.

In this period, Jamestown Blacks built their institutions undeterred. The Mt. Zion AME Church became a spiritual and social anchor. Benjamin and Lucy Morrell transformed their Jamestown real estate holdings into the *West View Cottage*, a summer resort for Black elites, including attorneys, physicians, entrepreneurs, and educators such as Booker T. Washington of the Tuskegee Institute. During this period, Andrew and Milissa Lodkey opened Jamestown's first Black-owned restaurant, while the Netter family operated successful, independent downtown businesses for three generations.

As millions fled Southern turmoil and poverty in the early years of the Great Migration, Jamestown's Black population peaked at 116 in 1905. By 1920, however, the nation's urban centers offered greater opportunity and the population dwindled. Even so, those who stayed continued to build and prosper. In 1920, just months after the ratification of the 19th Amendment, nine Black women in Jamestown voted, demonstrating a quiet resolve in a town once sustained by enslaved labor.

Jamestown was not without shortcomings. For generations, the town archives ignored the presence and contributions of Blacks. The Black community faced the prejudice, segregated employment, and low wages experienced by other Black communities, yet managed to mitigate the turmoil engulfing much of

America. For migrants arriving from slave states, Jamestown was a stepping stone; for multigenerational families like the Champlins, Rices, and Netters who settled, it was home—a place to celebrate family, own land, vote, worship, and bury their dead.

In the end, Jamestown's counter-narrative is instructive. In a time when America wavered in its promise of equality and opportunity, Jamestown's "peaceful patch of earth" proved to be a fertile testing ground for Black resilience. The community not only survived—which in itself is an accomplishment—but also built an enduring legacy. As Black leaders fought and agitated for rights and freedom on the national stage, on the local level, Jamestown Blacks accomplished their goals with quiet dignity and grace.

The achievements memorialized here may inform or inspire readers today, but above all, they must never be forgotten.

Appendix A

Maps—Black Households, Locations, and Structures, Jamestown, Rhode Island, 1850–1920

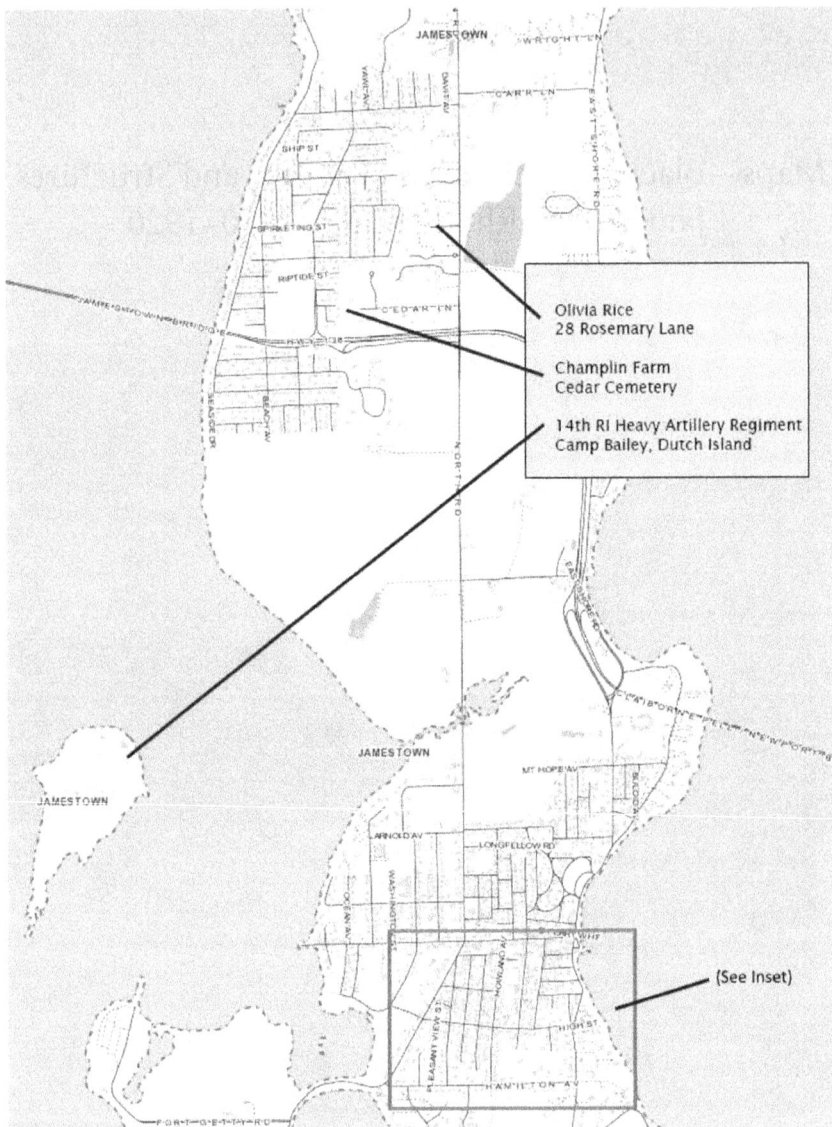

Black households, locations, and structures, Jamestown, Rhode Island, 1850–1920.

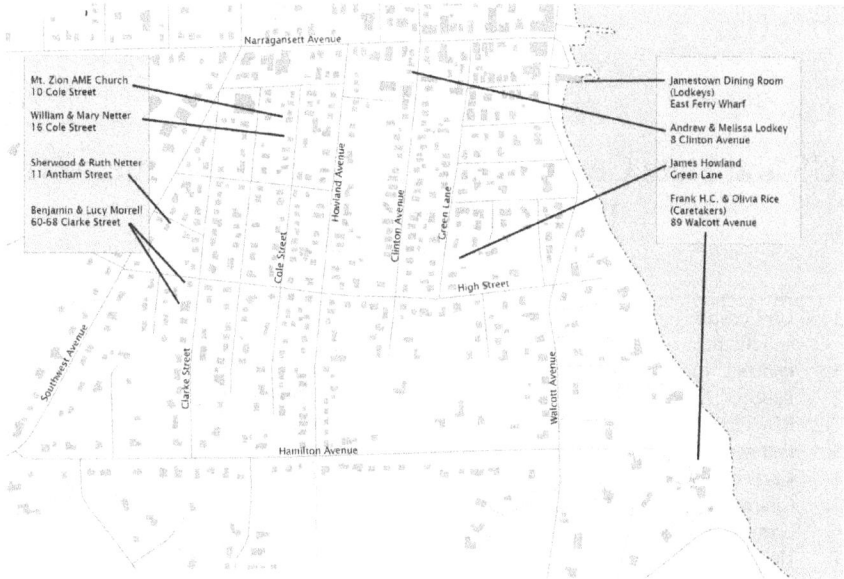

Mt. Zion AME Church
10 Cole Street

William & Mary Netter
16 Cole Street

Sherwood & Ruth Netter
11 Antham Street

Benjamin & Lucy Morrell
60-68 Clarke Street

Jamestown Dining Room
(Lodkeys)
East Ferry Wharf

Andrew & Melissa Lodkey
8 Clinton Avenue

James Howland
Green Lane

Frank H.C. & Olivia Rice
(Caretakers)
89 Walcott Avenue

Narragansett Avenue

Howland Avenue

Clinton Avenue

Green Lane

Cole Street

High Street

Southwest Avenue

Clarke Street

Walcott Avenue

Hamilton Avenue

Jamestown village inset.

Appendix B

US and State Census—Black Population—Jamestown, Rhode Island, 1850–1920

1850 US Census: Name, Age, Occupation, and Birthplace

1. Babcock, Isaac – 25 – Laborer – RI
2. Babcock, Moses Wm. – 27 – Laborer - RI
3. Battey, Orber – 78 – RI
4. Carpenter, Araminta – 70 – RI
5. Champlin, George – 28 – Laborer – RI
6. Gardner, Sarah – 25 – RI
7. Howland, James – 94 – Laborer - RI
8. Hull, Ann – 17 – RI
9. Perry, William – 26 – Laborer – RI
10. Potter, Rachel – 36 – CT
11. Spellman, John – 16 – Laborer – NY
12. Stephens, Mary – 56 – RI
13. Watson. Martha – 38 – RI
14. Weeden, Dorcas – 14 – RI

1860 US Census: Name, Age, Occupation, and Birthplace

1. Champlin, Alexander – 11 – RI
2. Champlin, Charles W. – 2 – RI
3. Champlin, George W. – 14 – RI
4. Champlin, George W. – 47 – Farm Laborer – RI
5. Champlin, Hannah – 5 – RI
6. Champlin, John H. – 44 – Farm Laborer – RI
7. Champlin, William H – 8 – RI
8. Frye, Sarah – 42 – RI
9. Hazard, James M. – 32 – Farm Laborer – RI
10. Johnston, Henry – 54 – Farm Laborer – RI
11. Potter, Rachel – 60 – Domestic – RI
12. Remington, Henry – 12 – Farm Laborer – RI
13. Warmsly, William – 18 – Farm Laborer – RI

1865 RI Census: Name, Age, Occupation, and Birthplace

1. Champlin, Alexander – 17 – Housekeeper – RI
2. Champlin, Charles W. – 6 – RI
3. Champlin, George W. – 13 – Servant – RI
4. Champlin, George W. – 55 – Farm Laborer – RI
5. Champlin, Hannah – 8 – RI
6. Champlin, John H. – 49 – Farm Laborer – RI
7. Champlin, William – 10 – RI
8. Colbert, Anna – 19 – Servant – NJ
9. Commons, Mary J. – 16 – Servant – RI
10. Corliss, Lewis – 13 – Servant – MA
11. Drummond, Alice – 16 – Servant – MA
12. Johnson, Henry – 60 – Farm Laborer – RI
13. Potter, Thomas – 18 – Farm Laborer – MA
14. Remington, Mary J. – 15 – Servant - RI
15. Rhodes, Thomas – 21 – Farm Laborer – RI
16. Warmsly, William – 25 – Farm Laborer – RI
17. Williams, Mary – 20 – Servant – VA

1870 US Census: Name, Age, Occupation, and Birthplace
1. Champlin, Alexander – 19 – Farm Laborer – RI
2. Champlin, Chas W. – 14 – At Home – RI
3. Champlin, George W. – 56 – Farm Laborer – RI
4. Champlin, Hannah E. – 15 – At Home - RI
5. Champlin, William H. – 16 – Farm Laborer – RI

6. Dodge, George – 21 – Farm Laborer – RI
7. Hareborn, Joseph – 17 – Farm Laborer – New Providence, Bahamas
8. Philips, Herbert – 15 – Farm Laborer – SC

1875 RI Census: Name, Age, Occupation, and Birthplace
1. Champlin, Alexander – 26 – Laborer – RI
2. Champlin, Chas W. – 18 – Laborer – RI
3. Champlin, Geo. W. – 64 – Laborer – RI
4. Champlin, Hannah E. – 19 – Servant – RI
5. Champlin, Henry – 61 – Laborer – RI
6. Champlin, William – 21 – Laborer – RI
7. Jones, Mary – 82 – Washing – MD
8. Moor, Annie – 40 – Servant – MD
9. Moor, Washington – 40 – Servant – MD

10. Talbot, Elizabeth – 16 – Servant – RI
11. Talbot, James – 9 – In School – RI
12. Talbot, Josephine – 30 – Housekeeper – MD
13. Talbot, Lizzie – 16 – Servant – RI
14. Talbot, Mary – 15 – MD
15. Talbot, William – 40 – Laborer – MD
16. Talbot, Wm. B. – 10 – In School – RI
17. Williams, James – 16 – Laborer – VA

1880 US Census: Name, Age, Occupation, and Birthplace
1. Artist, Thomas W. – 30 – Farm Laborer – VA
2. Bauldin, Francis F. – 41 – Washing – MD
3. Champlin, Alexander – 30 – Farm Laborer – RI
4. Champlin, Charles – 32 – Laborer – RI
5. Champlin, George W. – 35 – Farm Laborer – RI
6. Champlin, George W. – 67 – Laborer – RI
7. Champlin, Hannah – 23 – House Keeper – RI
8. Dodge, George C. – 40 – Farm Laborer – RI
9. Fairweather, John – 21 – Farm Laborer – RI

10. Rice, Claudine H. – 20 – At Home – RI
11. Rice, Frank C. – 11 – At Home – RI
12. Rice, Fred L. – 13 – At School – RI
13. Rice, Hannah – 49 – House Keeper – RI
14. Rice, Isaac – 49 – Carpenter – RI
15. Rice, Orman C. – 5 – At Home – RI
16. Rice, Rosa G. – 23 – House Keeper – RI
17. Ritter, William – 21 – Farm Laborer – RI
18. Tasker, Emily E. – 64 – Cook – MD

1885 RI Census: Name, Age, Occupation, and Birthplace

1. Baldwin, Francis T. – 40 – Washing – MD
2. Baldwin, Lavenia H. – 20 – Table Girl – VA
3. Champlin, Alexander – 32 – Servant – RI
4. Champlin, Charles W. – 28 – Servant – RI
5. Champlin, George W. – 72 – Laborer – RI
6. Champlin, Hannah – 28 – Housekeeper – RI
7. Davis, Elizabeth – 8 – At School – RI
8. Davis, Henry – 5 – At Home – RI
9. Davis, Mary – 3 – At Home – RI
10. Davis, Phoebe – 10 – At School – RI
11. Davis, Thomas – 46 – Laborer – VA
12. Dodge, George – 40 – Farm Helper – RI
13. Rice, Frank – 17 – Laborer – RI
14. Rice, Frederic – 18 – Farm Laborer – RI
15. Tasco, Emily L. – 69 – Cook – M

1900 US Census: Name, Age, Occupation, and Birthplace

1. Andrews, Mollie – 37 – Servant – VA
2. Berriman, James – 26 – Servant – GA
3. Bramer, Frank – 31 – Day Laborer – Western Isles
4. Broadus, Ellen – 25 – Servant – VA
5. Broadus, Lavinia – 23 – Servant – VA
6. Broadus, Melvin – 28 – Laborer – VA
7. Broadus, Willie – 33 – Farm Laborer - VA
8. Broadus, Willis – 30 – Farm Laborer – VA
9. Butler, Grace – 46 – Servant – GA
10. Campbell, Washington – 32 – Farm Hand – VA
11. Carpenter – 20 – Servant – VA
12. Carter, Marshall – 20 – Farm Hand – VA
13. Champlin, Charles – 40 – Farm Laborer – RI
14. Champlin, Hannah E. – 44 – Servant – RI
15. Clarke, Willard F. – 16 – Day Laborer – RI
16. Clifford, Alfred – Butler – MD
17. Coates, Evalina – 50 – Dressmaker – VA
18. Cole, Maria – 23 – Servant – MD
19. Colvert, John – 20 – Farm Laborer – VA
20. Davis, Henry – 20 – Stable Boy – RI
21. Davis, Irene – 47 – House Keeper – West Indies
22. Davis, Mary – 17 – In School – RI
23. Davis, Melissa – 60 – RI
24. Davis, Thomas – 41 – Mason
42. Johnson, Robert – 21 – Salesman – MD
43. Jones, Mary A.B. – 34 – Dressmaker – VA
44. Jones, William Z. – 45 – Servant – MD
45. Jordan, Rebecca P. – 30 – RI
46. Jordan, Walter – 55 – RI
47. Lawson, Wilfred – 22 – Farm Laborer – VA
48. Mahony, Benjamin – 15 – Servant – DC
49. Mahony, Henrietta – 39 – Servant – MD
50. Miller, Gabriel B. – 33 – Day Laborer – KY
51. Morrell, Benjamin F. – 52- Expressman – KY
52. Morrell, Nannie A. – 52 – NC
53. Netter, Edith – 8 – In School – RI
54. Netter, Lila – 12 – In School – RI
55. Netter, Mary F. – 58 – Laundress – MD
56. Netter, Sherwood – 10 – In School – RI
57. No Name – 48 – Farm Laborer – RI
58. No Name – 55 – Farm Laborer – RI
59. Parker, Powtan – 17 – Farm Laborer – VA
60. Payne, Almeda – 1 – RI
61. Payne, George L. – 26 – Fisherman – RI
62. Payne, Harris S. – 4 – RI
63. Payne, Sarah L. – 25 – VA
64. Robinson, John – 25 – Farm Hand – VA
65. Rose, Caroline – 37 – Laundress – VA
66. Rose, William S. – 34 – Carriage Keeper – VA
67. Scott, Dinna K – 35 – Cook – SC
68. Scott, James A. – 38 – Hotel Waiter – GA
69. Snowden, Samuel – 25 – Farm Laborer – MD
70. Stewart, Walter E. – 33 – Day Laborer – DC

25. Dodge, George C. – 53 – Day Laborer – RI
26. Dodge, Susie – 45 – RI
27. Dosia, Henrietta – 22 – Servant – GA
28. Dutton, Robert – 31 – Day Laborer – MD
29. Fitzhugh, Strother – 21 – Farm Laborer – VA
30. Grant, Monnie – 40 – Servant – VA
31. Holly, Charles – 26 – Day Laborer – MD
32. Holly, Florence – 22 – MD
33. J. Carpenter, J. – 28 – Farm Laborer – VA
34. Jackson, John – 24 – Laborer – Canada
35. Johnson, Alfred – 20 – Day Laborer – RI
36. Johnson, Annie – 17 – RI
37. Johnson, Earnest – 23 – MD
38. Johnson, Edward – 11
39. Johnson, Eliza – 45 – MD
40. Johnson, Isaac – 48 – Stone Mason – VA
41. Johnson, Rebecca – 15 – RI

1905 RI Census: Name, Age, Occupation, and Birthplace

1. Beander, Corra – 28 – Servant – VA
2. Berryman, James (Mrs.) – 28 – Laundress – VA
3. Berryman, James E. – 30 – Cook – VA
4. Black, Pheby – 47 – Laundress – SC
5. Brodeur, William – 28 – Farm Labor – VA
6. Brown, Emma – 11 – VA
7. Brown, Mattie – 16 – Waitress – NC
8. Brown, Sarah (Mrs.) – 43 – Laundress – NC
9. Butler, Grace E. (Mrs.) – 48 – Laundress – GA
10. Campbell, Anthony – 38 – Farm Labor – SC
11. Carter, James – 18 – Day Labor – VA
12. Carter, Lee – 20 – Day Labor – VA
13. Carter, Marshell, – 26 – Farm Labor – VA
14. Caswell, Mary – 26 – Housewife – RI
15. Cates, Evline T. – 57 – Dressmaking – VA
16. Champlin, Hannah – 42 – Domestic – RI
17. Clark, Marie – 31 – Laundress – SC
18. Colbert, Arron – 23 – Farm Labor – VA
19. Cole, Willer – 45 – Laundress – MD
20. Collins, Eliza – 36 – Laundress – RI

71. Tanner, Jane – 14 – Servant – VA
72. Thomas, Bertha L. – 3 – PA
73. Thomas, Quintina – 26 – MD
74. Thomas, Walter – 36 – Farm Laborer – MD
75. Walker, Lottie – 30 – Servant – RI
76. Washington, Minerva – 27 – Servant – VA
77. White, Frederick G. M. – 8 – In School – MT
78. Williams, Mary – 32 – Servant – MD
79. Wood, Fielding – 22 – Laborer – VA
80. Wright, Josephine – 22 – Servant – VA
81. Wright, Louis P. – 26 – Servant – VA
82. Young, Nathan – 23 – Farm Laborer – VA

59. Jones, William H. – 43 – Steward at Club – MD
60. Jones, William Alex – 21 – Day Labor – NC
61. Jordan, Eva P. (Mrs.) – 31 – Maid – RI
62. Jordan, Mary – 56 – Domestic – VA
63. Jordan, Walter – 48 – Grocers Salesman – RI
64. Jordan, William E. – 5 – RI
65. Kelly, N. – 23 – Servant – VA
66. Kendall, Louisa G. – 48 – Laundress Helper – MA
67. Lewellen, Ella – 38 – Housewife – NC
68. Lewis, Edward – 28 – Farm Labor – VA
69. Lindsy, Eliza – 27 – Servant – VA
70. Morrell, B. F. – 56 – Expressman – KY
71. Morrell, Fred G. – 13 – MN
72. Morton, David – 27 – Farm Labor – VA
73. Netter, Edith – 14 – RI
74. Netter, Lila – 17 – Laundress – RI
75. Netter, Mary F. – 42 – Laundress – RI
76. Netter, Sherwood – 15 – Teamster – RI
77. Netter, William H. – 50 – Day Labor – MD
78. Osburn, William – 45 – Day Labor – VA
79. Parker, Powtan – 22 – Farm Labor – VA
80. Payne, Almetta – 7 – RI
81. Payne, George L. – 33 – Day Labor – RI
82. Payne, Louis L. – 9 – Domestic – RI
83. Payne, Mary I. – 2 – RI
84. Payne, Ruth – 4 – RI
85. Payne, Sarah L. – 31 – VA

21. Crawford, Ephraim P. – 34 – Laundry Proprietor – NC
22. DeBois, Edward – 16 – Domestic (Ft. Greble) – PA
23. Dodge, Charles E. – 50 – Deck Hand – RI
24. Dodge, George C. – 53 – Day Labor – RI
25. Dodge, Susie (Mrs.) – 45 – RI
26. Edmonds, Nelson – 21 – Servant – VA
27. Elliott, John – 32 – Chauffeur – NC
28. Fields, Olivia – 27 – Domestic – VA
29. Fitzgerald, Junius H. – 30 – Teamster – VA
30. Fitzgerald, Mary – 56 – Laundress – VA
31. Gaines, D.C – 6 – NY
32. Gaines, Ellen T. – 42 – Housewife – VA
33. Gaines, Stephen – 48 – Express Labor – NY
34. Gallaway, Florence – 4 – MD
35. Galway, Lizzie – 23 – Domestic – MD
36. Green, Viola – 6 – RI
37. Greene, Frank, Jr. – 22 – Farm Labor – VA
38. Groos, George – 26 – Farm Labor – MD
39. Heathman, C. (Mrs.) – 46 – Laundress – RI
40. Henderson, Jessie – 19 – Domestic – VA
41. Holley, Ellen – 4 – PA
42. Holley – 32 – Coachman – NC
43. Holley, Lewtinsey – 2 – NC
44. Holley, Opencie – 2 – NC
45. Holley, Susie – 31 – Housework – NC
46. Hutton, Marrie – 9 – RI
47. Jackson, Fannie – 30 – Domestic – DE
48. Jackson, Floyd M. – 32 – Barber – GA
49. Jefferson, James – 30 – Farm Labor – VA
50. Johnson, Alfred – 24 – Day Labor – 24
51. Johnson, Annie – 23 – Laundress – RI
52. Johnson, Edward – 16 – Grocers Salesman – RI
53. Johnson, Eliza (Mrs.) – 53 – Laundress – MD
54. Johnson, Ernest – 26 – Teamster – MD
55. Johnson, Rebaca – 20 – Domestic – RI
56. Johnson, Rebeca – 20 – Domestic – RI
57. Jones, Mary A. (Mrs.) – 39 – Dressmaker – VA
58. Jones, Mattie J. – 16 – Nurse – NC
86. Penn, Better – 56 – Laundress Helper – VA
87. Perry, Laura (Mrs.) – 29 – GA
88. Respass, Matilda – 69 – Domestic – NC
89. Rester, Marie – 75 – MD
90. Richards, Charlott – 2 – RI
91. Richards, Thomas – 31 – Sailor – P.E.I., CAN
92. Richards, Thomas – 4 – RI
93. Richards, Thomas (Mrs.) – 30 – Laundress – NY
94. Robinson, John – 27 – Teamster – VA
95. Robinson, John – 27 – Teamster – VA
96. Robinson, John (Mrs.) – 20 – Laundress – VA
97. Robinson, Minnie – 30 – Domestic – VA
98. Rose, Emma T. – 33 – Cook – NY
99. Ross, E. Chas – 24 – Waiter – FL
100. Sayles, Elizabeth – 40 – Domestic – MD
101. Smith, Elizabeth (Mrs.) – 33 – Laundress – MD
102. Smith, George – 29 – Day Labor – VA
103. Spriggs, Caroline – 65 – Housewife – VA
104. Thomas, Berth – 8 – VA
105. Thomas, Steven – 29 – Farm Labor – MD
106. Thomas, Walter – 37 – Farmer – MD
107. Thomas, Walter (Mrs.) – 31 – MD
108. Tillman, Annie M. – 32 – Domestic – GA
109. Townsend, Ella – 22 – Domestic – SC
110. Turner, Annie – 30 – Laundress – VA
111. Walker, Lottie – 30 – House Work – VA
112. Washington, M. Miss – 35 – Domestic – VA
113. White, Charles – 14 – Domestic (Ft. Greble) – GA
114. Wood, Fielding – 30 – Farm Labor – VA
115. Wood, Thomas – 25 – Day Labor – VA
116. 116 Wright, Louis – 30 – Farm Labor – VA

1910 US Census: Name, Age, Occupation,
and Birthplace

1. Battle, Austin – 25 – Cook – NC
2. Beaufort, William – 30 – Driver – VA
3. Brown, Frank – 40 – Servant – FL
4. Butler, Henry – 29 – Farm Laborer – RI
5. Cannon, Earnest – 2 – PA
6. Cannon, Helen – 30 – MD
7. Cannon, John – 32 – Laborer – DE
8. Champlin, Hannah E. – 44 – Cook – RI
9. Coates, Evalina T. – 65 – Dressmaker – VA
10. Coleman, William – 19 – Farm Laborer – VA
11. Cross, Charles – 33 – Cook – WV
12. Currington, John – 22 – Orderly – PA
13. Dizzo, Edward – 50 – Dishwasher – MD
14. Drew, Carrie – 53 – Servant – LA
15. Dunn, Alice – 0 – VA
16. Dunn, Annie – 28 – VA
17. Dunn, Jennie – 3 – VA
18. Dunn, Mary – 2 – VA
19. Greene, Frank – 25 – Farm Laborer – VA
20. Henderson, Jesse – 21 – Farm Laborer – RI
21. Hutton, Marie – 13 – RI
22. Johnson, Alfred – 29 – Farm Laborer – VA
23. Johnson, Earnest – 31 – Ferry Boat Worker – VA
24. Johnson, Eliza A. – 59 – Laundress – MD
25. Johnson, Elsi – 26 – Servant – MD
26. Jones, Mary A. – 44 – Dressmaker – VA
27. Jones, Willie – 19 – Servant – NC
28. Langston, Benjamin B. – 19 – Farm Laborer – NC
29. Lewellen, Ella R.B. – 43 – NC
30. Lewellen, Robert B. – 37 – Driver – VA
31. Menke, Beulah – 19 – Housemaid – NJ
32. Minor, James – 23 – Farm Laborer – VA
33. Morrell, Benjamin F. – 60 – Ret. Officer – KY
34. Morrell, Lucy J. – 45 – VA
35. Netter, Edith – 18 – Laundress – RI
36. Netter, Mary F. – 48 – Laundress – MD
37. Netter, Sherwood – 19 – Driver – RI
38. Netter, William H. – 50 – Laborer – MD
39. Reaster, Maria – 82 – MD
40. Scott, Dianna – 40 – Cook – GA
41. Shinks, Mildred – 45 – Housekeeper – VA
42. Washington, Agnes – 19 – Housekeeper – VA
43. Whithead, Columbus – 19 – Servant – NC
44. Whithead, Hillard – 20 – Servant – NC
45. Williams, Majorie – 11 – NJ
46. Williams, Viola – 14 – Children's Nurse – DE
47. Wood, Fielding W. – 30 – Laborer – VA
48. Wood, John J. – 17 – Servant – VA
49. Wood, Richard A. – 21 – Farm Laborer – NC
50. Wood, Thomas L. – 25 – Servant – VA
51. Young, Edward – 1 – VA
52. Young, Rebecca – 25 – Waitress – RI
53. Young, Willetta – 1 – VA

1915 RI Census: Name, Age, Occupation
and Birthplace

1. Ashbey, Francis – 34 – Servant – US
2. Brain, Robert – 50 – US
3. Brinkley, Melten – 49 – Laborer – US
4. Butler, Grace A. – 50 – Dressmaker – US
5. Champlin, Hannah – 50 – Housekeeper – US
6. Coates, Evaline T. – 64 – Dressmaker – US
7. Dunn, Alice – 6 - In School – US
8. Dunn, Annie B. – 34 – Washing – US
9. Dunn, Jeannette – 8 – In School – US
10. Dunn, Mary – 7 – In School – US
11. Fielding, Jordan – 73 – Laborer – US
22. Jordon, Eva P. 38 – Washing – US
23. Jordon, William T. – 14 - In School – US
24. Lee, Flossie – 23 – Housekeeper – US
25. Lee, John H. 51 – Painter – US
26. Lee, Sarah H. – 30 – US
27. Lewellen, Ella B. – 43 – US
28. Lewellen, Robert B. – 37 – Livery – US
29. Lodkey, Andrew W. – 62 – Lunchroom – US
30. Lodkey, Melissa A. – 59 – US
31. Loofes, Ralph – 22 – Laborer – US
32. Madden, Howard – 30 – Laborer – US
33. Netter, Sherwood – 24 – Laborer – US
34. Rice, Frank C. – 45 – Carpenter – US
35. Rice, Lois – 2 – US

12. Green, Frank Jr. – 30 – Laborer – US
13. Haversham, Kenneth – 1 – US
14. Haversham, Mary – 20 – US
15. Haversham, Simon S. – 28 – Laborer – US
16. Heathman, Carrie B. – 47 – Housekeeper – US
17. Henderson, Faunsie – 23- Laborer – US
18. Johnson, Eliza – 64 – US
19. Johnson, Ernest J. – 36 – Ferryboat Fireman – US
20. Jones, Mary – 49 – Dressmaker – US
21. Jones, William H. – 51 – US

36. Rice, Olivia – 34 – US
37. Shannon, Nettie – 28 – Servant – US
38. Thomas, Bertha L. – 17 – In School – US
39. Thomas, Quintina – 41 – US
40. Walter, Thomas – 46 – Laborer – US
41. Wiggers, Ethel – 22 – Nurse – US
42. Wilson, Francis R. – 12 – In School – US

1920 US Census Name, Age, Occupation, and Birthplace

1. Butler, Grace – 60 – Laundress – GA
2. Lewellen, Ellen – 47 – NC
3. Lewellen, Robert – 48 – Express man – VA
4. Lir?fin, Lacill – 25 – Head Waiter – VA
5. Lodkey, Andrew – 66 – Restaurant Proprietor – GA
6. Lodkey, Melisa – 64 – GA
7. Lucker, Louisa – 65 – VA
8. Major, Isora – 15 – VA
9. Major, Silvester – 40 – VA
10. Major, Lucy – 42 – Servant – VA
11. Netter, Ella – 21 – AL
12. Netter, Mary – 55 – Laundress – MD
13. Netter, Mary Joseph – 11 – RI
14. Netter, Sherman – 29 – Chauffer – MD
15. Netter, William H. – 56 – Laborer – MD
16. Netter, William H. 3rd – 0 – RI
17. Netter, William Jr. – 40 – Cobbler – MD
18. Perkins, George – 34 – Laborer – NC
19. Perkins, Marion – 26 – Laundress – RI

Further Reading

"Minutes of the Newport Anti-Slavery Society, 1836–1841," Newport Historical Society Manuscript Collection, Newport, R.I.

Aptheker, Herbert. *American Negro Slave Revolts*. 5th ed. International Publishers, 1983.

Aptheker, Herbert. *Nat Turner's Slave Rebellion*. Humanities Press, 1966.

Armstead, Myra Beth. *Lord, Please Don't Take Me in August: African-Americans in Newport and Saratoga Springs, 1870–1930*. University of Illinois Press, 1999.

Bartlett, Irving H. *From Slave to Citizen: The Story of the Negro in Rhode Island*. Urban League of Greater Providence, 1954.

Bell, Andrew J. *An Assessment of Life in Rhode Island as an African American In the Era From 1918 to 1993*. Vantage Press, 1997.

Chaput, Erik J., and Russell J. DeSimone. "George T. Downing and the 'Fraternal Unity of Man': The Battle for an Abolition Democracy in Nineteenth-Century America." *Newport History* 100, no. 289 (2024): Article 2.

Clark-Pujara, Christy. "The Business of Slavery and Antislavery Sentiment in Rhode Island: The Case of Rowland Gibson Hazard – An Antislavery Negro Cloth Dealer." *Rhode Island History* 71, no. 2 (Summer/Fall 2013): 35–56.

Cottrol, Robert J. *Afro Yankees: Providence Black Community in the Antebellum Era*. Greenwood Press, 1982.

Cranston, Timothy, and Neil Dunay. *We Were Here Too: Selected Stories of Black History in North Kingstown*. N.p., 2005.

Dimmick, Robb. "Disappearing Ink: A Bibliography of Writings by and about Rhode Island African Americans with Occasional Annotation." 2022.

Douglass, Frederick. *Frederick Douglass: Selected Speeches and Writings*. Edited by Philip Sheldon Foner. Lawrence Hill Books, 1999.

Du Bois, W. E. B. *The Complete Published Works of W. E. B. Du Bois*. Edited by Herbert Aptheker. Kraus-Thomson, 1982.

Dyer, Brigadier-General Elisha. *Annual Report of the Adjutant General of the State of Rhode Island for the Year 1865*. Freeman & Son, 1895.

Foner, Eric. "A Historian Explains the Significance of the Fugitive Slave Act." *American Social History Project*, https://shec.ashp.cuny.edu/items/show/1489.

Gross, Carl Russell. "A Brief History on the Life of Matilda Sissieretta (Joynor) Jones 'The Black Patti' 1869-1933" (1966). Rhode Island College, Dr. Carl Russell Gross Collection. 8. https://www.riamco.org/render?eadid=US-RPRC-MSS.2&view=all.

Gross, Carl Russell. "The Negro and Events in Rhode Island, 1696–1968." Typescript. Rhode Island College and Rhode Island Historical Society, 1968.

Grossman, Lawrence. "George T. Downing and Desegregation of Rhode Island Public Schools, 1855–1866." *Rhode Island History* 36 (November 1977): 99–105.

Hooks, Edward K. *The Formation of the NAACP Providence Branch*. Rhode Island Black Heritage Society, 2013.

Lancaster, Jane. "'I Would Have Made Out Very Poorly Had It Not Been For Her'": The Life and Work of Christiana Bannister, Hair Doctress and Philanthropist." *Rhode Island History* 59, no. 4 (November 2001): 103–22. https://www.rihs.org/assetts/files/publications/2001_Nov.pdf.

National Archives. "The Great Migration—1910–1970." *African American Heritage*. https://www.archives.gov/research/african-americans/migrations/great-migration.

Oklahoma State Legislature, *Tulsa Race Riot Commission. Final Report*. Oklahoma State Legislature, 2001. https://www.okhistory.org/research/forms/freport.pdf.

Princess Redwing, Editor. *The Narragansett Dawn. 1935–1936*. https://digitalcommons.uri.edu/sc_pubs/5/.

Public Archeology Laboratory. "Survey Report African American Struggle for Civil Rights in Rhode Island: Pre-1900 Statewide Survey and National Register Evaluation." *Public Archeology Laboratory*, September 30, 2024. https://preservation.ri.gov/sites/g/files/xkgbur406/files/2024-11/RI%20Pre-1900%20Civil%20Rights%20Survey%20Report%20FINAL%20%28with%20inventory%20forms%29.pdf.

Rhode Island General Assembly. *Narraganset Tribe of Indians: Report of the Committee of Investigation, A Historical Sketch and Evidence Taken, House of Representatives, January Session 1880*. E.L. Freeman & Company Printers, 1880.

Rhode Island Historical Preservation & Heritage Commission. *Native American Archaeology In Rhode Island*. Rhode Island Historical Preservation & Heritage Commission, 2002.

Robinson, William H. *Blacks in 19th Century Rhode Island: An Overview*. Rhode Island Black Heritage Society, 1978.

Rubertone, Patricia E. *Native Providence: Memory, Community, and Survivance in the Northeast*. University of Nebraska Press, 2020. https://doi.org/10.2307/j.ctv17ppct6.8.

Simmons, William Scranton. *Cautantowwit's House: An Indian Burial Ground on the Island of Conanicut in Narragansett Bay*. Brown University Press, 1970.

Stensrud, Rockwell. *Newport: A Lively Experiment, 1639–1969*. Redwood Library and Athenaeum, 2007.

Stewart, Rowena and Andrew Bell. "Rhode Island Underground Railroad." In *Underground Railroad in New England*. American Revolution Bicentennial Administration, 1976.

Stewart, Rowena, et al. *Creative Survival: The Providence Black Community in the 19th Century*. Rhode Island Black Heritage Society, 1985.

Stokes, Keith W., and Theresa Guzmán Stokes. *A Matter of Truth: The Struggle for African Heritage & Indigenous People Equal Rights in Providence, Rhode Island (1620–2020)*. Rhode Island Black Heritage Society and 1696 Heritage Group, 2021.

United States Senate. "Landmark Legislation: Civil Rights Act of 1875." *US Senate*. https://www.senate.gov/artandhistory/history/common/generic/CivilRightsAct1875.htm.

United States Senate. "The Enforcement Acts of 1870 and 1871." *US Senate*. https://www.senate.gov/artandhistory/history/common/generic/EnforcementActs.htm

Veney, Bethany. *Aunt Betty's Story: The Narrative of Bethany Veney, A Slave Woman*. Press of Geo. H. Ellis, 1889.

Washington, S.A.M. *George Thomas Downing: A Sketch of His Life and Times*. The Milne Printery, 1910.

Weeden, John E. *Speech of J.E. Weeden, of Westerly, R.I., in the House of Representatives, January Session of the Legislature of Rhode Island, 1865, on the Equal School Rights of Colored Children*. A.C. Greene, 1865.

Williams, Roger. *A Key into the Language of America*. Edited by Howard M. Chapin. Applewood Books, 1936.

Yates, Josephine Silone. "The National Association of Colored Women." *Voice of the Negro* 1 (1904): 283–7; reprint. Negro University Press, 1969.

Bibliography

1696 Heritage Group. Keith Stokes, "No Strange Fruit for Newport." https://www
.1696heritage.com/no-strange-fruit-for-newport/.

African American Registry. "Mary Dickerson, Businesswoman,and Club Woman
born."https:aaregistry.org/story/mary-dickerson-business-and-club-woman-born/

"Agreement among the Colonists to Purchase Conanicut Island." Jamestown
Historical Society Archives. 1657. A2006.461.001.

American Battlefield Trust. "Slave Rebellions and Uprisings." Accessed 6/10/24,
https://www.battlefields.org/learn/articles/slave-rebellions-and-uprisings.

American Battlefield Trust. John Pierce, "The Reasons for Secession: A Documentary
Study." Accessed 12/27/23, https://www.battlefields.org/learn/articles/reasons
-secession.

American History Central. "General Orders, No. 20 (Headquarters of the Army)."
https://www.americanhistorycentral.com/entries/general-orders-no-20
-headquarters-of-the-army/.

American Social History Project. Eric Foner, "A Historian Explains the Significance
of the Fugitive Slave Act." https://shec.ashp.cuny.edu/items/show/1489.

Ancestry.com. "US Civil War Pension Index to Pension Files."

Ancestry.com. "US Naval Enlistment Rendezvous." NARA No. M1953, Roll 18,
Philadelphia, February 1, 1862.

Aptheker, Herbert. "Negro Casualties in the Civil War." *The Journal of Negro History*
32, no. 1 (January 1947): 10–80.

Armstead, Myra Beth Young. *The History of Blacks in Resort Towns: Newport, Rhode
Island and Saratoga Springs, New York, 1870 – 1930.* Doctoral Dissertation,
University of Chicago, Chicago, IL, 1987.

Arnold, Benedict. "Will of Benedict Arnold, of Jamestown, 1733." *Newport Historical
Magazine* 1, no. 4 (July 1883): 21–49. https://archive.org/details/newporthistoric
188384newp/page/n51/mode/2up.

Arnold, James N., ed. *Narragansett Historical Register* II, No. 1, 1883. Narragansett
Historical Publishing Co., 1883.

Arnold, Samuel Greene. *History of the State of Rhode Island and Providence
Plantations Vol. II.* Preston & Rounds, 1894.

Atlas Obscura. Lambeck, Briona. "The Double Life of New York's Black Oyster King." September 28, 2022. Accessed 12/21/23, https://www.atlasobscura.com/articles/new-york-oyster-history.

Atlas of Southern Rhode Island, Jamestown and Prudence Island. Everts and Richards, 1895.

Bates, W. Lincoln. "Slavery Days in Rhode Island." *Bulletin of the Jamestown Historical Society, No. 2*, November 1921.

Battle, Charles A. *Negroes on the Island of Rhode Island.* 1932. Republished by Newport's Black Museum, 1971.

Beck, Hamilton. "W.E.B. Du Bois as a Student Abroad in Germany 1892- 1894." *Frontiers: The Interdisciplinary Journal of Study Abroad* 2, no. 1 (1996): 45–63. https://doi.org/10.36366/frontiers.v2i1.25.

Beckert, Sven. "Empire of Cotton." *The Atlantic,* December 12, 2014. https://www.theatlantic.com/business/archive/2014/12/empire-of-cotton/383660/.

Benbow, Mark E. "Birth of a Quotation: Woodrow Wilson and 'Like Writing History with Lightning'." *The Journal of the Gilded Age and Progressive Era* 9, no. 4 (2010): 509–33. https://doi.org/10.1017/S1537781400004242.

Berlin, Ira, Joseph P. Reidy, and Leslie S. Rowland. *Freedom: A Documentary History of Emancipation: 1861-1867, Series II, The Black Military Experience.* Cambridge University Press, 1982.

Biography.com. "Marcus Garvey was a prominent activist whoadvocated for Black separatism and nationalism via his namesake ideology,Garveyism." Catherine Caruso, January 25, 2025.https://www.biography.com/activists/marcus-garvey.

Black Past. Nate Christensen, "Mahlon Van Horne, 1840-1910,"June 3, 2011. https://blackpast.org/african-american-history/van-horne-mahlon-1840-1910/.

Boutin, Cameron. "The First Rhode Island Regiment and Revolutionary – America's Lost Opportunity, The War Years 1775 – 1783." *Journal of American Revolution,* January 17, 2018. https://allthingsliberty.com/2018/01/1st-rhode-island-regiment-revolutionary-americas-lost-opportunity/.

Brackett, Jeffrey R. *The Negro in Maryland: A Study of Slavery.* Johns Hopkins University, 1889.

Britannica. "Thaddeus Stevens - American Politician." https://www.britannica.com/biography/Thaddeus-Stevens.

Britannica. "Republican Party - Political Party, United States [1854-Present]." Accessed 7/28/23, https://www..britannica.com/topic/Republican-Party.

Britannica. "Ida B. Wells-Barnett: American Journalist and Social Reformer." Accessed 8/7/23, https://www.britannica.com/biography/Ida-B-Wells-Barnett.

Britannica. "How the West was Won." https://www.britannica.com/topic/American
-frontier/How-the-West-was-won.

Britannica. "Daniel Hale Williams, American Physician." https://www.britannica.com
/biography/Daniel-Hale-Williams.

Britannica. "Confiscation Acts - United States History [1861-1864]." https://www
.britannica.com/event/Confiscation-Acts.

Brooks, Lisa. *Our Beloved Kin: A New History of King Philip's War*. Yale University
Press, 2019.

Brown, William. *The Life of William Brown of Providence*. University of New
Hampshire Press, 2006.

Butler, Sana. *Sugar of the Crop – My Journey to Find the Children of Slaves*. The Lyons
Press, 2009. https://archive.org/details/sugarofcropmyjou0000butl.

Byman, Daniel. "White Supremacy, Terrorism, and the Failure of Reconstruction in
the United States." *International Security* 46, no. 1 (Summer 2021): 53–103. https://
doi.org/10.1162/isec_a_00410.

California State Library. Ancestry.com. U.S., Adjutant General Military Records,
1631-1976. Provo, UT, USA: Ancestry.com Operations, Inc., 2011.

Cardona, Nina. "50 Years Before Rosa Parks, A Bold Nashville Streetcar Protest
Defied Segregation." September 22, 2015. https://wpln.org/post/50-years-before
-rosa-parks-a-bold-nashville-streetcar-protest-defied-segregation/.

Carlson, Kenneth S. "Black & White, The Third & Fourteenth Rhode Island Heavy
Artillery Regiments 1861 – 1865." *Rhode Island College*, 1992.

Carr. Edson I. *The Carr Family Records: Embacing [sic] the Record of the First Families
who Settled in America and their Descendants*. Herald Printing House, 1894.

Center for Black Digital Research, Pennsylvania State University. "Colored
Conventions Project." Accessed 12/20/23, https://coloredconventions.org/.

Charles, Safiya. "2,000 more Lynching Victims Brought to Light in EJI's New
Reconstruction Era Report," Montgomery Advertiser, June 15, 2020. https://
www.montgomeryadvertiser.com/story/news/2020/06/16/equal-justice-initiative
-reconstruction-era-reports-2000-more-lynching-victims-found-emancipation
/3196140001.

Chenery, William H. *The Fourteenth Regiment Rhode Island Heavy Artillery (Colored)
in the War to Preserve the Union, 1861-1865*. Snow & Farnham, 1898.

Clark-Pujara, Christy. *Dark Work: The Business of Slavery in Rhode Island*. New York
University Press, 2016.

Colored Conventions Project. "Mary Ann Shadd Cary – Herstory in the Colored
Conventions - 1855 National Convention of Colored People held in Philadelphia,
PA." Accessed 12/20/23, https://coloredconventions.org/mary-ann-shadd-cary/.

Coppedge, Clay. "Bass Reeves, Lawman Extraordinaire - Could the West's first African American Deputy Marshal have inspired the Lone Ranger?" Texas Coop Power, October, 2018. Accessed 11/13/23, https://texascooppower.com/bass -reeves-lawman-extraordinaire/.

Coughtry, Jay. *The Notorious Triangle: Rhode Island and the African Slave Trade, 1700-1807.* Temple University Press, 1981.

Creech, Margaret. *Three Centuries of Poor Law Administration: A Study of Legislation in Rhode Island.* University of Chicago Press, 1936.

Cromwell, Adelaide. *The Other Brahmins: Boston's Black Upper Class 1750-1950.* University of Arkansas Press, 1994.

Davis-Marks, Isis. "The Little-Known Story of America's Deadliest Election Day Massacre," Smithsonian Magazine, November 13, 2020. Accessed 8/18/23, https:// www.smithsonianmag.com/smart-news/new-exhibition-florida-honors-victims -bloodiest-election-massacre-american-history-180976283/.

DeFrancesco, Joey La Neve. "Abolition and Anti-Abolition in Newport, Rhode Island, 1835-1866." *Newport History* 92, no. 281 (2020): Article 2. https://digitalcommons .salve.edu/newporthistory/vol92/iss281/2.

Desrosiers, Marian Mathison. *John Banister of Newport: The life and Accounts of a Colonial Merchant.* McFarland & Company, Inc., 2017.

Dorman, Franklin. *Twenty Families of Color in Mass.* New England Historic Genealogical Society, 1998.

Douglass, Frederick. "I Denounce the So-Called Emancipation as a Stupendous Fraud," History Is A Weapon. https://www.historyisaweapon.com/defcon1/ douglassfraud.html.

Du Bois, W.E. Burghardt. "Reviewed Work: Race Traits and Tendencies of the American Negro by Frederick L. Hoffman." *The Annals of the American Academy of Political and Social Science* 9 (1897): 127–33. http://www.jstor.org/stable /1009520.

Du Bois, William Edward Burghardt. *The Souls of Black Folk: Essays and Sketches.* A.C. McClurg & Co., 1903. https://archive.org/details/cu31924024920492/page/n7 /mode/2up.

Dumpson, Kimberly Conway. Author communications. October 10, 2020.

Dumpson, Kimberly Conway. "Olivia Johns Rice in Stories In Stone." Jamestown Historical Society Archive, #A2021.132.002, October 2021.

Eltis, David. *Slave Voyages: The Trans-Atlantic Slave Trade Database.* Accessed 11/19/24, https://www.slavevoyages.org/voyage/database.

Encyclopedia Virginia. "Racial Integrity Law (1924 – 1930)." https://encyclopedi avirginia.org/entries/racial-integrity-laws-1924-1930/.

Encyclopedia Virginia, Virginia Humanities. "Anthony Burns (1834–1862)." Accessed 7/28/23, https://encyclopediavirginia.org/entries/burns-anthony-1834-1862/.

Enright, Rosemary, and Sue Maden. *Historic Tales of Jamestown.* Acadia Publishing, 2016.

Enright, Rosemary, and Sue Maden. "Jamestown Historical Society 100 years: The Civil War at Home." *Jamestown Press,* July 26, 2012. https://www.jamestownpress .com/articles/jamestown-historical-society-100-years-the-civil-war-at-home/.

Enright, Rosemary, and Sue Maden. "JHS 100 Years: Jamestowners in the Civil War." *Jamestown Press,* July 12, 2012. https://www.jamestownpress.com/articles/jhs-100 -years-jamestowners-in-the-civil-war/.

Enright, Rosemary, and Susan Maden, "Societies Offered up Lively Debates." *Jamestown Press*, May 13, 2021. https://www.jamestownpress.com/articles/ societies-offered-up-lively-debates/.

Equal Justice Initiative. "On this day Sep 04, 1875 - Massacre by White Mob in Clinton, Mississippi, Leaves Dozens of Black People Dead." https://calendar.eji.org /racial-injustice/sep/04.

Equal Justice Initiative. "A History of Racial Injustice - President Wilson Authorizes Segregation within Federal Government." https://calendar.eji.org/racial-injustice/ apr/11.

Equal Justice Initiative. "Reconstruction in America: Racial Violence after the Civil War, 1865-1876." https://eji.org/report/reconstruction-in-america/.

Federal Reserve Bank of Kansas City. Dell and Chad Wilkerson, "The Past, Present and Future of Black Wall Street." https://www.kansascityfed.org/oklahomacity/ oklahoma-economist/oklahoma-economist-the-past-present-and-future-of-black -wall-street.

Fishers Island Oyster Farm. Malinowski Sarah, "Thomas Downing - NYC Oyster King & Abolitionist." Accessed 12/21/23, https://www.fishersislandoysters.com/ blog/2021/2/22/thomas-downing.

Foner, Eric. *A Short History of Reconstruction, 1863-1877.* Harper, 2015.

Foner, Eric, and Olivia Mahoney, *America's Reconstruction: People and Politics after the Civil War.* Louisiana State University, 1995. https://archive.org/details/america sreconstr0000fone.

Gaines, Kevin and Beth Parkhurst. *African-Americans in Newport, 1660-1960.* Report to the Rhode Island Black Heritage Society. N.p., 1992.

George Washington's Mount Vernon. "Militia Acts of 1792." Accessed 4/24/23, https://www.mountvernon.org/education/primary-source-collections/primary -source-collections/article/militia-act-of-1792/.

Gilder Lehrman Institute of American History. "FrederickDouglass on the disfranchisement of Black Voters, 1880." https://www.gilderlehrman.org/history -resources/spotlight-primary-source/frederick-douglass-disfranchisement-black -voters-1888.

Gilder Lehrman Institute. "Historical Context: Facts about the Slave Trade and Slavery." Accessed 7/28/23, https://www.gilderlehrman.org/history-resources/ teacher-resources/historical-context-facts-about-slave-trade-and-slavery.

Gould, J.J., "Longfellow's Antislavery Poem 'Paul Revere's Ride' Turns 150," The Atlantic, December 20, 2021. https://:www..theatlantic.com/entertainment/archive /2010/12/longfellows-anti-slavery-poem-paul-reveres-ride-turns-150/68279.

Groves, Stephen. "State senate urges inquiry into Wounded Knee Medals of Honor." Associated Press, February 22, 2021. https://apnews.com/general-neews-1ffb1c5 fe6dd8a33af7bcb94d3c9095d

Greene, Evarts, and Virginia Harrington. *American Population Before the Federal Census of 1790.* Columbia University Press, 1932.

Hannah-Jones, Nikole. *The 1619 Project: A New Origin Story.* New York Times Company, 2021.

Harris, Leslie M. *In the Shadow of Slavery: African Americans in New York City, 1626-1863.* University of Chicago Press, 2003.

Historic and Architectural Resources of Jamestown, Rhode Island. Rhode Island Historical Preservation & Heritage Commission, 1995.

History.com. "After the Underground Railroad, Harriet Tubman Led a Brazen Civil War Raid." https:www.history.com/news/harriet-tubman-combahee-ferry-raid-civil-war.

History.com. "Apartheid." https://www.history.com/articles/apartheid.

History.com. "Creation of the Freedmen's Bureau." https://www.history.com/articles/ freedmens-bureau.

History.com. "The Short-Lived Promise of '40 acres and a Mule." Nadra Kareem Nittle, November 9, 2022. https://www.history.com/news/40-acres-mule-promise.

History.com. "Slavery Persisted in New England Until the 19th Century - Becky Little." Accessed 3/22/23: https://www.history.com/news/slavery-new-england -rhode-island.

Hoffman, Frederick L. "The Race Traits and Tendencies of the American Negro." *Publications of the American Economic Association* 11, no. 1/3 (Jan-Mar-May, 1896): 1–329. Accessed 12/20/23, https://www.jstor.org/stable/2560438.

Horton, James Oliver, and Lois E. Horton. *In Hope of Liberty, Culture, Community and Protest Among Northern Free Blacks, 1700 -1860.* Oxford University Press, 1977.

Illinois Periodicals Online. Roberta Senechal, "The Springfield Race Riot of 1908." https://www.lib.niu.edu/1996/iht329622.html.

Immigration History. "People v. Hall (1854)." https://immigrationhistory.org/item/people-v-hall/.

Jamestown Historical Society Archives, Jamestown, R.I.

Jeter, Henry N. *Pastor Henry N. Jeter's Twenty-five Years Experience with the Shiloh Baptist Church and Her History, Corner School and Mary Streets, Newport, RI.* Remington Printing Co., 1901.

Jones, Melissa Janczewski. "The Clinton Riot of 1875: From Riot to Massacre," Mississippi History Now, September 2015. https://www.mshistorynow.mdah.ms.gov/issue/the-clinton-riot-of-1875-from-riot-to-massacre.

King, Shannon. *Whose Harlem is This, Anyway?* New York University Press, 2017.

Lanham, Andrew. "When W.E.B. Du Bois Was 'Un-American.'" *Boston Review,* January 13, 2017. https://www.bostonreview.net/articles/when-civil-rights-were-un-american/.

LaRoche, Cheryl Janifer. *Free Black Communities and the Underground Railroad.* University of Illinois Press, 2014.

Lemons, J. Stanley, and Diane Lambert. "John Carter Minkins: Pioneering African-American Newspaperman." *The New England Quarterly* 76, no. 3 (2003): 413–38. https://www.jstor.org/stable/1559809.

Levin, Kevin M. "Why 'Glory' Still Resonates More Than Three Decades Later." *Smithsonian Magazine,* September 14, 2020. https://www.smithsonianmag.com/history/why-glory-still-resonates-more-three-decades-later-180975794/.

Library of Congress. "The African American Odyssey: A Quest for Full Citizenship Reconstruction and Its Aftermath." https://www.loc.gov/exhibits/african-american-odyssey/reconstruction.html.

Library of Congress. "Compromise of 1850." Accessed 5/21/2021, https://guides.loc.gov/compromise-1850.

Library of Congress. "Narrative of the Life of Frederick Douglass, an American Slave." https://www.loc.gov/resource/lhbcb.25385/?sp=2&st=text.

Library of Congress. "Primary Documents in American History - Abraham Lincoln's Second Inaugural Address." https://www.loc.gov/rr/program/bib/ourdocs/lincoln2nd.html.

Library of Congress. "Public Law. 31-60, 31st US Congress, Sept. 16, 1850, Ch. 60." Fugitive Slave Act. https://tile.loc.gov/storage-services/service/ll/llsl/llsl-c31/llsl-c31.pdf#page=42.

Library of Congress. "Roosevelt's Hostility to the Colored People of the United States. The Record of the Discharge of the Colored Soldiers at Brownsville, 1906." https://www.loc.gov/resource/rbpe.24001000/?sp=1&st=text.

Library of Congress. "Secession States." Accessed 11/27/23, https://www.loc.gov/rr/geogmap/placesinhistory/archive/2011/20110314_secession.htm.

Library of Congress. "With Malice Toward None, The Abraham Lincoln Bicentennial Exhibition, The Run for President." Accessed 12/26/23, https://www.loc.gov/exhibits/lincoln/the-run-for-president.html.

Lin, Rachel Chernos. "The Rhode Island Slave-Traders: Butchers, Bakers and Candlestick-Makers." *Slavery & Abolition* 23, no. 3 (2002): 21–38. https://www.tandfonline.com/doi/abs/10.1080/714005253.

Lincoln University Biographical Catalogue. New Era Printing, 1918. Accessed 1/10/2025, https://www.lincoln.edu/_files/langston-hughes-memorial-library/Library%20Alumni%20Directories/1918.pdf.

Lindert, Peter H., and Richard Sutch. "Consumer Price Indexes, for All Items: 1774-2003." In *Historical Statistics of the United States, Millennial Edition.* Cambridge University Press, 2006.

Mark Stelzer, and Sven Beckert. "The Contribution of Enslaved Workers to Output and Growth in the Antebellum United States." *Economic History Review* 77, no. 1 (February 2024): 137–59. https://equitablegrowth.org/working-papers/the-contribution-of-enslaved-workers-to-output-and-growth-in-the-antebellum-united-states/.

Maryland State Archives. "Legacy of Slavery in Maryland." *Accommodation Docket*, April 19, 1842. Accessed 4/28/21, http://slavery2.msa.maryland.gov/pages/Search.aspx.

Mason, Nancy Caswell Bailey. "A Brief Historical Survey of Central Baptist Church." Central Baptist Church of Jamestown, R.I. Accessed 7/30/20, http://www.cbcjamestown.com/ABriefHistoricalSurveyofCentralBaptistChurch.pdf.

McBurney, Christian M. "Freedom for African Americans in British-Occupied Newport, 1776-1779 and 'The Book of Negroes.'" *Newport History* 87, no. 276 (2017): 7.

McWhirter, Cameron. *Red Summer – The Summer of 1919 and the Awakening of Black America.* St. Martin's Griffin, 2012.

Melish, Joanne, *Disowning Slavery: Gradual Emancipation and Race in New England, 1780–1860.* Cornell University Press, 1998.

Miller, G. Wayne. "'Away From Home' Exhibit Tells the Story of Native Children Stripped of their Identity." *Providence Journal,* November 10, 2021. https://www

.providencejournal.com/story/news/local/2021/11/10/away-from-home-exhibit-tells-of-native-children-forcibly-removed-to-american-indian-boarding-schools/6353102001/.

Miller, Richard F. *States at War, Volume 1 - A Reference Guide for Connecticut, Maine, Massachusetts, New Hampshire, Rhode Island, and Vermont in the Civil War.* University Press of New England, 2013.

Minutes of the Rhode Island Baptist Anniversaries, 1906. Remington Printing Co, 1906.

Muhammad, Khalil Gibran. "Sugar." In *The 1619 Project – A New Origin Story*, edited by Nikole Hannah-Jones. New York Times Company, Penguin Random House, LLC, 2021.

Muhammad, Khalil Gibran. "The Condemnation of Blackness: Race, Crime, and the Making of Modern Urban America." In *Racism in America – A Reader.* Harvard University Press, 2020. https://doi.org/10.4159/9780674251656-009.

Mystic Seaport Museum. "Register of Seaman's Certificates." Accessed 1/26/20, https://research.mysticseaport.org/databases/protection/.

Narragansett Indian Tribe. "Perseverance." Accessed 6/21/2025. https://narragansettindiannation.org/history/perseverance/.

National Archives. "14th Amendment to the US Constitution." https://www.archives.gov/milestone-documents/14th-amendment.

National Archives. "19th Amendment to the U.S. Constitution: Women's Right to Vote." https://www.archives.gov/historical-docs/19th-amendment.

National Archives. "25th Infantry Scrapbook, I:145." Records of US Regular Army Mobile Units, 1821-1942, Record Group 391.

National Archives. "Black Soldiers in the U.S. Military During the Civil War." https://www.archives.gov/education/lessons/blacks-civil-war.

National Archives. "Dred Scott v. Sandford, 1857." https://www.archives.gov/milestone-documents/dred-scott-v-sandford.

National Archives. "The Emancipation Proclamation." https://www.archives.gov/exhibits/featured-documents/emancipation-proclamation .

National Archives. "The Freedmen's Bureau." https://www.archives.gov/research/african-americans/freedmens-bureau.

National Archives. "Records of the Adjutant General's Office, 1780's-1917." Record Group 94.

National Archives. "US Army, Register of Enlistments, 1798-1914." Microfilm Publication M233, 246.

National Association of Black Military Women. "Cathay Williams, The First African-American Woman To Enlist in The Army and the only female member of the Buffalo Soldiers." Accessed 9/7/23, https://www.nabmw.org/cathay-williams.

National Constitution Center. "South Carolina Declaration of Secession (1860)." Accessed 12/27/23, https://constitutioncenter.org/the-constitution/historic-document-library/detail/south-carolina-declaration-of-secession-1860.

National Museum of African American History and Culture. "Nat Turner's Rebellion." https://nmaahc.si.edu/explore/stories/nat-turners-rebellion.

National Park Service. "The 54th Massachusetts and the Second Battle of Fort Wagner." https://www.nps.gov/articles/the-54th-massachusetts-and-the-second-battle-of-fort-wagner.htm.

National Park Service. "The 54th Massachusetts Regiment." https://www.nps.gov/articles/54th-massachusetts-regiment.htm.

National Park Service. "Aboard the Underground Railroad - Mary Ann Shadd Cary." Accessed 12/22/23, https://www.nps.gov/nr/travel/underground/dc2.htm.

National Park Service. "An Absolute Massacre – The New Orleans Slaughter of July 30, 1866." https://www.nps.gov/articles/000/neworleansmassacre.htm.

National Park Service. "African Americans in the Revolutionary War." Accessed 11/25/2024, https://www.nps.gov/chyo/learn/historyculture/african-americans-in-the-revolutionary-war.htm.

National Park Service. "Cathay Williams." https://www.nps.gov/people/cwilliams.htm.

National Park Service. "The Civil War's Black Soldiers - Black Officers." Accessed 1/22/23, https://www.nps.gov/parkhistory/online_books/civil_war_series/2/sec14.htm.

National Park Service. "Frederick Douglass." Accessed 2/17/22, https://www.nps.gov/frdo/learn/historyculture/frederickdouglass.htm.

National Park Service. "Harriet Tubman and the Underground Railroad." https://www.nps.gov/articles/harriet-tubman-and-the-underground-railroad.htm.

National Park Service. "Hiram Rhodes Revels." https://www.nps.gov/people/hiram-rhodes-revels.htm.

National Park Service. "Ida B. Wells." https://www.nps.gov/people/idabwells.htm.

National Park Service. "John Brown's Raid." https://www.nps.gov/articles/john-browns-raid.htm.

National Park Service. King Philip's War, 1675–1678." Accessed 11/29/23, https://www.nps.gov/rowi/learn/historyculture/kingphilip.htm.

National Park Service. "War Declared: States Secede from the Union!" https://www.nps.gov/kemo/learn/historyculture/wardeclared.htm.

National Public Radio. "After Slavery, Searching for LovedOnes in Wanted Ads," Ari Shapiro and Maureen Pao, 2017. https://www.npr.org/sections/codeswitch/2017 /02/22/516651689/after-slavery-searching-for-loved-ones-in-wanted-ads.

National Trust for Historic Preservation. Nicholas Som, "4 African American Women's Clubs That Helped Write History," 2019. Accessed 8/7/23, https:// savingplaces.org/stories/4-african-american-womens-clubs-that-helped-write -history.

National Women's Hall of Fame. "Mary Ann Shadd Cary." Accessed 12/21/23, https:// www.womenofthehall.org/inductee/mary-ann-shadd-cary/.

National Women's History Museum. Arlisha R. Norwood, "Ida B. Wells-Barnett, 1862-1931." Accessed 8/5/23, https://www.womenshistory.org/education -resources/biographies/ida-b-wells-barnett.

National Women's History Museum. Debra Michals, "Sojourner Truth, 1797-1883." https://www.womenshistory.org/education-resources/biographies/sojourner -truth.

The National World War I Museum and Memorial. "African-AmericanWomen and WWI." https://www.theworldwar.org/learn/about-wwi/african-american-women -and-wwi.

New England Historical Society. "The New London Race Riots of 1919 Follow a Pandemic." https://newenglandhistoricalsociety.com/the-new-london-race-riots -of-1919-follow-a-pandemic/.

New Georgia Encyclopedia. "Sherman's Field Order No. 15." https://www .georgiaencyclopedia.org/articles/history-archaeology/shermans-field-order-no -15/.

New Jersey State Census, Newark, NJ, 1885.

Newport Mansions. "The Gilded Age Newport in Color." https://www .newportmansions.org/events/gilded-age-newport-in-color/.

North Carolina Digital Collections. LeRae Umfleet, "1989 Wilmington Race Riot Report." Accessed 11/18/24, https://digital.ncdcr.gov/Documents/Detail/1898 -wilmington-race-riot-report/2257408?item=2277536.

North Carolina Office of Archives and History. "Red ShirtViolence, Election Fraud, and the Demise of the Populist Party in NorthCarolina's Third Congressional District, 1900," James M. Beeby. *The North Carolina Historical Review 84*, no. 1 (2008): 1–28.https://jstor.org/stable/23523367.

Online Review of Rhode Island History. Patrick T. Conley, "George T. Downing: Rhode Island's Most Prominent African American Leader." Accessed 11/18/23,

https://smallstatebighistory.com/george-t-downing-rhode-islands-most
-prominent-african-american-leader/.

Palmer, Colin A. *Passageways: An Interpretive History of Black America, Volume I,
1619–1863.* Wadsworth Group, 2002, http://nationalhumanitiescenter.org/pds/
maai/enslavement/text3/text3read.htm.

Pew Research Center. "More than half of states willrecognize Juneteenth as an
official public holiday in 2023," KatherineSchaeffer, June 9, 2023. https://www
.pewresearch.org/short-reads/2023/06/09/more-than-half-of-states-now
-recognize-juneteenth-as-an-official-holiday/.

Plante, Trevor K. "Researching African Americans in the U.S. Army, 1866-1890,
Buffalo Soldiers and Black Infantrymen." *Prologue Magazine,* National Archives
33, no. 1 (Spring 2001): 56–61. https://www.archives.gov/publications/prologue
/2001/spring/buffalo-soldiers.html.

Preserve Rhode Island. "African Heritage and Historical Sites in Rhode Island."
https://www.preserveri.org/african-heritage-sites.

Proceedings of the Rhode Island Historical Society, 1873-74. Rhode Island Historical
Society, 1874.

Project Gutenberg. Ida B. Wells-Barnett. "Southern Horrors: Lynch Law in All Its
Phases." Accessed 6/1/2025, https://www.gutenberg.org/files/14975/14975-h
/14975-h.htm.

Public Archeology Laboratory. "Survey Report - African American Struggle for
Civil Rights in Rhode Island: The Twentieth Century Phase 2: Statewide Survey
and National Register Evaluation." 2019. https://preservation.ri.gov/pdfs_zips
_downloads/resources_pdfs/2019twentiethc_ri_afam-civil-rights_report.pdf.

Quattromani, Shirley Teixeira. *History of the Portuguese of Conanicut Island.* Edited
by Catherine M. Wright. Jamestown Philomenian Library, 1980.

Rhode Island. *Acts and Resolves passed by the General Assembly of the State of Rhode
Island and Providence Plantations, May Session 1897.* E.L. Freeman & Sons, 1897.

Rhode Island. *Report on the Committee on Finance of the House of Representatives on
Bounty Frauds, etc.* H. H. Thomas & Co., 1865.

Rhode Island Archival and Manuscript Collections Online. "Guide to the Rhode
Island 11th United States Heavy Artillery (Colored), 1853-1913." Accessed
6/19/20, https://www.riamco.org/render?eadid=US-RPPC-us11regiment.

Rhode Island College. Kimberly Dumpson, "The Power of the Story." Accessed
5/27/2021, https://www.ric.edu/news-events/news/power-story.

Rhode Island General Assembly. "An Act authorizing the Manumission of Negroes,
Mulattoes and Others, and for the Gradual Abolition of Slavery, February

1784." Rhode Island State Archives Repository. Accessed 5/14/23, https://sosri
.access.preservica.com/uncategorized/digitalFile_cb907aee-887d-4c77-9cdd
-88ac56b0ec9c/.

Rhode Island General Assembly. *Report of the Commission on the Affairs of the
Narragansett Indians Made to the General Assembly, 1881.* E.L. Freeman & Co.,
1881.

Rhode Island Historical Cemetery Database. "Rhode Island Historic Cemeteries,
#JM002." Accessed 11/27/23, https://rihistoriccemeteries.org/newsearchcemete
rydetail.aspx?ceme_no=JM002.

Rhode Island State Archives. *Marriages Registered in the City of Providence.*

Rhode Island State Census, 1865, 1875, 1885, 1905, 1915, 1925.

Rhode Tour. May Wijaya, "The World was his Oyster - George T. Downing." https://
rhodetour.org/items/show/41.

Rice, John M. "Frederick Douglass and His Abolitionist Friends in Newport and New
Bedford." *Newport History* 97, no. 286 (2022): Article 2. https://digitalcommons
.salve.edu/newporthistory/vol97/iss286/2.

Rockman, Seth. "Negro Cloth: Mastering the Market of Slave Clothing in Antebellum
America." In *American Capitalism: New Histories.* Columbia University Press,
2018. https://www.degruyter.com/document/doi/10.7312/beck18524-008/html.

The Roys Report. "Christian Hymn, Anthem of Civil Rights andBlack Churches,
Marks 125 Years." Adelle Banks, June 24, 2025.https://julieroys.com/christian
-hymn-anthem-civil-rights-black-churches-marks-125-years/.

Sanborn Map Co. *Atlas of Newport, Jamestown, Middletown and Portsmouth, RI
from Actual Surveys and City Records.* Sanborn Map Company, 1921. Accessed
2/1/2025, https://repository.library.brown.edu/studio/item/bdr:384505/.

Schroder, Walter K. *Dutch Island and Fort Greble.* Acadia Publishing, 1998.

Schubert, Frank N. *On The Trail of the Buffalo Soldier: Biographies of African
Americans in the US Army 1866-1917.* Scarecrow Press, 1995.

Slavery in the North. Douglas Harper, "Slavery in Rhode Island." Accessed 6/24/23,
http://slavenorth.com/rhodeisland.htm.

Smith, Jesse Carney, ed. "Mahlon Von Horne, 1840-1910." In *Notable Black American
men. Book II* (Thomson Gale, 2007). Accessed 7/1/2025, https://archive.org/details
/notableblackamer0002unse/page/653.

Smithsonian Institution, National Museum of African American History and
Culture. "Buffalo Soldiers – Legend and Legacy." https://nmaahc.si.edu/explore/
stories/buffalo-soldiers.

Smithsonian Institution, National Museum of African American History and Culture. "The Combahee Ferry Raid." https://nmaahc.si.edu/explore/stories/combahee-ferry-raid.

Smithsonian Institution, National Museum of African AmericanHistory and Culture. "The Historical Legacy of Juneteenth," June 19, 2019. https://nmaahc.si.edu/explore/stories/historical-legacy-juneteenth.

Snodgrass, Mary Ellen. *The Underground Railroad: An Encyclopedia of People, Places, and Operations.* Routledge, 2015.

Southern Family Archives, Jamestown, RI. "Oral History – Mattie R. Southern." August 24, 2020.

Stewart, Rowena. *A Heritage Discovered: Blacks in Rhode Island.* Rhode Island Black Heritage Society, 1975.

Still, William. *The Underground Railroad Records – The Hardships, Hairbreadth Escapes and Death Struggles of the Slaves in their Efforts for Freedom.* Philadelphia, 1886. https://www.google.com/books/edition/Still_s_Underground_Rail_Road_Records/KD9LAAAAYAAJ.

Tamakloe, Nelson. "Sarah Charles, Josias Budgel, Her Husband, And Their Children." *Rhode Island Roots* 39, no. 4 (December 2013): 177–80.

Tax Assessment of the City of Newport, 1915. Mercury Publishing Co., 1915.

Thaddeus Stevens College of Technology. "Legacy of ThaddeusStevens." https://www.stevenscollege.edu/about/history/.

Texas State Historical Association. "Brownsville Raid of1906 - A Historical Overview." Garna Christian. https://www.tshaonline.org/handbook/entries/brownsville-raid-of-1906.

The African American Experience in Massachusetts Courts. "1854 Anthony Burns and the Fugitive Slave Act." Accessed 7/28/23, http://www.longroadtojustice.org/topics/slavery/anthony-burns.php.

The American Presidency Project. "Abraham Lincoln, 16th President of the United States, 1861 - 1865: Remarks to Committee of the Republican National Convention Accepting the Presidential Nomination, May 19, 1860." Accessed 12/26/23, https://www.presidency.ucsb.edu/documents/remarks-committee-the-republican-national-convention-accepting-the-presidential-nomination.

The Art Story. "Edmonia Lewis, African and Native American Sculptor." https://www.theartstory.org/artist/lewis-edmonia.

The Southern Workman and Hampton School Record, Vol. 28. Hampton Normal and Agricultural Institute, 1899.

The White House Historical Association. Sarah Fling, "The Formerly Enslaved Household of the Grant Family." https://www.whitehousehistory.org/the-formerly -enslaved-household-of-the-grant-family.

Town of Jamestown. Comprehensive Community Plan, 2015.

Town of Jamestown. Death Registry.

Town of Jamestown. Jamestown Land Evidence.

Town of Jamestown. Jamestown Probate Records.

Town of Jamestown. Jamestown Town Council and Probate Records.

Town of Jamestown, Rhode Island. *2015 Comprehensive Community Plan*. Town of Jamestown, 2015.

Town of Jamestown. Tax Assessor Database.

Town of Jamestown. *Tax List of the Town of Jamestown, RI.* Gladding Print, 1921.

Town of Jamestown. Voter Roster, 1883, 1885, 1920, 1921.

United States Agricultural Census, Jamestown, RI, 1880

United States Census, Fort McKarett, Menard County, Texas.

United States Census, Jamestown, R.I., 1850–1920.

United States Census, Slave Schedule.

United States Census, South Kingstown, R.I.

United States Congress. "H.R.55 - Emmett Till Antilynching Act, 2022." https://www .congress.gov/bill/117th-congress/house-bill/55.

United States Senate. "Kansas-Nebraska Act." https://www.senate.gov/artandhistory/ history/minute/Kansas_Nebraska_Act.htm.

United States Senate. "The Caning of Senator Charles Sumner, May 22, 1856." https:// www.senate.gov/artandhistory/history/minute/The_Caning_of_Senator_Charles _Sumner.htm.

United States Senate. "The Civil War: The Senate's Story." https://www.senate.gov/ artandhistory/history/common/civil_war/VictoryTragedyReconstruction.htm.

United States Senate. "Kansas-Nebraska Act."https://www.senate.gov/artandhistory/ history/minute/Kansas Nebraska Act.htm.

University of Arkansas-Little Rock. "Healing the Land:Elaine." Anderson Institute on Race and Ethnicity. Accessed 8/23/23,https://ualr.edu/race-ethnicity/healing-the -land-elaine/.

University of Chicago Press. "The New York City Draft Riots of 1863." Accessed 4/19/23, https://press.uchicago.edu/Misc/Chicago/317749.html.

University of Hartford, Digital History. "What was Life Like Under Slavery." https:// www.digitalhistory.uh.edu/disp_textbook.cfm?smtid=2&psid=3040.

University of Maryland, University Libraries. "1851 Indian Appropriations Act."
University of Maryland, University Libraries, Research Guide. Accessed 8/2/23,
https://lib.guides.umd.edu/c.php?g=1261350&p=9246797.

University of Rochester. "Frederick Douglass Project." The Frederick Douglass
Institute and Department of Rare Books and Special Collections. Accessed
12/26/23, https://rbscp.lib.rochester.edu/2509.

US Hastings College of the Law Library. "Anti-Chinese California Laws,1858, Cal.
Stat. 295." Accessed 7/24/23, http://libraryweb.uchastings.edu/library/research/
special-collections/wong-kim-ark/laws3.htm.

Virginia Commonwealth University, Social Welfare History Project. Catherine A.
Paul, "Fugitive Slave Act of 1850." Accessed 8/2/23, https://socialwelfare.library
.vcu.edu/federal/fugitive-slave-act-of-1850.

W.E.B. Du Bois Papers (MS 312), Special Collections and University Archives,
University of Massachusetts Amherst Libraries.

Warfare History Network. Eric Niderost, "The Dakota War of 1862: What Caused the
Great Sioux Uprising." https://warfarehistorynetwork.com/article/dakota-war-of
-1862-what-caused-the-great-sioux-uprising/.

Washington, Booker T. *The Story of My Life and Work.* J.L. Nichols & Company, 1901.

Washington Center for Equitable Growth. Kathryn Zickuhr, "New Research Shows
Slavery's Central Role in U.S. Economic Growth Leading up to the Civil War."
https://equitablegrowth.org/new-research-shows-slaverys-central-role-in-u-s
-economic-growth-leading-up-to-the-civil-war/.

Watson, Daniel. "Map of Conanicut Island, opposite Newport, Rhode-Island in
Narragansett Bay." Daniel Watson publisher, 1875. Accessed 3/22/21, https://
digitalcollections.nypl.org/items/7c302910-c546-0134-f338-00505686a51c.

Watson, Walter Leon. *The History of Jamestown on Conanicut Island in the State of
Rhode Island.* John F. Greene, 1949.

Waxman, Olivia B., "America's First Anti-Slavery Statute Was Passed in 1652. Here's
Why It Was Ignored," Time Magazine, May 18, 2017, https://time.com/4782885/
rhode-island-antislavery/.

Western Rhode Island Civic Historical Society. "Underground Railroad in Coventry,
RI." Pawtuxet Valley Preservation and Historical Society. Accessed 8/6/23, http://
www.westernrihistory.org/underground-railroad-in-coventry-ri-by-pawtuxet
-valley-preservation-and-historical-society.

Westwood, Howard. *Black Troops, White Commanders, and Freedmen during the Civil
War.* Southern Illinois University Press, 2008.

Wickenden, Dorothy. *The Agitators–Three Friends who Fought for Abolition and Women's Rights.* Scriber, 2021.

Work Projects Administration. *Inventory of the Church Archives of Rhode Island: Baptist.* Historical Records Survey, 1941.

Wright, Richard R., Jr. *Centennial Encyclopedia of the African Methodist Episcopal Church.* Book Concern of the A.M.E. Church, 1916.

Youngken, Richard C. *African Americans in Newport. An introduction to the Heritage of African Americans in Newport, Rhode Island, 1700–1945.* Rhode Island Historical Preservation and Heritage Commission and Rhode Island Black Heritage Society, 2nd Printing, 1998.

Index

About the Authors

Peter Fay For twenty-five years, Peter Fay has explored secrets hidden in dozens of historical archives across New England. He publishes columns uncovering never-before-known histories of Rhode Island Black Revolutionary War veterans and early mariners, town governments selling slaves after the Revolution, and one of the first Black Rhode Island farms which was donated to create Cedar Cemetery. He leads public art and history projects as a public historian at universities, libraries, and public forums across New England, presented from a Marxist perspective.

He unearths stories on Black labor in the early textile industry, Black and Indigenous whalers, the early socialist labor movement, and the history of the slave trade. He has developed tours of Newport colonial history and created *Makonde: Art and Community* about the Makonde people of Mozambique during the Newport slave trade to East Africa.

Mr. Fay is a co-founder of the Newport Middle Passage Project, the Friends of Jamestown Black History, and sits on the Board of the Jamestown Historical Society and Battle of Rhode Island Association. He retired in 2021 after a thirty-year career in software engineering in commercial and educational institutions, most recently at Brown University.

Valerie J. Southern and her family have lived in Jamestown for over sixty years. She attended Jamestown Elementary School, St. Catherine Academy in Newport, and earned bachelor's and master's degrees from the University of Rhode Island where, in her undergraduate years, she was founder and editor of *Black Gold*, the university's first Black student newspaper. She later earned a master's degree from

Harvard University where she served as a founder and president of the first Harvard Kennedy School Black Alumni Association.

Ms. Southern is the first and only person of color (to date) to have been elected to the Jamestown Town Council and the first woman of color to run for statewide office in Rhode Island. Her appointments and awards include Kahn Fellow from Harvard University, Toll Fellow from the Council of State Governments, Business Person of the Year from the Issaquah Chamber of Commerce, and Achievement Honoree from the *Providence Business News*.

Ms. Southern is currently the president of her transportation planning and engineering consulting practice located in Jamestown. She has published technical transportation studies for the National Academy of Sciences and locally for the State of Rhode Island and for cities such as Newport and Providence. This is her first foray into researching and writing historical narrative on the Black experience. The effort was inspired by her love for her family, her unique experiences as a Black child growing up in Jamestown, and by her desire to preserve the history of the island's Black community. She is co-founder of the Friends of Jamestown Black History.

www.ingramcontent.com/pod-product-compliance
Lightning Source LLC
Chambersburg PA
CBHW072004090426
42740CB00011B/2086